MARKETS NOT STAKES

MARKETS NOT STAKES

The Triumph of Capitalism and the Stakeholder Fallacy

PATRICK MINFORD

ORION
BUSINESS
BOOKS

This edition first published in Great Britain in 1998 by
Orion Business
An imprint of The Orion Publishing Group Ltd
Orion House, 5 Upper St Martin's Lane, London WC2H 9EA

A CIP catalogue record for this book is available
from the British Library.

ISBN 0-75281-172-X

Typeset by Selwood Systems
Printed in Great Britain by
Butler & Tanner Ltd, Frome and London

This book is dedicated to my mother, Patricia Martin.

CONTENTS

LIST OF FIGURES

LIST OF TABLES

Chapter 8

PREFACE

When one agrees to write a book, as I did this one when Martin Liu, Orion's persuasive business editor, kindly suggested it, one is forcing oneself to do something unwelcome at the time and yet ultimately a relief. This book is the product of work over the past ten years, and bringing it all together and forming it into what I hope will seem to the reader to be a coherent whole has been just as that first sentence puts it.

I am an applied economist and happiest constructing and explaining models of what is, or has been, going on. Yet this book demanded more: for applied economics to be put into the context of values and politics. So I have written about these, as I had to in order to make explicit just why I believe the politics and applied economics set out here do make sense for a typical democratic people. I am no philosopher or politician – God forbid: may the laws of comparative advantage prevail – but I have trespassed because I had to. I have done so honestly and openly, I trust; I have said what I think works in society and politics. The essence of my remarks is this: free market economics works to enrich economies, and the people in those economies – once they have absorbed how it works – mostly accept it, freely and with all its distributional consequences. Too bad that some 'left-wing intellectuals' and others regard that popular judgement with moral disdain: that is their problem.

I am deeply indebted to the many economists who have developed these themes before. The writings of Milton Friedman and Friedrich Hayek, who are of course household names, have greatly influenced me, as they have so many others. More personally, my own teachers have included Harry Johnson and Alan Walters at the LSE and, at Balliol, Paul Streeten – he was the first to introduce me to classical economic thought, not a fashionable area in the Oxford of the early sixties. At Manchester I met David Laidler, Michael Parkin and Jack Johnston. Soon after I met Karl Brunner and Allan Meltzer at their Konstanz Seminar on monetary theory and policy which I have attended ever since. In the late 1970s I met Ralph Harris and Arthur Seldon at the Institute of Economic Affairs. The influence of all of them runs through this book.

Much of the applied work reported here has been carried out in conjunction with my colleagues in the Liverpool Research Group in Macroeconomics, whose members are spread across several universities, especially Liverpool and Cardiff Business School in the University of Wales, Cardiff. This sort of applied work is a team effort in the broadest sense – mutual help, exchange of ideas and much else. I am grateful to Paul Ashton, Kent Matthews, Eric Nowell, Jonathan Riley and Bruce Webb for a great deal of joint work (the references to our published joint efforts are set out in full in the text). Kent Matthews, David Peel and Michael Wickens have spent many hours discussing the issues in this book with me over the years: latterly they have been joined by Laurence Copeland and James Davidson at Cardiff. Samuel Brittan and Alan Walters kindly commented on parts of the manuscript.

I acknowledge gratefully permission from the publishers, MIT Press, to reproduce much of the material in my chapter 'Reconstruction and the UK post-war welfare state: false start and new beginning', from *Postwar Economic Reconstruction and Lessons for the East Today*, edited by Rudiger Dornbusch, Wilhelm Nolling and Richard Layard (1993). I also gratefully acknowledge permission from the Fraser Institute to reproduce from their publication *Economic Freedom of the World*, 1997 (eds. J. Gwartney and R. Lawson) the two charts shown herein as Figures 1.1 and 1.2.

I would also like to thank Simon Blackman, Jane Francis and, again, Paul Ashton and Jonathan Riley for their assistance in gathering up and putting all the material into its typeset form. And last but not least I thank my wife, Rosie, our family and my sister Deborah's family for putting up with my many antisocial moments during this past summer; and my mother for relentlessly nagging me to 'get on with it'. This book is dedicated to her: like me, she originally had an Oxford (PPE) education. I cannot imagine a starting point further from the position of this book – for me to arrive here has been an exercise in intellectual masochism and self-purification – but she too has made the journey with me over the years and our discussions have been a source of support and illumination to me.

CHAPTER ONE

Introduction

AT THE HEART of this book is a vision of freedom under a law that restricts itself to the minimum necessary for the avoidance or resolution of conflict – a 'free society' in short. Freedom is a 'pro' word, with good connotations. So it has been appropriated to advocate its opposite: the regulation of people's lives for their own good. Rousseau used the word for what Sir Isaiah Berlin defined as 'positive freedom' – freedom 'to' enjoy things such as food, shelter, leisure. This is a misleading use of the word, as Sir Isaiah Berlin argued, which has led over the ages to many abuses of state power, including fascism and communism.

It is the contention of this book that a society that is free in the proper sense is preferred by its citizens to one which is not, that is, one where a government redistributes resources and controls activities in order to create 'positive freedoms'. A modern version of this latter society is a 'stakeholding economy'. This is defined by regulations, explicit or implicit, that compel firms and individuals to act against their own interests in order to give advantage to some group with which they deal – for example employees, customers, suppliers. The notion is no different in essence from that of using taxation to redistribute resources to such groups; its only difference is its lesser transparency and consequent subtlety.

In an age when old socialism is no longer fashionable, having demonstrably failed in Eastern Europe, stakeholderism seems more acceptable. But it is as much taxation and redistribution concealed by the regulative form that forces people to transfer resources directly to other groups. When such regulation is suggested, appeal is usually made to a 'public good' – something good for all that would be underprovided if charged for normally under the market and so must be provided by the state. So, supposedly, a minimum wage and workers' rights prevent exploitation and insecurity; supplier consultation spreads technology; customer rights to 'fair prices' reduce monopoly power; and so on.

We can evaluate regulations – in principle – by whether they raise or lower overall costs. Good regulation can be defined as the sort that lowers costs, in that the benefits it creates indirectly (the public good element) reduces the prices firms will charge or the wages workers will accept. Such benefits could, for example, be a reduction in 'information search costs' for a worker who knows – because of some health and safety standard – that any firm he joins will be safe to work in; otherwise he would have to spend time and energy checking each one out. Or (another example) the general practice of posting prices on goods can save the 'transaction costs' of endless bazaar haggling, where the true price is not revealed until you have left the shop two or three times. If good regulation then is in something firms or workers will pay for, bad regulation is not; it raises costs overall because its indirect benefits are less than its direct costs.

In practice, such an evaluation of regulation is hard to carry out; the indirect benefits that may be conferred are too widely diffused and mixed up with the effects of other factors. We are therefore driven back to comparisons of the overall economic performance of different economic systems.

No doubt some people will gain from such regulations in some limited time period; and it is possible that some effects of the type claimed occur. There is no way of organising society that avoids identifiable errors, that is episodes where things could have been unambiguously better had government done or not done something. However, such a way is not on offer: the choice we have is between systems. By 'system' we mean a set of rules, written or implicit, defining what can and cannot be done. Because people make plans in the light of the system, any alteration in it will have long-term effects. Therefore, if one system has been chosen, it makes it impossible to act in particular episodes in particular ways without altering the system itself. For example, suppose a law has been passed outlawing beggars on the grounds that begging is an undesirable industry; then even though a particular beggar is highly deserving, it is impossible to allow people to give to him without changing the system and violating its intention.

When commenting on a system, people often fall into the fallacy of citing such particular episodes as evidence for or against it. Yet to evaluate a system we clearly must look at its average performance over very long periods of time. When I claimed earlier that a system based on freedom under a minimal law was preferred by its citizens, I meant it in this sense. The citizens would have a consensus that over long periods the system of freedom would benefit themselves, their current families, and their descendants.

In a later chapter, I sketch out a theory of social consent based on the idea that groups can block the working of a society they hate. This has never been more obvious than today when the instruments of terror and disruption are available to very small groups and have huge effects in a highly interdependent economy. By 'consent', therefore, I mean that no group exists that is willing to obstruct the system because it believes another is sufficiently better for it. History is full of examples of systems changed by the challenge of certain groups. In this spirit, I argue that minimalist capitalism is the system towards which we shall evolve as the one least open to this sort of challenge.

This is a large claim and it will take the whole of this book to substantiate it. It is not 'provable', needless to say – not logically because it involves experience, not empirically because too much diverse experience is involved for me to be able to adduce it all even if I knew it all. Rather, my aim is to bring together a combination of theory and experience that will, I hope, prove persuasive. The experience I shall appeal to most, partly because I know it best but mainly because it most clearly and dramatically demonstrates the effect, pure and simple, of changing systems, is that of the UK. This country, having pursued a fairly radical socialist experiment from 1945, underwent an equally radical experiment from 1979 of restoring market freedom. The theory I shall use is what economists call 'general equilibrium theory' – where we ask what may result from the full effects, direct and indirect, of interference in a set of simultaneous relationships between millions of independent people going about their business.

However, before we get too deep into reflections on the nature of man and society, into episodes of comparative history and of attempted reform, and into sketches of future possible reform, let us spend the rest of this chapter discussing some examples of 'stakeholder' alternatives to a free society and trying to define, partly by elimination and contrast, what a free society might look like.

STAKEHOLDING AND THE FREE SOCIETY – SOME EXAMPLES

The most plausible definition of stakeholding is, on the one hand, the idea that private firms should give rights to workers, customers, and the general public as well as to shareholders, and, on the other, the idea that the government should provide rights (such as to social support for unemployment, poverty, sickness and old age) in return for responsibilities (such as availability for work, providing as far as possible for oneself and one's family, and co-operating in tests of whether one is meeting those responsibilities). A general case for this approach is made by Will Hutton in his well known book, *The State We're In*.

The latter idea is fairly generally shared across the political spectrum within the Western world, whether by the UK's New Labour, the Labour parties of Australia and New Zealand, Mr Clinton's Democrats in the United States, or, indeed, the UK's Conservative party and most Conservative parties around the world. However, there are significant exceptions: among the OECD countries Japan has a substantially smaller welfare state than most (although it has increased with the rising burden of their state pensions). Among other countries, South-East Asian countries generally have little, or no welfare state; many of them have grown rapidly in the past two decades, even if very recently they have been hit by problems of economic overheating and consequent speculative attacks on their currencies and stock markets.

It is something on which we will focus in our later discussion of the welfare state. I shall argue that it is in fact more effective for people to provide for themselves and their families privately, with a resulting drop in the level of taxation. In earlier versions of Western European welfare statism, there was little practical emphasis on responsibilities or on the state's role in disciplining those who failed in such responsibilities. Furthermore, there was also an intent to use taxes to redistribute resources from rich to poor in a vigorous way. I would argue that although the modern, more disciplinarian approach is an improvement on this older, explicitly socialist approach, it remains seriously flawed. The reason is that less well-paid people have poor incentives to provide adequately for themselves, while better-paid people also have poor incentives, because of taxation, to work as hard and as effectively as they could. The economy is therefore poorer overall.

We will return later to the question of how the welfare state in the West can be rebuilt to conform better to the notion of a free society. I will argue that, in this dimension, those countries of the Far East have much to teach the West. They have shown how unnecessary it is for the state to intrude on this area of human interaction, how well the individual and his family can deal with the vicissitudes of life without state insurance and its accompanying tax burdens.

Now consider the second idea, that of private-sector stakes. Under company law, shareholders own the firm, just as you and I own our lawnmowers – or, more precisely, as we would jointly own the same lawnmower. Now, are we to give a say to our gardener, our spare parts supplier, the moles and our neighbours in how that lawnmower is used or disposed of? A sensible plan, you may say. In gardening it is wise to take all these views into account, or you may have endless trouble – witness the case of the hedge the neighbour chopped down. Professor John Kay of the London Business School has argued plausibly that attention to these stakeholders' views is wise corporate practice. Yes, indeed, it is wise; but is it mandatory to obey them? That is where ownership comes in.

It is reminiscent of the debate about free will and determinism: for much of the time I may well behave as if compelled by forces of necessity. But I have the choice to act otherwise and occasionally I do so – perhaps because I take a strategic view of my interests.

This is an important distinction. Am I, the owner or representative of the owners (shareholders), to decide? Or is the government to compel me to behave in the way it (and Professor Kay) thinks I should? Leave aside any moral issues: just ask whether or not the economy is best served. First, who has the best information and judgement? Secondly, if I am overruled, how will I and those like me decide to use their money in the future? Thirdly, if those who disagree with Kay et al are prevented from doing business their way, how will business practices develop over time in the economy?

The answer to the first question is plain. I have the best information and I am therefore in the best position to judge. Should the government happen to have some piece of information I should know, its best course is to divulge it to me. This includes advice on how to act. The alternative is worse because even where the government had superior information to me and acted better on it on my behalf, it could achieve the same result by telling me without the costs of its having to act.

As serious is the answer to the second question. The possibility of overruling owners suggests to those who can invest in the economy that it would be dangerous to do so because they too may be compelled to do things that would reduce the return on their investment.

Consider, finally, the third question. Kay's 'communitarian' police would stop those they disliked doing business. So business practice would fossilise in the Kay mould. In a recent pamphlet (1997), Kay gives some examples of business practices of which he disapproves: ICI after the Hanson takeover bid; BTR's Intermed subsidiary (which supplied artificial limbs); Robert Maxwell; a Mr Mole whose petrol prices outside Manchester were said to be exorbitant; and Titan Business Club (which offered rewards to members for recruiting more members in a chain letter style). One may or may not disagree with him, but his point is that businessmen should be forced by general opinion (peer pressure, subtle or brutal social sanctions, and so on) not to act in these ways. Businesses of which he (and so we) disapprove should simply not have access to normal business services. For example, lawyers (and economists!) should refuse to advise them, or assist them in court; they 'should not be touched with a bargepole'.[1]

This is quite inconsistent with British common law, which entitles all to conduct business as they please and to defend themselves before the law in acting as they have, with access to lawyers and other advisers, until and unless proved guilty. Were this not to be so, business practice would be set in a mould created by the great and good opinion Kay defines. It may well be that in particular cases we could all agree, at least after the event, that a certain business practice was wrong; but if we proscribe, as a matter of general procedure, any practice of which such opinion disapproves, we create a fossilised economy in which experimentation will be stunted (like the Mastersingers that Wagner parodied in his opera). This regulation by disapproval makes a poor system for business evolution. As Kay himself concedes earlier in the same pamphlet, economic practice evolves by a process akin to Darwinian selection in biology. For this purpose, it requires plenty of mutations from which to select. Kay and his communitarian value-setters would deprive the economy of mutations; they would be setting themselves up as a super-Darwinian selection mechanism. Forget the moral outrage that the average businessman might feel at this restriction of business freedom; merely consider how bad such procedures would be for economic selection.

Let us turn now to some evidence of how it works. There are many economies where these stakeholders have powers by law, especially in mainland Europe where the Social Charter or Social/Christian Democrat ideas reign supreme. In Spain, for example, firing workers

[1] This point is made by Kay *ad hominem*, as I gave professional economic advice to Titan in the course of their court cases and attempts at dialogue with British officialdom. On the substantive issues, Kay fails to rebut the arguments I raised in a widely circulated paper, as well as two articles in the *Daily Telegraph*. In any case, he implicitly rebukes me (and presumably the lawyers that Titan hired) for agreeing to help them. Yet, as argued in the text, it is a basic principle of British justice that people should have access to professional help; this is routinely accepted in the case of lawyers, and economists or any other professionals for that matter (doctors, actuaries) can be no different.

costs huge amounts; in France, the minimum wage runs at around half average earnings; and in Germany, unions have overwhelming powers to set wages across their industries and are represented on boards. Of these, Germany is held up as the role model. President Clinton did so in his original programme, now almost totally abandoned. New Labour repeatedly tells us of the German miracle. So we should look closely.

But before we do so, we should remember the case of the Soviet Union, and then of Sweden. These have each in their time been held up to us by the Left as models of how we should do things. First, full-blooded communism collapsed in ruins. Then we were told that Sweden was the middle way, with its taxes at 70% of national income and its cradle-to-grave socialism – no sooner admired by our fickle leftists than it too collapsed and Sweden is as a result in the process of far-reaching capitalist reforms. Now comes Germany: once thought by the Left to be, in its post-war Erhard version, a capitalism hook and claw, it is now seen in its social charterism of the past two decades as pleasantly left-wing or 'middle way' (between socialism and laissez-faire capitalism). Socialists, too, must move with the times.

Alas, the curse of leftist admiration strikes again. Germany's labour costs per hour are two-and-a-half times the UK's, six times Korea's, and twenty times Poland's. There are many excellent engineers and entrepreneurs in Germany – the fabled *Mittelstand* of small and medium-sized firms – and they have a labour force well-trained in craft skills. For years, these firms commanded monopoly power in the markets for capital goods and consumer durables such as cars and washing machines. But price matters when others can obtain the same technology, and wage costs matter when those firms themselves are deciding where to have the products made.

There is in 1997 an unemployment crisis in Germany. The explicit unemployment rate is 11.6%. On top of that, there is low employment of women and youngsters; and there is underemployment at work, with average working hours in manufacturing 20% lower than in the UK or the US. Industry is relocating as much as it can outside Germany, and where possible into Poland and the Czech Republic, importing components to be assembled as 'made in Germany'. This process could be devastating to employment in manufacturing (35% of Germany's output and 45% of its employment).

The implications are that the social charter philosophy is coming under acute questioning in Germany, just as the Left in the UK is uncritically embracing it. We have already seen, and will continue to see, a collapse of the deutschmark (and the French franc with it) as policy-makers panic to improve competitiveness. Then, as in Sweden too, we shall see the difficult changes in social rights brought in on the grounds of reluctant realism.

'Stakes' sound as cosy and caring as the 'middle way' (the same idea) once did. But such stakes are not only a violation of property rights but, unsurprisingly, do not work either. We just have to accept that capitalism, for all its 'unacceptable faces', by giving people the fruits of their efforts and ingenuity, delivers the results. Whenever tyrants, planners or social do-gooders take over, the economy suffers in the end.

THE SHAPE OF A FREE SOCIETY

I have already mentioned that in matters of welfare, Far-Eastern economies provide us with examples of how people can provide for themselves necessary insurance against life's vicissitudes without sacrificing freedom to the state. I shall elaborate later on how this element of additional freedom can be incorporated into modern capitalism. But let us here identify a model of capitalism that minimises regulation of this 'stakeholder' variety. For this, we have examples mainly from the Anglo-Saxon world of how people and businesses can operate freely under the law. Anglo-Saxon 'capitalism' is simply the extension of the common law from the protection of the individual to the protection of business within the economy.

The principles involved are well enough known and have originated from English common law. In general, businesses are expected to conduct themselves individually as they please and to develop their own practices and standards, which may include the agreements made within trade associations. Only when these arrangements cause disagreement between businesses themselves (civil law disputes), are criminal (eg, fraud), or operate 'against the public interest' (as defined in statutes from time to time) such that the public prosecution authorities take them to court are they potentially prevented. Notice that when these preventatives are attempted, they are still only put into practice after due legal process. Examples of public interest infringement are monopolies and restrictive trade practices; others are health and safety regulations, environmental protection, and planning controls.

I conceded earlier that there were 'public good' elements in the economy for which state control and subsidy or other intervention might be required. These elements are defined by whether private action alone produces waste: for example, if we allowed competition between railway tracks, we would be wasting resources in having multiple parallel railway tracks. Now, often competition does generate waste in the sense that one can see, certainly after the event, excessive production, but we put up with that because we gain from the trial and error that competition makes possible. For example, in the early days of video recorders, two main systems were in competition (VHS and Betamax) and when in the end just one (VHS) became the popular standard, massive duplication of effort had occurred in developing the other also (though it retains a professional niche). Yet better this waste than have one system imposed without the trial of strength that determines which is the most fitted. This is similar to the waste that occurs in Darwinian selection.

Nevertheless, we may wish to draw the line if we can gather enough information to take a group choice where large costs are imposed by such competition. Essentially, what we are doing in these cases is intruding an additional cost into the social calculation that is not properly reflected in the marketplace. Having made the social calculation we then interfere somehow – by law, subsidy, tax or whatever – to force the private actions into line with the outcome of that calculation.

In a free society, one would ideally like to dispense with such interference by getting market prices to reflect all costs – but it might not be practicable. For instance, in the case of railway tracks the cost of duplication not reflected in the private calculations would be the congestion of the territory, the environmental deprivation of land for other purposes. These costs are widely spread among people using this land for uncharged purposes – recreation say. We could make such use of land chargeable: farmers could levy a toll on walkers, birdwatchers and others, which currently they cannot as such use is protected under the common law. Then the land value would be greater, reflecting these tolls; and then the railway companies would have to pay more, making them more likely to agree on a joint railway track.

The pioneering, and in many ways definitive, work on this issue was that of Ronald Coase (1960), an economist whose life's work has been the study of the interaction between law and economics. He argued that where the 'transactions costs' of awarding such property rights (above the ability to levy a toll on users of land) were low, they were a method of getting the optimal (non-wasteful) use of resources and thus made state intervention unnecessary. These transactions costs are the 'hassle' essentially of levying the charges in our example; they are the costs of carrying out business (transactions) in this way.

Here we have the nub of the case for state intervention in these 'public good' elements. If the assigning of property rights is just too much trouble ('imposes excessive transactions costs'), then the state can legitimately intervene to 'correct' the private misallocation of resources. But notice that even in this case it still has to establish that the waste is not justified by considerations of natural selection – what we may call 'dynamic' considerations – because in the long run you get less resources overall (and so less growth and dynamism) if you suppress the waste involved in competition.

A free society therefore imposes on itself a double test for intervention. First, it checks that it has used prices (via the assignation of property rights) as much as is justified by transaction costs. Secondly, it checks that any waste apparent because that process has been to some extent prevented is not justified by the potential end-result of the process of competition. These two checks then define the 'minimal state' in these matters of economic intervention.

Have we any examples? It is hard to feel that any country in the world has got to this purely minimalist level. Clearly, within Europe, the UK is an example of low regulation in both goods and labour markets, as documented in a recent study by Koedijk and Kremers (1996), which also shows that there has been a correlation between low regulation and higher growth in the past few decades. The UK's practices are broadly true of Anglo-Saxon countries generally, no doubt because of their shared common law tradition.

Nevertheless, we can insist on the rigorous application of our two principles to proposed regulations and other interventions as a way of reducing further the level of regulation. The technology of transactions is constantly changing, making possible more imaginative methods of assigning property rights (that is, in effect, charging for things). A good example is road charging, which can now (or very soon will, once teething troubles are ironed out) be made to deal finely with urban and motorway congestion – something only possible because of the computer revolution. (Chips with everything and now in our very roads!) We have seen UK privatisations that managed to create competition in previously unheard-of areas by ingenious institutional invention – for instance, electricity generation, and the 'electricity pool' of daily generated electricity, which acts as an auction market within the UK's national grid for tranches of generation capacity. Property rights can be spread wider and wider as a consequence. Hence the possibilities are ever increasing for a reduction in the scope of state regulation and a corresponding increase in the scope of the market.

THE EFFICIENCY GAIN OF A FREE SOCIETY

A free society has obvious purely political attractions; to be left alone to pursue our lives according to our own choices is itself a huge enhancement of them. We hate to be bossed around, even when the bosses are telling us to do what we would have freely chosen (Sutherland, 1992, pp 115–17). But there is also an economic gain from freedom (which in turn, of course, adds to its political attractions). It comes from the fact that the efficiency of the economy is reduced, the higher is taxation and the more there is state redistribution in cash and kind from taxpayers to those identified as 'poor', because these things reduce incentives among both taxpayers and the poor themselves.

There are two types of efficiency to be distinguished. One, 'static efficiency', concerns the amount of output that can be produced with available knowledge and the effectiveness of its use. Better incentives to work will induce more people into the labour market and more work from those within it, and this in turn will induce more investment to take advantage of it, and more is therefore produced. At the same time, what is produced should be better used by consumers, who know their own needs, than by a remote government on their behalf. Static efficiency therefore improves on what can be produced and used within the limits of knowledge from available resources: mainly skilled and unskilled labour and land in the economy, plus any capital and raw materials brought in to supplement those locally available.

But there is also 'dynamic efficiency'. This concerns the rapidity with which knowledge accumulates and so raises productivity growth. A dynamic society is one in which those who have the talent to acquire and spread knowledge (usually by application) are strongly motivated to do so by consequential rewards. These need not be monetary, but of course money is the most generally effective of them because it can be turned into any form the recipient wants. Status rewards (honours, titles, social esteem, etc) are also effective up to a point, but they do not work for all and their method of allocation (committees of the 'great and good', for instance) do not always appeal to potential innovators.

We all know what is meant by a dynamic society. Hong Kong and the US spring to mind. In them, it is possible to make a fortune from innovation; taxes and government interference are low. Statistical demonstration that these are the causes of dynamism is difficult because of the plethora of factors that might be at work. However, we can appeal to a wealth of experience from economic history (explored, for example, by North in a series of studies, eg, 1990), which confirms what economic theory would suggest to us – that the greater the reward, the greater the innovatory effort by those who have the potential, and therefore the greater the likelihood of innovatory results. What is even more difficult is to quantify the connection between lower taxes, say, and a faster rate of innovation. But that there is an important connection would be dangerous (if not impossible) to deny.

What I will do in the remainder of this chapter is to gather together the crude statistical evidence available over all countries and episodes of history to check the prediction of the hypothesis that the freer a society is, the greater its static and dynamic efficiency. I check first dynamic efficiency by correlating an index of freedom for a country over a period of history with its per capita growth rate over the same period, and I do this across all country-periods we can find data for. Secondly, I check total (static and dynamic) efficiency by correlating the same index of freedom (averaged now over the full country's recorded history) with its current level of per capita income. The point of the latter test is that the longer a country has been relatively free, the more years of higher growth (dynamic efficiency) it has clocked up and the longer it has had to generate static efficiency in the use of available resources. Similar tests can be found in Scully (1992) and Gwartney and Lawson (1997).

The latter two authors' work is of particular interest. They have brought together a consortium of 47 free-market institutes around the world under the auspices of the Fraser Institute in Canada to compile an agreed index of economic freedom, together with other general economic statistics. Figures 1.1 and 1.2 show their results by quintile for per capita growth during 1986–96 and per capita GNP in 1996 against an index of economic freedom in 1995. Figure 1.3 shows a scatter diagram by country for its growth during 1985–94 against the average of its economic-freedom index during this period (1985, 1990 and 1995), as suggested in our test. Figure 1.4 shows the scatter by country of GNP per capita in 1995 against the same average economic freedom index. Table 1.1 shows a variety of statistical relationships along the lines shown within these figures.

These correlations are tests of our (monocausal) theory: that freedom via corresponding incentives generates both faster innovation in knowledge and greater utilisation of available resources, given existing knowledge. This theory is a 'deep' or 'high-level' one (according to one's taste in hierarchies). In other words, it is not about the mechanics, the 'proximate' determinants, of growth – what inputs in what quantities and combinations, including such things as capital, technology, skill and education, are needed to produce what output (the concern of much of 'growth theory') – but rather it is about the institutions that produce these inputs in greater quantity and at higher quality. In effect, it is a theory of the economic energy that gets turned into inputs: institutions

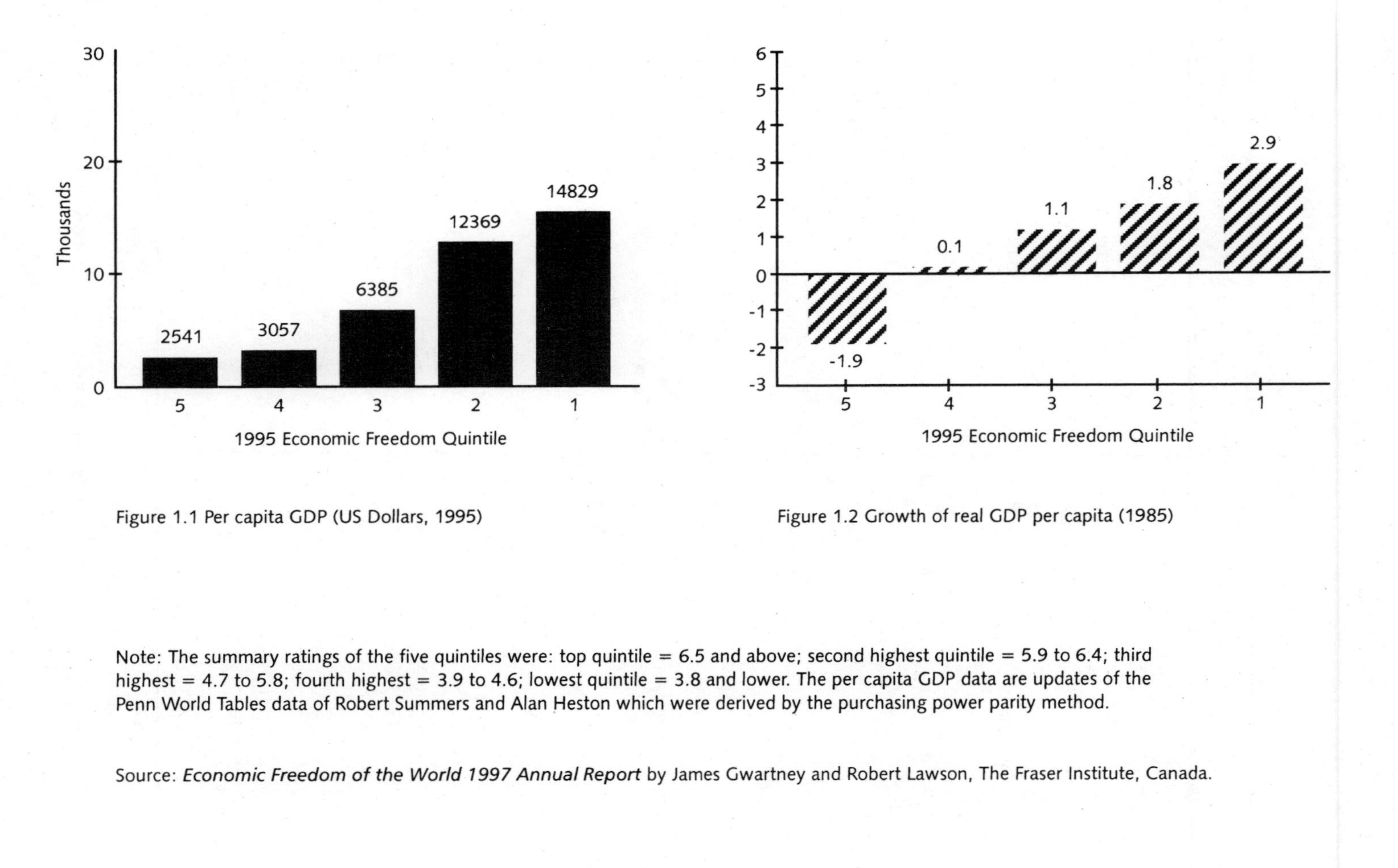

Figure 1.1 Per capita GDP (US Dollars, 1995)

Figure 1.2 Growth of real GDP per capita (1985)

Note: The summary ratings of the five quintiles were: top quintile = 6.5 and above; second highest quintile = 5.9 to 6.4; third highest = 4.7 to 5.8; fourth highest = 3.9 to 4.6; lowest quintile = 3.8 and lower. The per capita GDP data are updates of the Penn World Tables data of Robert Summers and Alan Heston which were derived by the purchasing power parity method.

Source: *Economic Freedom of the World 1997 Annual Report* by James Gwartney and Robert Lawson, The Fraser Institute, Canada.

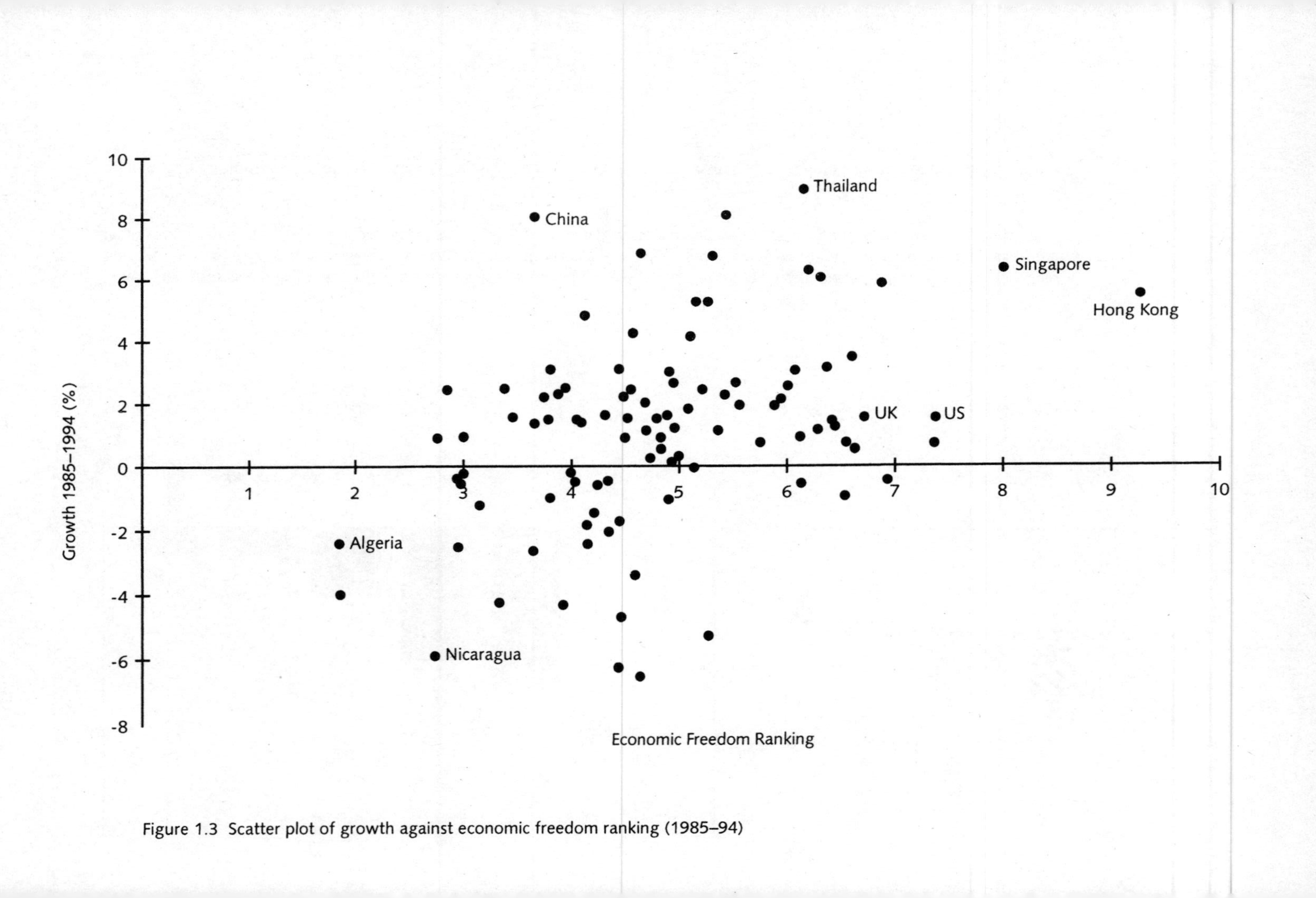

Figure 1.3 Scatter plot of growth against economic freedom ranking (1985–94)

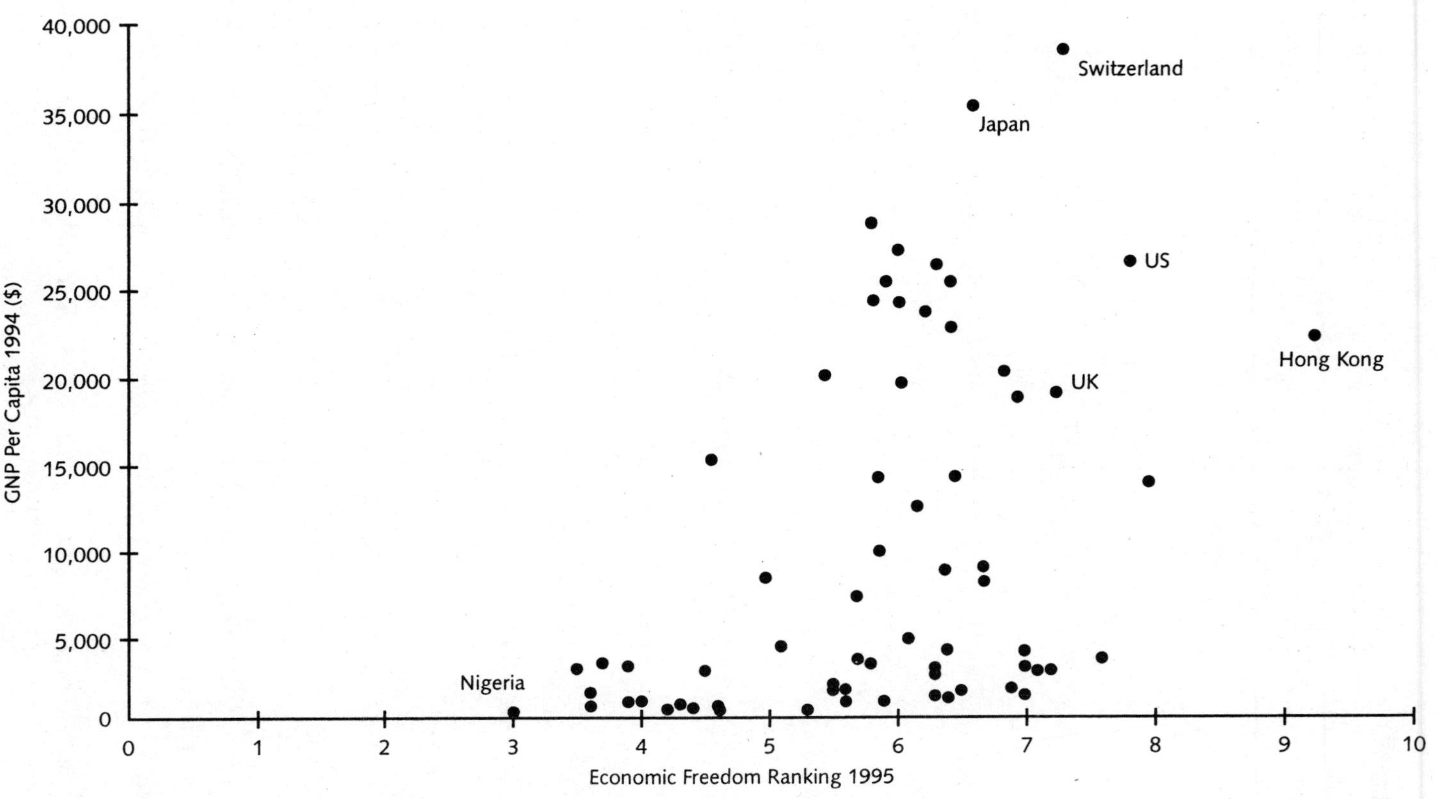

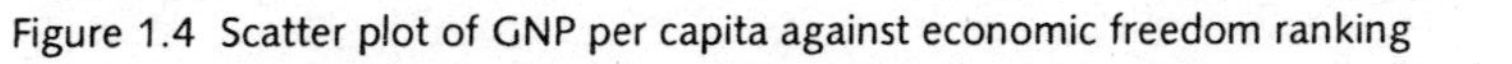
Figure 1.4 Scatter plot of GNP per capita against economic freedom ranking

Dependent Variable	Constant	Independent Variable		Number of Countries	R^2
G8594	-3.25 (1.19)	0.87 (0.23)	ECFR8595	95	0.13
G8594	-4.95 (1.12)	1.10 (0.20)	ECFR95	95	0.25
G8096	-0.37 (1.06)	0.39 (0.20)	ECFR8095	69	0.05
G8096	-1.26 (1.18)	0.48 (0.20)	ECFR95	69	0.08
LPCGNP94	0.85 (0.81)	4.10 (0.48)	LFR95	96	0.43
LPCGNP94	1.97 (0.87)	3.64 (0.54)	LFR8595	96	0.32
LPCGNP94	2.47 (0.89)	3.39 (0.57)	LFR8095	96	0.27

Notation:		
	G8594	Growth % p.a. 1985–94
	G8096	Growth % p.a. 1980–96
	LPCGNP94	Log of per capita GNP 1994
	ECFR8095	Economic Freedom Index, average of 1980, 1985, 1990, 1995
	ECFR8595	Economic Freedom Index, average of 1985, 1990, 1995
	ECFR95	Economic Freedom Index for 1995
	(LFR95 etc. Log of economic freedom indices as above)	

Table 1.1 Statistically estimated relationship between growth, per capita GNP and Economic Freedom Index[+]

Sources: *World Bank World Development Report data tapes*; Gwartney and Lawson (1977)

[+] Ordinary least squares regression of dependent variable growth, or per capita GDP, on a constant and independent variable, Economic Freedom Index:
dependent variable=constant + coefficient x independent variable
Figures in parenthesis are standard errors

that are free and so embody larger rewards for individual effort and initiative produce more economic energy. As by-products of this process, one would expect to see more skill, more education, more capital, better technology and so forth; but these are not the basic causes of the growth.

The statistical correlations of course prove nothing. Other researchers with different pet ideas could no doubt find correlations between growth and some X-factor. The problem we have in these statistical correlations is that other factors are not held constant and that therefore it is possible that some such factor is also correlated with growth. There may be many such good correlations between growth and different X-factors – we know, for instance, that growth is associated with more education, better health, and so on. Although we would argue here that these are the result of higher growth, it is open to others to argue that they are the causes of higher growth; plainly there is no way of distinguishing statistically between these associations. So my point is merely to show that the statistics are not inconsistent with our theory, which I put forward as reasonable in its own terms. By this I mean that I believe I can persuade others to believe it, whereas I might have more difficulty doing so with some other putative X-factor – say, culture or genetic make-up.

More serious tests of the theory will be presented in later chapters, when we examine the evidence from the UK, where a marked policy shift, first towards socialism and then sharply away from it towards a free society, gives us an opportunity to see the effects of the institutional shift largely unobscured by movements in other factors. Further, we will examine the evidence from the European mainland (such as Germany, which we have already briefly discussed) where policies of a 'stakeholder' variety have systematically been adopted in the past few decades, and indeed to a greater or lesser extent through most of their history – although Germany had an instructive episode after the Second World War when it adopted much freer institutions in the famous *Wirtschaftswunder* period ushered in by Erhard and Adenauer.

This sort of evidence is that on which we place the greatest emphasis. Nevertheless the crude international correlations are of interest, at least in the negative sense that they demonstrate that the theory is not inconsistent with the data.

References

Berlin, Sir Isaiah (1967) 'Two Concepts of Liberty', *Political Philosophy*, ed. A. Quinton (Oxford Readings in Philosophy), Oxford University Press, Oxford.

Coase, R. (1960) 'The Problem of Social Cost', *The Journal of Law and Economics*, 3, pp 1–44.

Gwartney, J. and Lawson, R. (1997) *Economic Freedom of the World 1997*, co-published by Fraser Institute, Vancouver, BC, Canada, and free-market institutes in 46 other countries.

Hutton, W. (1995) *The State We're In*, Jonathan Cape, London.

Kay, J. (1997) *Community Values and the Market Economy*, Social Market Foundation, London.

Koedijk, K. and Kremers, J.J.M. (1996) *Market Opening, Regulation and Growth in Europe*, Research Memorandum 9607, OCFEB, Research Centre for Economic Policy, Erasmus University, Rotterdam.

North, D. (1990) *Institutions, Institutional Change and Economic Performance*, Cambridge University Press, New York.

Scully, G. W. (1992) *Constitutional Environments and Economic Growth*, Princeton University Press, Princeton.

Sutherland, S. (1992) *Irrationality – the Enemy Within*, Constable, London.

CHAPTER TWO

The moral and political fundamentals of a free society

THIS CHAPTER ATTEMPTS to tackle the difficult questions of value that are often raised about capitalism by its critics. Capitalism allows, by definition, wages and prices to be determined by market forces; hence the distribution of income, via the fortunes of workers and of shareholders, is set by the market. Its critics typically argue that this will in general violate the demands of morality and social justice. Let us for the present leave aside issues of just how capitalist systems behave, as modified or not by different systems of social insurance. What I wish to focus on in this chapter is just what principles we appeal to when we accept or reject such systems.

There is of course nothing to stop you, me, or anyone else, including professors of moral philosophy (as happened to me in one debate), telling the world what we believe to be right or wrong, moral or immoral, socially just or unjust. The difficulty lies in the weight these statements carry: some are widely assented to, others are ignored by the great mass of people. And it is what the great mass of people accept that determines what actually happens, the system we actually have. Nothing I can say in this book will ever convince a left-wing professor of moral philosophy that capitalism is 'right'; that is not my purpose. Rather, it is to argue that capitalism has the ability to attract the support of the great mass of people.

This ability – this long-term political attractiveness and survival capacity – is partly the result of how capitalist systems behave, partly the result of people's actual values, and partly the result of how people – usually in groups – interact in society. Most of this book is about how capitalist systems behave. But this chapter is an attempt to consider people's actual values and their social interaction. 'What people will accept' is therefore its topic: this is the important question. And it is not necessarily the same as 'what people believe to be morally right', although obviously one would expect there to be a large overlap. The point is that people take decisions not merely on explicitly moral grounds.

Suppose that we establish a certain sort of system as to what people tend to accept; and then someone argues, on grounds culled from a value system (for example invoking Rawls' 'veil of ignorance' principle), that this system is wrong – as Robin Marris has in a recent book (1996). What do we say? I suggest that this person's views are legitimate but irrelevant to 'the acceptability' of the system. In short, if people want it, they will get it even if there are some demonstrable moral grounds on which they should not want it – and morality cannot anyway be 'demonstrated' in such a way. The most that one could say would be that if enough people became convinced that the system was wrong, then its acceptability could fade. It is really only in this sense that moral issues are relevant to what we are assessing here, which is to repeat what people will actually accept.

Finally, how do I intend to approach this question? I fear very simply, simplistically even. I propose to record my own impressions based partly on general argument but mainly on observation. There is nothing here that could be dignified by the term 'philosophy' – moral or political; I leave that to my academic colleagues. Rather, I want to put together an account of what we observe in political and social practice and provide a rationale for it. Inevitably, my observation is concentrated on UK experience; but then that is quite informative since it contains so much experiment.

It is tempting, in a book such as this mainly about economics and economic policy, to ignore all political and social practice and go straight on to economic material, as if it was obvious what people value in this domain. Some readers may wish to do just that and skip to the next chapter. But manifestly values are a matter of wide controversy and other readers will want to pause to consider just why it is appropriate to proceed as we do in later chapters. Hence this chapter on values.

MORALS

In this section, I set out the facts as I see them about people's values: what people want from their lives and therefore what will guide them in accepting or rejecting political and economic systems. I am concerned with values of the generality of people. This means that, in an age when many are not religious in the conventional sense, we must discuss the values of those who are not religious as well – I shall call them 'humanist'. I begin with them; but I will argue that they share in all essentials the values of the religious.

Write down a series of deep philosophical questions. What is the meaning of life? What is good? What is truth? Those religiously inclined answer them by assuming an overarching power in the universe, whose designs man is part of. The power may be good (the Christian God), evil (the 'cruel' god of the Iago in Verdi's *Otello*), or indifferent (as in Buddhism); but power it is and man ignores it at his peril. From it are derived principles of conduct, canons of truth, and purposes of life.

The humanist is defined as one who, even though denying the existence of such a power, attempts to answer these questions otherwise, namely by reference to the condition of man. The existentialist, for example, argues that man, by virtue of his brief life, only lives for the moment, and therefore should make the most of each moment (Camus, 1942). Closely related is the Epicurean principle (following Epicurus in the fourth century BC): maximising the pleasure/profit/'utility' from actions. The Kantian derives from the structure of man's discourse the principles by which he is guided (Kant, 1788): the 'moral imperative', for example, comes from the universalist language of moral statements. Oxford 'linguistic' philosophy follows in that tradition: it answers the questions linguistically – what do we in practice mean by 'truth' etc (eg, Austin, 1961)? Then there is Nietzsche, who argued (eg, 1883-91) that man's role was perfectibility: by improving himself (and through eugenics, we might say today, his genetic material), he could attain the status of god on earth. Modern genetics have told us that this is no longer a cranky idea, and we shall return to this matter after investigating more promising humanist avenues.

Another way of approaching the matter from a humanist viewpoint is to ask what people actually do. That is, we may learn something from the actions and revealed purposes of people. For the moment, then, we will abandon the questions of what people ought to do, what is good, what is the proper purpose of life, in favour of the more humdrum, limited question: what *do* people do, what is their actual purpose as revealed by their actions?

Immediate puzzles present themselves for the existentialist and the epicurean. People sacrifice themselves for their country, for their children. People labour to produce artistic end-products – music, poetry, pictures – for little gain, but apparently hoping that future generations will prize them. We educate our children, often at great expense, we devote resources to them in their upbringing and entertainment: why? It is a cost, and they will often desert us before too long.

We value the good opinions of our colleagues and our neighbours. We value our reputations. Why? As Falstaff puts it in *Henry IV, Part 1*, 'What is honour? Mere air, mere words.' It does not fit with any ideas of self-indulgence. In George Eliot's *Middlemarch*, the businessman Bulstrode is utterly devastated when his neighbours discover his dreadful past, and they shun him in spite of his good works for the community. He is of course a fictional character, and if one is critical of Eliot it would be to ask why this man, while aiming to create a position for himself as local benefactor, would take the risk of doing base acts which must surely in the end be exposed, if only after his death? The ruin of Bulstrode serves to point up the futility of deceit in the attempt to achieve a measure of immortality.

The politician wishes to 'write himself or herself into the history books', the actor to become another Irving or Olivier, commemorated in legend or video, the singer a Joan Sutherland, and so on.

Before we get carried away, we also note our human's propensity to mere pleasure or other self-indulgence. He or she gets distracted from the noble aim of immortality by the brute desires of the moment – shouts in anger at a treasured colleague, sleeps around, and so on. The process seems to mirror exactly the struggles of Bunyan's Pilgrim, gripped by the religious battle between godliness and sin.

This is irony indeed. Humanists, freed from religious scruple, observe that humanity is obsessed, first, by a desire to do good that will be recognised for some time at least by fellow humans but, secondly, also by guilt from regular failure. Let us call these two modes of action the duty and the pleasure principles. We all know examples of people driven more by the one than the other: 'he never relaxes', 'she let herself go and now life is all golf and bridge'. Most manage some sort of balance, tilting one way or the other – to do a good job, to have grateful clients or students or children, to be remembered with liking and respect by colleagues, friends, family and acquaintances, and then to have a good time, to eat, drink and be merry, for tomorrow... 'You cannot take it with you: enjoy it.' 'Life's but a poor player that struts and frets his hour upon the stage and then is heard no more. It is a tale told by an idiot, full of sound and fury, signifying nothing.'

The latter are the desperate and insincere words of those who failed in the duty principle. Shakespeare's Macbeth, after all, strove for the crown, so hoping for his respected place in history. He failed, then spoke those words. The writer of the hedonistic Arabian verses (such as Omar Khayyam, 1048-1122, whose *Rubaiyat* was made famous by Edward Fitzgerald's translation in 1859) was playing out a fashionable role for the rich aristocrats of Arabia. Sure of their place in society and its history, their hedonism was a way of adding elegance and spectacle to their passing show. Thus even in the heart of the pleasure principle, one finds the effects of the duty principle.

Nor can there be any doubt which takes precedence in our minds: duty, of course. Pleasure is all right in its place – necessary relaxation to ensure the proper functioning of body and soul, but no more. More is indulgence.

This is the crudest of descriptions of human behaviour; no doubt we could enrich it greatly. The point is that we justify our actions to ourselves in terms of the duty principle – we are acting for the good of our family, we are doing something useful for our community, for the human race, we will leave something behind us that we will be remembered by, and other such. The pleasure principle intrudes – we like to enjoy ourselves but if the enjoyment goes beyond some (let us call it) 'maintenance' level, we feel guilt, which is of course the manifestation of the dominance of the duty principle.

The duty principle is therefore the ultimate organising principle of human conduct. This, I am suggesting, is a fact. It is in no way inconsistent with Adam Smith's idea that people pursue self-interest and that the market co-ordinates their actions so that they thereby contribute to the interests of others. The point here is that the 'self-interest' Smith is talking about is the actual objectives of the individual: these are justified by him to himself in the terms that I have described – family, ambition, and so on. Of course, by the same argument, those individuals who do work that is explicitly charitable are not particularly to be distinguished in their motivation from those who do not. This is an astonishing thing. The butcher, the baker, the candlestick maker, all are engaged in doing things that they feel will leave their mark – in whatever way, be it ever so small – on their society.

And what then of the 'alienated' – the criminal, the hooligan, those who get pleasure from destroying what others have or are creating – be it the pleasant streets that they litter, the houses that they rob, or the peaceful atmosphere that they fill with noise? Are they inspired by the duty principle? Clearly, in a direct sense they are not; they are rejecting it explicitly in favour of outright pleasure. But are they not reacting to a situation, as they perceive it, where there is no possibility for them to carry out any 'duty'? Iago, their Shakespearean standard-bearer, has been passed over for justified promotion, he feels bitter, rejected. Leave aside the difficulty of making this character plausible, one sees what Shakespeare was trying to depict.

The apparent irrationality, often violent, of people who react in this way can perhaps be explained in terms of their frustration at being unable to do any duty. Denied their defining human activity, they succumb to despairing anger. Duty is sovereign, after all – most so when she gives no opportunity to obey her.

This view of human behaviour seems quite consistent with the survival instinct attributed by some biologists to DNA – as argued by Richard Dawkins (1995). According to this view, genes are instructed by their DNA to act in a way that ensures the greatest probability of the DNA's survival. If that were so, it would not be surprising if human actions tended to ensure the interests of the species. They would be obeying deep-seated instincts.

I am not committed to any such 'reductionist' position. The genetic explanation is interesting but not essential. The fact seems to be that this is how we behave. We might want to ask how it is that we go to war, or put one group's interests above another's. But this is not obviously a problem: we identify with communities in some hierarchy (family, tribe, country, continent and so on – as pointed out by Samuel Brittan, 1996, pp.78–80), and no doubt genes have some similar species hierarchy.

Now, if this is a good description of our behaviour, it does not follow that we *ought* to behave like this. Logically, an 'ought' statement differs from an 'is' statement, as Hume first pointed out. However, suppose we had discovered a law of nature – such as the law that we must all die. Then the question of 'ought' does not arise. One cannot say: 'You ought not to die' or even 'You ought to try not to die' (as opposed to 'You should not expose yourself to the danger of dying early'). If something is out of our control, then its morality does not arise.

It might be said that a general tendency to certain behaviour could not amount to such a law. After all, as we have seen, not everyone obeys the duty principle. Nevertheless most do, and those who do not often appear to flaunt their rejection of it out of frustration. To compel those who do by some moral command not to do so would be bizarre, equivalent to saying to someone, 'Thou shalt harm thyself'. They would not take any notice.

Therefore, there is a sense in which it does not arise. The sense is that although it would be possible, in a physical sense, for people to act against their nature, they would not in practice be willing to do so. Such a 'morality' would have no shelf life. Of course, what we frequently find is that morality reinforces people's normal actions. This is not surprising, since morality that was regularly transgressed would cease to command respect – much as laws of that sort lose credibility.

In sum, we observe that people actually pursue the duty principle. What is more, they regard actions that are consistent with that principle as right, and feel guilt if such actions instead are overridden by the pleasure principle – that is, such overruling is regarded by them as wrong. We cannot conclude from these observations that such actions are right and that their overruling is wrong; for indeed one cannot deduce an 'ought' from an 'is', as a matter of logic. But if we were to say that such actions were right etc, no one would disagree with us, it seems.

Let us therefore state that moral principles as enunciated by people reinforce the duty principle. As noted earlier, there seems to be little difference between the moral statements made by humanists and those who are religious (within most religions practised by most people at any rate). Religious people also prize what will produce permanent benefits to mankind. Sometimes their hierarchies within mankind will differ, but not much in practice – during wars each antagonist thinks God is on his side, hence confirming that even the religious follow their natural hierarchy.

The values of permanent achievement for which people strive and which they regard as right give us a helpful yardstick for evaluating economic systems in a way that will command wide agreement, including moral assent. This yardstick implies that 'time preference' (more preferred now than later) does not apply to decisions comparing the effects on future generations with current effects. For example, someone who sacrifices their current living standard in order to provide for the education of their children and their grandchildren is showing 'negative time preference' across his own and the next generations. This suggests that the very long-term effects of policy changes – if they can be established – will command wide interest. This is most obviously relevant to taxes such as inheritance tax that affect one generation's behaviour towards long-term issues; but it is, as we shall argue, a key factor in the acceptability of free market policies generally, since these often have their main effects in the very long term.

THE POLITICALLY SUCCESSFUL SOCIETY [1]

We now turn from the matter of personal values to the matter of social

[1] This section is adapted and abridged from 'A positive theory of rights', which appeared as Chapter 16 in my *The Supply Side Revolution in Britain* (Edward Elgar, 1991).

organisation and political values: how do people interact and to what sort of political structures does this create a tendency? We do this in order to understand what it is that makes policies acceptable to people, in the sense that they endure within a society: this is what is meant by 'political success'. We start by considering the basic social notion of 'rights'.

The concept of rights

What is a man's right? Does he have a right to a job? Does he have a right to enjoy clean air? To be spared loud noises by passers-by in the middle of the night? To commit suicide? To pass his property on to his children without penal taxation? To be protected against theft and physical threats? To have a vote? To vote in a referendum on some major issue – or on all issues? To have any religious beliefs he pleases? To have any beliefs? To avoid fighting as a conscript for his country on any grounds, on grounds of 'conscientious objection', or not at all?'

What is immediately clear when one asks these questions about randomly chosen 'rights' is that the answers, where they are agreed, differ across countries – even within parts of some countries – and they have differed over time within the same country. Further, the answers are not, in many cases, agreed at all in many places.

Considerations of morality may well be associated with particular rights at a particular time and place, but 'what is morally right' and 'what is right' are different classes of things. It may be my right, say, because it is within the province of my 'private life', to break a promise to my children, but it may equally well not be morally right to do so. It may be morally right for me to help someone to commit suicide, but I may not have a right to do so. I seek not a 'normative' but a 'positive' theory of rights; in fact, I will argue later that the role of morals in political success is essentially secondary, that what is politically acceptable is based on people's interests, and that these too dictate the structure of actual rights.

Suppose a woman wishes to establish what her rights are; how does she set about doing so? The answer to this is quite straightforward. She must find out how the law stands. Her rights are what the law permits and enforces. Just to be quite clear about this, let me answer, in order, the questions posed in our first paragraph, even though my answers will be tentative (I am not a lawyer and, in any case, they may need to be tested in a court) and will be special to the UK in 1997 (even, in some cases, England). Our theoretical person does not have a right to a job; she cannot force anyone, any corporation, or the state, to provide her with one. She may offer herself for any job that is, or she thinks may be, available, but that is all. And so we could go on – enumerating the scope and provenance of the law of the land.

A person's 'rights' – or 'the law' – are those things that person is permitted to do by the civil power, whatever that may be. That civil power can take many forms, from the autocratic whim of a sole ruler all the way to the complex and divided powers of a modern democracy.

Our enquiry could now take two directions. First, we could ask, 'What is good law?', 'What rights ought a person to have?' and similar questions which, among other things, involve the morality of different laws or rights. Secondly, we could ask, 'What sort of civil power will occur, permitting what sort of rights?', 'What are the sources of civil power?' and similar questions concerned with the causality of different laws or rights.

We shall take the second direction, that of causality. Causality is logically prior to morality, for what is good must be conditioned by what is possible. As we saw above, death cannot be bad or good; it simply is inevitable and the 'morality' of it does not arise. Nor will it be any use decrying a particular form of power or state if it cannot be avoided. Furthermore, before we recommend that a particular form should occur, we must know how it could be brought into being, what difficulties this would involve, etc.

Many authors have considered what states, rights and laws ought to exist. We will speculate only on what states are, are likely to be, and why. To do so, we have to argue in a more abstract way than up to now, when considering people's personal values. One reason is that we are too familiar with current society (ie, modern democratic society) to think easily about why it is like it is. The other reason is that there are all sorts of societies – not all Western, and not all democratic. So we must perforce launch ourselves into a more theoretical discussion. Again, I refer the impatient reader onwards to the next chapter.

The basis of civil power

Civil power, henceforth 'power' for short, is the subject of much art (particularly drama), usually describing the evils produced for those wielding it, as well as for those over whom it is wielded. 'Power corrupts; absolute power corrupts absolutely', we have been told.

In Wagner's *The Ring of the Nibelungen*, first performed in 1876, Richard Wagner allegorises power in the ring forged from the Rhinegold. Gods, dwarves, giants and men struggle for possession of the ring. Originally, it is won from its keepers in the Rhine by the swearing of an unnatural oath ('to forswear love'). Then it is stolen from the winner, and this illegitimate act brings a curse on the ring, which dominates the story to its ending in the destruction of the old world and the power of the old gods. The ring returns to its keepers in the Rhine, and the world to a new beginning. The implication is that power, seized unnaturally from its dormant state in nature, falls into the wrong hands and causes great evil, ultimately destroying itself and all who attempt to control it. Only a state of nature, in which power is not wielded – at least in a manner that involves 'domination', whatever that may be – will cause no harm and survive.

Contrast this vision with that of Thomas Hobbes (1651): in the state of nature, life is 'nasty, brutish, and short'. Power is necessary to prevent men from killing and thieving from each other. Individuals give it to some person or body of people for this purpose. Robert Nozick's argument (1974) follows the same lines as Hobbes'. Men surrender some of their 'natural rights' (ie they submit to a civil power) in order to achieve protection for their remaining rights.

There are three questions I should like to answer about power:

1. Must it exist at all, and if so, why?
2. What type of person or group will hold it and why?
3. How much power will he or they have, and why?

The first question is one to which many great minds have addressed themselves, namely the existence of power or the 'state' at all and its reasons. The widespread answer that has emerged has been the theory of the social contract, as set out, for example, in Nozick and summarised above.

The second and third questions have been addressed less often and less systematically. Clearly, they form a large part of the subject matter of history, but historians have preferred (perhaps rightly) to chronicle the particular and not to seek general explanations. Political theorists, too, have tended to concentrate on the answers for given institutions, mostly in modern times those of democracy and, in earlier times, those of monarchy (in Greek times those of the 'city state'). One general theory has been proposed by Michael Oakeshott (1975). He argues that if a society is composed for the most part of independent-minded people who prize their self-fulfilment, it will tend to be a *societas* where the citizens have submitted merely to a set of rules in the pursuit of their own interests. If it is composed of people who value security above self-fulfilment, it will tend to be a *universitas*, where the citizens regard the state as the active provider of common economic and physical security. To Oakeshott, the nature of the state thus derives from the character of its citizens. We shall consider this seminal idea further below.

We shall attempt to find general answers. These will necessarily be about long-run tendencies, not particular (short-run) situations. We shall try to formulate 'laws' of the form: 'such and such will happen in the long run under such and such (rather general) conditions'. This type of theorising is common in economics when 'equilibrium outcomes' are investigated – ie, outcomes which, once arrived at, are self-perpetuating (as distinct from others which are self-destructive). We shall also have something to say – though probably rather sketchily – about whether these equilibrium outcomes are likely to be arrived at and, if so, how; what in economics is commonly described as 'stability analysis', in other words an analysis of whether or not a political system will be driven towards the 'stable', self-perpetuating state or away from it into a series of self-destructive states.

The conditions for power to emerge

The question, 'Must power exist?' is generally taken to be co-extensive with 'Can a state of nature (in which there is no power) be self-perpetuating?' We shall see later that the questions are *not* the same but we shall start as if they are.

The usual answer to the latter question is, 'No, a state of nature cannot survive.' But this does not seem to be correct.[2] Let us begin by constructing a counter-example. Imagine a community of smallholders where each family farms their own plot. With given-sized plots, each farms this plot to the point where the extra crops yielded by a given effort (a diminishing output) just equals the pain of that extra effort.

Each is concerned to protect their possessions, so they buy weapons, dogs etc, sufficient to deter any other farming family from thieving or taking anything forcibly. Now we seem to get in a difficulty. Must a farmer not guard against a combination, by all the others, to despoil him and divide up his possessions between them? That indeed he must do, for if he does not, the others have an incentive to pick him off. This is the worst aggression (internally within the community) he can face. So he arms himself sufficiently to deal with it.

The farmer may do this in various ways. He may buy powerful enough weaponry, for himself and his family to operate. Or he may enter into a private alliance with other farmers (at most, half of them would be enough) for mutual defence in this contingency. Or he may enter into an alliance with a few farmers and invest in less powerful weaponry.

[2] Anthony de Jasay's *The State* (1985) makes this point powerfully. *See also* his *Against Politics* (1977).

How will such an alliance be 'policed' by its members? It is policed by itself; each member comes to the help of a threatened member because if he fails to do so, the agreement is that he will cease to obtain the help of the alliance. With such an agreement, it pays no member to avoid helping the threatened member; for if he helps, he is one of many risking little, whereas if he does not, he loses the help of the others and risks being threatened himself without help. Since it pays each to behave so, then the others will expect this behaviour from each other and they will then have confidence in the agreement. By this means, the agreement will be kept and expected by all to be kept, so providing security.

Exactly how large such alliances will be will depend on the costs of forming them relative to the costs of sole defence through weaponry alone. Technology and geography will have much to do with it. Suppose there is a super-automatic machine-gun-cum-mortar which, in the hands of one family, can rapidly destroy a large attacking force from a place that cannot be reciprocally attacked. Suppose too that farms are separated by large distances across mountainous country. Then alliances will be minimal and weaponry will be the principal defence of each farmer. There is no 'power' in such a community; it is in a state of nature.

We must now consider the external aspects of the community. Suppose, now, that there is a 'community' in a contiguous region; to make it meaningful, suppose that it is separated by a large mountain range, so that contact is rare and difficult. How does our typical farmer react to this? Does be say, 'Now, not only could all the farmers in my community gang up on me, but so could they plus those in the next community'? How would he modify his defence plan?

He will argue that the members of the other community will also be in a state of mutual deterrence. They will therefore have no incentive to attack each other, but they will have an incentive to join and attack members of his community, including him, if those members are inadequately defended against such a concerted attack. His own alliance-cum-weaponry is designed to counter an internal threat; the agreement does not cover external threat (it could not, because the chances of defeat are too great for the members to have an incentive to deliver help, rather than to surrender or combine with the attacking outsiders). He must therefore install further defences. This time, the maximum threat is of all the members of the other community plus those members of his own community who are not in his alliance, plus at worst (under pressure from such strength) even members of his own alliance.

Can this massive threat be countered without power? Surely it can. For he needs merely to supplement his alliance and weapons with a super-alliance between the alliances within his community. (Grant that technology is unlikely to provide weaponry sufficient for him alone to take on the maximum threat described in the last paragraph.) This super-alliance is an agreement about external threat only; it is subject to the same policing as that of the single alliance. This super-alliance may also specify additional weaponry to be held by members of each alliance.

The super-alliance agreement would specify that if any alliance is attacked by an 'outsider', the other alliances will come to their aid. We now have specified mutual deterrence, both between members of a community, and between communities. Our state of nature is governed by the principle of mutual deterrence. There is still no 'power' in this set-up; no president, no council, no one who can give orders to anyone else. There is therefore no 'state', only a state of nature in which the balance of terror keeps the peace. (There is however 'law', as we shall see.) Compare with this idealised equilibrium the present state of international relations. Here too there is no international government or 'power'. The peace is kept, if it is kept, by mutual deterrence of nations.[3]

According to Locke (1690), there are 'inconveniences of the state of nature', which lead men to create a civil power. What are they? After all, nations can coexist, without an international civil power, with alliances (NATO, Warsaw Pact, CENTO, etc) and through mutual deterrence. Why then cannot individuals? My argument is that it is possible to imagine a community where a state of nature is an equilibrium state. Such a community consists of a set of alliances within a super-alliance (of alliances); the alliances mutually deter individual acts of aggression, and the super-alliance deters external acts of aggression.

To fix this state in our mind's eye as a state of equilibrium, let us depict the life of a typical farmer therein. He goes about his private business, working his plot of land (his 'ranch'), going to market to buy tools, animals and materials, and to sell produce. In these activities, he knows that if his possessions are stolen or he is attacked, he has his weapons and his alliance to call on. Suppose this community is fairly recent; then he will go about his business with some trepidation. When he goes to remote parts of his property or away to market, he may go well-armed and take his most ferocious dog with him, or even only go with his grown-up son or a neighbour.

However, suppose the community has been in existence a long time (he was born into it). People have learned that it does not pay to rob or

[3] Again, de Jasay (1985) makes this point.

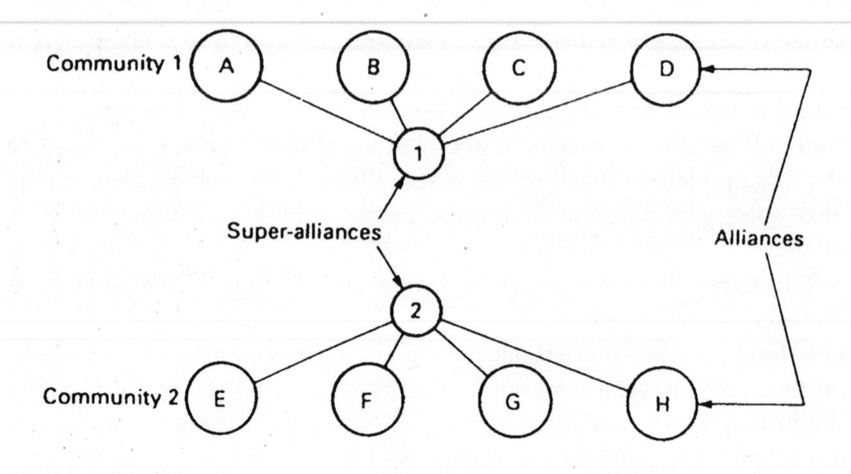

A, B, C, D = groups of citizens forming alliances in Community 1
E, F, G, H = groups of citizens forming alliances in Community 2
1, 2 = super-alliances of A, B, C, D and E, F, G, H

Figure 2.1 Alliance configurations illustrated

attack because the results are unpleasant – for instance, restitution and retribution exerted by the victim's allies. Our farmer now has a sense of security. He will go about his business with little protection (only enough for the outside chance that some fool or newcomer who does not understand the set-up will go for him) or even none at all (he may decide to give in if attacked, secure in the knowledge that his allies will get his property back for him later). We seem to have here, if not a Utopia, at least some sort of Arcadia. Farmers go about their business protected only by 'deterrence'. There are no private armies on the streets or out in the ranches; our farmers do not ride shotgun everywhere. There is but a stock of weaponry at home, to be used in mutual action by an alliance if one of its members is robbed or attacked. Our farmers own things in the state of nature which they turn into other things (produce) and voluntarily exchange with others for things they need.

Widening the Argument

Our argument so far has been strictly confined to the development of a narrow case as a counter-example to the idea that the state of nature cannot be self-perpetuating, namely a geographical area peopled by farmers with a rather primitive technology. The case yielded the result that within this area there would be alliances, linked into super-alliances (communities for self-defence purposes), and that there would be a common law enforced by the people themselves acting within the agreements that formed the alliances. We can distinguish the features of this result from those that others have alleged about the state of nature, especially Nozick with whom our argument has the closest affinity.

But can our argument be generalised, or at least widened in applicability beyond this rather special (and probably untypical) society? We have been trying for our narrow case to give an 'invisible hand' explanation of the law, as Nozick puts it. In other words, our argument has taken the following form:

1. Assume nothing about these farmers, except their initial geographical location, their initial knowledge (technology), and their initial supply of capital (tools, weapons, etc.)
2. Demonstrate that they would be organised (after a time, from whatever initial state) into a common law, not because anyone or any group intended to produce such an outcome but just by the promptings of their own individual interests.

Thus, for our narrow case, the state of nature includes law as one of the manifestations of 'natural', 'unhindered' activity by individuals. This state of nature is an equilibrium, it is self-perpetuating. It is reached from any initial state in which there are no constraints (other than endowments and geography) on persons' actions (ie, from any 'natural' initial stage); it is therefore stable within an unconstrained world, in other words within the set of states of nature.

Would a similar set of statements be possible for any set of people, in any initial geographical location, with any initial knowledge and capital endowment? There was nothing in our argument that hinged on the people being farmers, or on where they were located (plains, mountains), or on what weapons they had access to, or on what tools (with what strength and capability) they would use, or on what knowledge they possessed. We did say that these things would affect the size of alliances (whether, for example, someone could securely go it alone without an alliance at all) and, no doubt, also the nature of the agreements (for example, if fences can be mended by a remotely placed device at low cost and with speed, then breaking fences would not be a violation of rights that would be punished severely, if at all, by an alliance).

It was, in fact, quite easy to explain our argument in terms of farms (ranches) and so on because we all have a common and coherent mental picture (whether derived from Hollywood, from Kipling, from experience, or whatever) of simple agrarian societies. Many of us would find it hard to follow the same steps if we were talking about computer operators, lawyers, bankers and so on realistically coexisting in a complex modern city; the interrelationships would be too complex, for some unfamiliar, and for many hard to imagine shorn of the frequently found constraints on natural activity (whether tyrannical emperors or big-city bureaucrats).

In case the reader is unpersuaded, let us set down an imagined scene in just such a modern city, Londago, but without such constraints. Our heroine, the local hairdresser, lives in a high rise block of flats in Londago; it is guarded by a neighbourhood police force which mounts a 24-hour patrol around the area. Periodically she takes her turn in a roster of 'officers' of this force, to keep an eye on the activities of the hired security men who are unskilled and low paid. Her hairdressing salon is in another part of town, to which she travels by subway; the subway fare includes an element to pay for subway security (a system of alarms, closed-circuit TV and patrols). Arriving at her shop, she enters another neighbourhood protection zone to which she also pays dues; this being mainly a commercial neighbourhood, the technology of protection here is heavier than at home (more like the subway system), with more emphasis on alarms than patrols. Yet, again, she may contribute to a roster of 'officers' of the patrol force.

Her customers generally pay their accounts and if they complain about the quality of haircut or any products she sells, she will generally pay them off (even for some barely justified complaints) for the sake of business goodwill. If a customer perseveres in not paying an account after the usual two or three demands spaced at monthly intervals, the commercial-zone police in which she has a share will take up the case, approaching the customer directly in the first instance. Usually this is enough, but on occasions where nothing happens, the zone police refer the case to the customer's zone police force. The case then is usually referred by the two forces to a local arbitration house with which many of these forces have a contract for settlement of disputes.

Our various zone police forces have at times considered a merger into a full-time professional force to do all duties, since the hairdresser and some others have complained half-seriously about the hours spent in tedious and 'unproductive' protection duties. They have turned the idea down because of the fear that such a force could get out of control of its citizens, perhaps be corrupted by enemies, and even attempt to pursue the interests of its own commanders to acquire property and power. Nevertheless, various zone forces have merged into larger forces to save costs, taking a risk on these other aspects.

And so on. The features we found in our simple agrarian state of nature reproduce themselves here in a more complex form. Our argument is perfectly general for the explanation of law emerging within a state of nature.

Accounting for other states

However, we are still far from a full explanation of rights. That 'the law will emerge from a state of nature of whatever form' is a useful statement. But we wish to know also the following:

a. Why are other forms of power also found, side by side with the law, in many societies?
b. Can this power emerge from a state of nature? Put another way, is there an 'invisible hand' explanation of power?
c. Is an 'invisible hand' explanation of power and/or the law a complete explanation? In other words, would such a combination of power and the law emerge over time whatever the initial stage, including 'unnatural' ones? (For example, would law and freedom, as in our farming society, emerge if the society started out under the domination of one ranch-owner and his henchmen imposing their will as the law?) This is to ask whether the equilibrium we describe is globally stable, or only stable locally (ie, within the set of 'natural' states).

I shall begin by attempting an 'invisible hand' explanation of power. Let us return to our simple agrarian case, but view it now as illustrative of our wider argument. Suppose that for a farmer to leave his farm and do a roster spell on security patrol, or a longer period (a year?) as an army regular, is very costly – say farming requires continuous attendance (as it normally does) or else these spells of patrol duty occur at crucial periods. Then, although the farmer will realise the risks of transferring security and army activities to an independent unit, he will be willing to run these risks to save the high costs of his personal involvement. There will also be gains in efficiency from specialisation in security/army work (as Nozick argues).

Each farmers' alliance will no doubt set up a security council to supervise the alliance police force, and the alliances will set up an army council to supervise the super-alliance's army. The members of these councils will now have civil power, as will the operational heads of the police and army. Thus, 'power' will come about because of economic costs/benefits;

it too will in fact be part then of the state of nature. It is delegated by the citizens to individuals in order to economise on functions they previously had to share out among themselves as 'amateurs'. The citizens then devise ways to limit the abuse of power by these individuals.

How far will this creation of civil power go? How concentrated will it be? Again, this will be a matter of economics. Power is the outcome of economic specialisation in the exercise of the protective functions of the law.

Our answers to the first two questions (a) and (b) above can then be derived from this general hypothesis. Power emerges – people are vested with power – because it is cheaper, even after allowing for the risks and difficulties of supervising their exercise of it, to give them power than for all to engage in the protective function. The varieties of power forms occur because of the variety of costs and benefits attaching to the exercise of the protective function.

Let us consider just two examples of power forms.

In Athens of the fifth century BC, the citizens gave power to an elected leader but controlled his power by a system of frequent referenda on council issues. The citizens gathered in the marketplace, listened to the arguments from their leader and the opposition, and then voted. This was a cost-effective activity because it was physically possible for all citizens to gather together to enforce this highly participative form of control, while for efficiency they needed a single leader to organise the military and other functions of a highly civilised and advanced city–state. The idea of federating with other Greek city–states and creating federal power did not appeal to the Athenians; they merely had a super-alliance with them in case of external threat (invoked notably in the Persian invasion). The economic gains from amalgamating these states' military forces (already formidable) into one did not offset the loss in control that would be implied with the technology of those days; with the rugged geography of Greece, it was hard for the citizens of Athens to check what was going on in Thrace and vice versa. A federal army and navy would be costly to check on and there would be a risk of it becoming an uncontrolled force. Notice in this example how the technology of communications enters crucially into the calculations.

Now consider the case of Tsarist Russia, a country of plains interrupted only at the Urals, a mountain range in any case of easy traversability. Nomad tribes of horsemen moved freely across this expanse of plain. As long as they alone constituted the population, they remained in tribal units, with a tribal power structure (namely very limited power for the leader, with constant and visible checking from his fellow-tribesmen). With no external threats except from other marauding tribes, federal power was unnecessary; super-alliances with other friendly tribes were enough, if even that. Yet, of course, as settled agricultural communities grew up in the west of Russia, the settlers required effective defence against these roaming tribesmen. As settlers busy in the fields, their effectiveness against surprise attack could only be purchased by costly sacrifice of time in the fields. Furthermore, to counteract an invasion from afar by large groups of horsemen would require a super-alliance with rapid response times, with the technology of the horse operating in the geography of the steppe. Co-ordination of separate communities' military units against such invasion would be expensive indeed. A federal force offered the cheapest solution; hence the central ruler or chief, the Tsar. As for citizen supervision, the federal state of Russia was so far-flung that formal referenda on voting would have been costly. Checks on the Tsar's power were provided by two means: first, by sheer distance, as no Tsar could keep effective control against the will of countries a thousand miles from Moscow; and, secondly, by the contestability of the Tsar's power by 'pretenders' who could capitalise on discontent.

In answering our first two questions, I have argued that there is no general bar to the existence of power in a state of nature. Power emerges in a state of nature for economic reasons – it is consistent with individual agents' voluntary agreement and simply a convenient extension of the mechanisms of their alliances. When power is of this form, I will call it 'natural' power or 'power in a state of nature'.

This brings us to the hardest of our three questions. Suppose we can in this way show that, if the economics dictate it, a state of nature will yield power as well as law and that it will yield it in different forms suited to the tastes, technology and constraints of the citizens. Can we also show that a non-natural state would yield the same power in the same form? Suppose, as in the story of the Ring, that something goes wrong, that power falls into the wrong hands and is abused, with the citizens' sanction being overridden. Clearly this is possible, for the citizens recognise the risk, and every so often the chances of abuse will be actually realised.

Let us now imagine the two states: the equilibrium (or 'natural') state, where citizens are content, and the non-natural state, which is any other. We now need to define rather carefully the 'contentment' involved in the equilibrium state. It is what economists know as the 'core'; it is a state such that no coalition of citizens can be created that desires to, and can, prevent it in any aspect. Contentment of a citizen therefore consists in this knowledge, that he cannot change the state by joining any coalition (including, of course, acting on his own, this being a coalition of one).

By this definition, we have implicitly answered our question. The equilibrium state results from the state of nature; that is to say, a state of nature will always turn into the equilibrium state. A non-natural state must be one in which some coalition could, and wishes to, frustrate it. It will therefore not survive, for that coalition will frustrate it.

But answering via a definition is not enough. We need to show that the power of coalitions to frustrate does not alter in such a volatile manner that the 'core' is a volatile concept and so of trivial use.

What I now assert, as an empirical hypothesis, is that the power of citizens' coalitions to frustrate is derived from their power in the state of nature. I refer to this as the 'fundamental' power distribution. I argue that any actual power distribution will be forced eventually to conform to the fundamental power distribution. This comes about through the activity of competitive intermediaries, the supply of whom is inexhaustible. They will perceive the profit from organising a blocking coalition of citizens, using their fundamental power. What then is the 'power of citizens in a state of nature'? If this hypothesis is to be genuinely testable, as opposed to merely a restatement of a definition, this concept must be carefully delineated.

What we require is a concept of power to which neither initial conditions nor capital stock contribute. For these two elements are arbitrary and can be changed by human effort. Remember, too, that skills, both mental and physical, are acquired and therefore must be included in 'capital stock' as 'human' capital.

If these elements are stripped away when we consider any set of citizens (not necessarily all of the same 'country', for a 'country' is already a particular power structure, which may not be 'fundamental'), we are left with their individual natural capacities, the natural constraints of their environment, and the technology available to them. (We will assume that any technology anywhere that can be applied in their situation is 'available', in the sense that if it is technology, ie, it comprises known processes, it can be acquired at some cost by them or by their intermediary.)

Suppose these elements can be listed in some necessarily incomplete way ('capacities', for example, is the set of all possible states to which our citizen may attain), can we make any sense of the concept of their power? What I have in mind is the result of a social optimisation plan by an intermediary, or 'political entrepreneur', looking at this situation. Such an intermediary will assess the possibilities of improving the welfare of a set of citizens, compute the costs (including his own required profit), and then sell the plan to the citizens if he feels it is worth pursuing.

In this plan, there will be a cost in blocking the existing power structure – the initial conditions. However, the capital stock that needs to be used in the plan will cost the same whether the citizens have it or not. If they do not have it and must acquire it, its cost is obvious (it is the interest and maintenance expense of leasing it for the time required); but if they already have it, they must divert it from its existing use, where it earns an economic return, to its use in the plan. Either way, the economic cost is the same, and so capital stock held by the citizens does not affect the plan's profitability.

The problem with the way that I have set up the plan is that its viability may depend on the initial conditions. If the existing power structure is repressive, then the costs of blocking it may be very high and make an otherwise profitable plan unprofitable. Yet my concept of 'fundamental' power rules out the role of initial conditions.

To deal with this problem formally, I shall use a technical trick from economics: we discuss shortly what this means in practice. Formally, we will assume that the economy in which our citizens are placed is in steady state with a zero real (marginal) rate of return on capital (ie, the capital stock is invested up to the point where an additional unit of capital yields no extra return), its citizens have a zero rate of time preference (ie they value the welfare of their descendants equally with their own), and our political entrepreneur views the situation likewise. This implies that if the plan yields a steady flow of profit year in year out without counting capital costs or the once-for-all costs of blocking the existing power structure, then it is profitable to undertake.

To put this now into practical human terms, this means that if a group of citizens can be shown a steady (permanent) future for themselves or their descendants that will be more attractive than a steady continuation of their present state, they will embrace it in spite of the transitory costs and turmoil required to bring the new state about. These costs and turmoil include:

- the diversion of capital stock;
- the acquisition, at cost, of necessary technology; and
- the effort, bloodshed or cost, required to block the existing state.

Our scenario is, of course, somewhat unrealistic: rates of time preference and real rates of return on capital are generally positive. So at any actual point of time, such a plan may not be embraced because these latter costs, when set against the discounted benefits of the future against the present, make the plan unattractive. The current set of citizens will in effect shrug their shoulders and put it off. 'Our descendants,' they may say to themselves, 'will perhaps have a real chance, but we do not.'

However, this lack of realism is necessary to define clearly the notion of 'fundamental power'. For what we have done is to define an opportunity waiting to happen when discount rates, etc, permit. Chance will eventually cause it to happen because of the following:

a. Discount rates have a statistical distribution which includes zero.
b. The costs of blocking a given power structure also have a distribution; in other words, power structures have periods of weakness as well as strength.
c. Costs of technology vary over time; indeed, they steadily fall as knowledge accumulates.

Hence, although the chance of the fundamental power being asserted at any given point of time is small, it is positive and therefore the chances of it being asserted at some point in time tend to certainty over the indefinite future.

It may be objected that the tyrant who has usurped or hijacked power will always have an incentive to bribe the outside intermediary to back off, and this is true. It might seem that in a bribery competition between tyrant and revolutionaries, the tyrant must come off best for, merely by oppressing his people more, he can offer a substantial slice of the country's GDP without cutting into his own personal fortune. The revolutionaries, however, must reduce their own supporters' returns to produce their bribe; all the people will recapture their rights after the tyrant's overthrow, but the revolutionaries' ability to 'tax' their supporters will nevertheless be limited. Whatever they can raise by voluntary contributions, furthermore, can surely be topped by the tyrant with compulsory contributions. Better, therefore, for the revolutionaries to stop negotiations with an intermediary, since that way the tyrant too will stop and not require these supererogatory extractions from the populace.

The key objection to this line of argument is that there is an infinite supply of intermediaries at some 'price' representing the return on their activities (supplying technology, organising weapons, shipments etc). Suppose this price is set at a not inconsiderable £y. The revolutionaries approach A offering £y. A seeks £y times 1.01 from the tyrant, who buys him off. The revolutionaries, losing A, offer their £y to B. He too is bought off by the tyrant, who has now paid out £2.02y. The revolutionaries continue down the list until eventually the tyrant's resources are exhausted and they get an intermediary, and so the tyrant cannot win this game and, unless completely foolish, is therefore unlikely to engage in a bribery competition at all.

What if the tyrant, seeing his predicament, puts himself under the protection of a greater power in return for policy subservience (eg, Husak and the USSR in Czechoslovakia)? This does not actually change the problem but merely transfers it to the greater power, which must deploy its resources to combat the revolutionaries. Because it may have greater resources, this may put off the critical time of overthrow, but that is the only effect (think here of Russian difficulties in Afghanistan or, as it later turned out, Soviet ones in Czechoslovakia).

To conclude, then, I must emphasise that this hypothesis does not predict that, at any given time, power is disposed according to its fundamental distribution. Rather, it predicts that over a (possibly very long) period, it tends towards this distribution. That this distribution is not volatile should be clear; for it does not depend on initial conditions or capital costs or the cost of acquiring available technology, all of which will vary continuously. It does depend, however, on the preferences of the citizens, on the natural constraints of their environment, and on the available technology. These latter will of course change; nothing is immutable nor, therefore, is the fundamental distribution itself immutable, but the changes in these are likely to be very gradual, and so we can think of this distribution as following some slowly moving trend. Actual power distributions, if they are different from this, may from time to time change discontinuously as volatile elements trigger a blocking coalition; or they too may converge continuously on the fundamental distribution as the threat of these coalitions is perceived by the temporarily dominant coalition.

In a recent monograph, Mancur Olson (who sadly died a few months ago), started as it were, from the other end and emphasised all the many ways in which power can be hijacked, whether by tyrants, warring oligarchs, or strong vested interests. He contrasts such a realistic approach with the Panglossian approach, based on extending Coase's (1960) optimising bargain between holders of property rights, that people will converge on efficient institutions. What I have argued here can be regarded as a very long-run version of the latter approach; essentially my point is that the Coasean bargain (the fundamental power distribution, as I have called it) is always lying around ready for a political entrepreneur to discover it and sell it to the people. Eventually this will occur, with 100% probability in the very long run.

What we have done here, in effect, is to define the core with reference to a steady-state world. The path by which it is reached we have left rather vague, noting that it depends on both chance possibilities and anticipation of such possibilities, but we have shown that it must be eventually reached because of the cumulative statistical probability that a blocking coalition will be mounted. Our world is determined by the preferences of the citizens (as in Oakeshott's theory) interacting with technology and natural constraints.

This analysis was originally written – in 1987 – before the recent overthrow of the Marcos regime in the Philippines by a largely unarmed proletariat with the help of overseas, especially US, moral support and some specific backing well short of physical intervention. It was also written before the developments in Eastern Europe that led to the overthrow of Soviet Communism, and before the overthrow of apartheid and white minority rule in South Africa. The original text pondered the 'puzzle' of continued Soviet (and Chinese) communist rule. It also speculated that a rational white regime could survive in South Africa if it abandoned apartheid, conceded proper citizenship rights to blacks, and entrenched property rights for entrepreneurs, white or black, so achieving economic gains through inward investment that would compensate blacks for not exercising a short-sighted majority tyranny. Since then, democracy in the Philippines has been reasserted; Soviet communism has disintegrated; Chinese communism has embraced capitalism (but not democracy) – the puzzle remains there; and power in South Africa has gone to a coalition government of blacks and whites under Nelson Mandela whose policies (at least in intent) may well approximate to the description above. The theory appears to have some reasonable predictive power for recent events.

SOME CONCLUSIONS ABOUT RIGHTS

I have argued that rights derive from what is enforceable, that is the (active) law of the land. Power to enforce the law will normally be vested in specialised agencies because of economic constraints, though it need not be in principle; such civil power will be subject to a structure of checks. 'Power structure' in turn tends towards a fundamental distribution; we have identified this as that which no blocking coalition would (ultimately) prevent. This is also the state of nature, in the sense that it will occur (in time) naturally and inevitably. Notice that in this state of nature, civil power – including a 'state' – can, and typically will, exist because of economic constraints. However, at a given point of time, there is no necessity that such a state of nature or equilibrium will occur; some of my arguments earlier in this essay were couched in terms of a pastoral society in which the plausibility of the state of nature occurring at all times was made to be as great as possible.

That presentation was useful in developing my case; but we can now see that it was somewhat misleading. The hijacking of power can occur at any time, and the rules of chance further dictate that it may occur in any society at any time. However, chance dictates too that the fundamental power distribution must reassert itself, discontinuously (when the hijacker's powers are temporarily weak) or gradually (as the hijacker recognises the inevitable and graciously yields up over time the reins of power).

I began by refusing to discuss morality, arguing that rights in the sense discussed were not derived from morality; what is morally right is not necessarily 'a right', nor is 'a right' necessarily morally right. I end by reflecting briefly on possible connections between rights and morality. Notice first that the fundamental power distribution is, if our hypothesis is correct, inevitable. Therefore, like nature, it just is. The 'rights' it gives (or will eventually give) are also inevitable; one could reasonably call them 'natural rights' (but perhaps should not because of the varieties of this phrase's usage). In that sense, they are primary, fixed points, beyond control, beyond the vagaries of custom and – dare we say – morals. This implies that what is morally right is dominated by these (fundamental) rights, just as when lightning strikes someone, it is an accident and not wrong even though that person may have a moral right to survive to old age.

Let us take another example. Two people may have differing views on the morality of redistributive taxation; one may say 'taxation is theft' and argue in favour of voluntary giving to the poor, while the other may argue that it is everyone's duty and so they should be compelled by taxation to do so. This question, however, will be settled by the evolution of power; the moral discussion will be dominated, will be irrelevant. It is of course possible – even probable, I would venture – that once the nature of these evolved rights has become apparent, they come to be dignified also by the status of moral rightness. But if so, then that is merely a form of decoration and in no way indicates their derivation or basis.

THE IMPLICATIONS FOR POLICY

In the previous two sections of this chapter, I set out a picture first of human motivation and secondly of human organisation.

I argued in the first that people aim to create long-term benefits by their actions, benefits that they judge partly by a hierarchy of closeness to themselves. Hence they care greatly about any effects on, for example, their descendants.

In the second, I argued that human organisations evolve through failing to be blocked by some internal coalition; democracy is an effective organisation because its voting procedures allow decisions to be blocked before enactment so that the whole organisation is not brought down. In modern society, the mechanisms available to quite small groups to block decisions are various and potent because of high interdependence and the cheapness of powerful technologies (such as terrorist weapons and communications).

Let us now consider the implications of these two ideas for policy. Again I have no interest here in what 'ought' in some moral sense to be done by policy makers; rather, the question is what policy makers must do in order to succeed and for their policies to survive.

The implication of my blocking theory of human organisation is that, in the long term, society will get the policies that will survive, what I have called the fundamental power distribution. This immediately gives us a clue as to what policies are best. They are those that get society most quickly to such a position. 'Bad' policies are those that will in the end self-destruct even if it may take a very long time.

The criterion that this implies for good policy is the negative one: good policies are those that will not be blocked by a coalition. This criterion is quite different from what one often encounters in discussions of policy, namely appeals to 'social welfare'. Attempts are made to evaluate some definition of this, say the monetary income of all households, weighted in some way. But of course this tells us nothing about whether the policy will succeed. Our criterion requires evaluation of the power of different groups and of their attitude (related no doubt to some measure of that group's welfare) to the policy.

In practice, because so many groups can block, this leads one to a 'no losers' principle side-by-side with demonstrable benefits to at least some group and preferably to as large a number of groups of as large a size as possible. This is a practical restatement of Pareto's (1906) principle of improvement – that some should gain while no one should lose – but given in group form, where groups are defined by their power to block and their commonality of response to the policy.

It follows that the art of policy making in economic matters in particular is the finding of improvements in economic efficiency – by which I mean that more value is produced from the same resources – and then the varying of the exact form of these improvements in order to avoid damage to politically dangerous groups, often a wide class. The first part of this problem is often the easiest; it is the second part that poses the biggest challenge without sacrificing too much of the efficiency gain.

However, three things can help. First, the increase in freedom is itself attractive to most people, who do not like to be compelled; as we noted above, psychologists have discovered (Sutherland, 1992) that people even take a dislike to situations they would voluntarily have chosen, if they are forced into them. It follows that there is a premium of attractiveness attached to what is freely chosen.

Secondly, people's long-term horizon will often help. If people can see that their children will benefit from the higher efficiency, they will weigh this against the damage to themselves. Hence if one can show that changes will produce, for example, faster long-term growth, that can be a powerful argument for reducing opposition among immediate losers.

A third useful element is to recognise 'grandfather rights'. These are the existing benefits enjoyed by interested groups – such as sitting tenants under controlled rents. They can be granted continued enjoyment of these benefits for their own lives until they give them up voluntarily (eg, by moving); but they cannot pass the benefits on. They are likely to accept change – for example rent decontrol – because they themselves will not lose and their children would quite possibly not have much wanted to inherit the benefit (for instance, because their circumstances will be different from their parents') nor gain from the better operation of the economy. Therefore the policy will apply to new entrants only; this plainly defers the full efficiency gain, but it preserves some of it in the short term (often the most important part, since new entrants will be the most active economically) and all of it in the long term. There were many examples of this sort of policy engineering in the British reforms of 1979–97, notably the issue of free or subsidised shares to employees of privatised industries and the rent decontrol in the Housing Act 1988, which only applied to new tenancies.

These points are well known to civil servants and indeed politicians. But they often surprise economists and other social scientists who focus on measures of social welfare and expect these to carry all before them. As we have seen, measures of general improvement of efficiency are relevant – although these are not the same as many proposed measures of social welfare. Social scientists can advise on these and also on the modifications that can make a policy acceptable to blocking groups without removing the overall gains entirely. This is an important role to which the modern tools of social science can make a big contribution.

In what follows we focus in considerable detail on the policy-making experience of the UK. We begin with the UK's post-war policies of heavy state intervention, contrasting them with the relatively free market policies of (West) Germany at that time. We then carefully review the free-market reforms introduced from 1979 by Margaret Thatcher's governments and then John Major's. This was an ambitious programme of reform designed to move the UK much closer to a free society. How successful was this programme? Does the contrast between its results and those of vastly different post-war policies of statism bear out the thesis proposed in Chapter 1, that the freer a society, the more efficient its economy? The evidence from this is most important in evaluating this thesis, because here we can genuinely test the effects of policy and institutional changes, essentially on their own – it would be hard indeed to maintain that in a mere few decades the British people could have changed genetically, or that the environment itself had become more or less favourable to them relative to other advanced countries. In economics, 'controlled' experiments (where all other 'nuisance' factors are held constant) are impossible; so an episode like this – where an 'uncontrolled' experiment occurred involving such a sharp change that other factors could be considered constant in relative terms – is evidence of great value. Such an episode is unparalleled perhaps in modern times (although similar evidence will in time be forthcoming from the transition in Eastern Europe).

NOTE

I have benefited from comments made at seminars of the Oxford Hayek Society and of Liverpool students. I thank Dale Benest particularly for pressing me on the question of tyrant bribery.

References

Austin, J.L. (1961) *Philosophical Papers,* J.O. Urmston and G.J. Warnock, eds., Clarendon Press, Oxford.

Brittan, S. (1996) *Capitalism with a human face*, Fontana Press, HarperCollins, London.

Camus, A. (1942) *L'Étranger.*

Dawkins, R. (1995) *River out of Eden*, Weidenfeld and Nicolson, London.

de Jasay, A. (1997), *Against Politics: on Government, Anarchy and Politics,* Routledge, London.

de Jasay, A. (1985), *The State*, Blackwell, Oxford.

Hobbes, T. (1651), *Leviathan.*

Hume, D. (1737) *Treatise of Human Nature.*

Kant, I. (1788) *The Critique of Practical Reason.*

Locke, J. (1690), *The Two Treatises of Government.*

Marris, R. (1996) *How to Save the Underclass*, Macmillan, London.

Nietzsche, F. (1883-91) *Thus Spake Zarathustra.*

Nozick, R. (1974), *Anarchy, State and Utopia*, Basic Books and Blackwell, Oxford.

Oakeshott, M. (1975), *On Human Conduct* (essay 'On the character of a modern European State'), Oxford University Press, Oxford.

Olson, M. (1996) *Capitalism, Socialism and Dictatorship – Outgrowing Communist and Capitalist Dictatorships*, mimeograph, University of Maryland, Dept of Economics, College Park, MD 20742, USA.

Pareto, V. (1906) *Manual of Political Economy.*

Sutherland, S. (1992) *Irrationality – the Enemy Within*, Constable, London.

CHAPTER THREE

Reconstruction and the UK welfare state – the origins of the UK's post-war debacle

IN THIS CHAPTER, we go back to the origins of the severe problems the UK faced in 1949 – the post-war installation of the welfare state by the Atlee government. This installation was partly the result of the socialist thinking of leading intellectuals of that time, partly a response to general feelings of collectivism on the part of British soldiers returning from war. So deep-rooted did it become that the Conservatives who ousted Atlee in 1951 did not seek to reverse the changes; instead, they sought to work within them, achieving only modest liberalisation at the edges. The result was a system that enjoyed over 30 years of life, by which time its malign results could finally no longer be denied. It is important to understand how it came to enjoy this lease of life. It is a good example of how a society can make errors – creating a sort of policy hijack (in this case largely for reasons of intellectual error) that can take many years to reverse. This chapter is, if you like, a gigantic negative against which we can better evaluate the positive.

The Second World War was fought by Britain under what was largely a command economy. Hayek (1988) has commented that socialism has its attraction because it reminds us of our tribal roots and it is essentially the organisational mode of the tribe. Britain during World War 2 was organised on tribal lines. The Chiefs in Whitehall allocated resources to the war machine, and then to private consumption with a virtually universal rationing system; what was not rationed was taxed heavily by the inflation tax, which fell on the large government bond issue (which eventually reached 300% of GDP) as well as money. Production was directed to 'the patriotic war effort', with unions induced to co-operate by a combination of threats (of action for treasonable behaviour) and promises (of post-war rewards, not clearly specified, though the government coalition included Labour, whose aims were clear). Finally, mass democratic mobilisation was underwritten by a similar implicit promise: that after the war, the masses would be 'looked after'.

It is perhaps no wonder that after the war, with no external force able to override these institutions or implicit commitments (as in Japan, for example), the British establishment set about running a peacetime economy along socialist lines. A Labour government was voted in, but only because it was in tune with the popular and intellectual mood of the times. The Civil Service and the rest of the establishment shared the general view that they could do as good a job of running the peacetime economy as they felt they had of the war machine. Having 'won for freedom' they also shared the general view that men and women of goodwill must build the good life that so many lives had been sacrificed to make possible.

It was in such an atmosphere that many intellectuals felt that 'Joe' Stalin was rather a good chap, and some of them – their antecedents having fought in the Spanish civil war on the communist side – sold him security secrets, most often out of idealism.

For example, in 1945 J.B. Priestley wrote in *Letter to a Returning Serviceman* (quoted in Howarth, 1985): 'Whatever their faults, the Bolsheviks had put their hand to the great task and were trying to lift the load of want, ignorance, fear and misery from their dumb millions, while the Americans – as they fully admit now – were living in a fool's paradise of money-for-nothing and Martinis, and we were shuffling and shambling along, listening to our Tory politicians talking their old twaddle.'

In a similar vein, A.J.P. Taylor, in a broadcast after the 1945 election, announced that 'nobody in Europe believes in the American way of life – that is, in private enterprise; or rather, those who believe in it are a defeated party which seems to have no more future than the Jacobites in England after 1688.' (Howarth, 1985).

Nor was the Conservative Party of the day immune from the atmosphere, though it did remain attached to a highly diluted and 'pragmatic' market philosophy. Churchill and Butler made no attempt to reverse the institutions of the welfare state put in place by the Atlee Labour government of 1945–51. They gradually eliminated rationing, but this was something that the Labour government had started and would have continued. They did bring down taxes somewhat. But in many other ways they were merely a less doctrinaire group of interventionists and so gave rise to the phrase 'Butskellism', the composite interventionist economic philosophy of the two Chancellors of the Exchequer in the early 1950s, real and shadow, Butler (Conservative) and Gaitskell (Labour).

From the viewpoint of what we know today about the efficient operation of modern economies, it is hard to understand the naive utopianism of this post-war era. This is why I have spent a few paragraphs attempting to conjure up the spirit of the age. Those who disbelieve me should read Tom Howarth's 'Prospect and Reality' (1985), a book that quotes amply from the thinkers of the day, themselves products of the Fabian movement and the Webbs.

The main theme of this chapter is that after the Second World War Britain – out of intellectual error – took a wrong turning that needed three and a half decades of stumbling incompetence to induce it to make a new beginning in 1979. The reason that the UK's experience is of so much interest today all over the world, and in particular in Eastern Europe (where a more extreme socialism flourished by conquest, again after a pre-war regime of free markets), lies precisely in this curious history. Eastern Europeans see close parallels between the decay induced by the UK's socialist experiment and that in their own economies, and they desire to understand how that can be reversed, as so much of it was by the governments of Margaret Thatcher.

Another theme of this chapter is that economic decay and success depend crucially on the institutions that create or eliminate incentives for the people to employ their native wit and energy. Sheer investment of money in such things as infrastructure and manufacturing capital are necessary but not sufficient conditions for success: it is useless building roads and subsidised factories for a lethargic people, but an energised people will induce the roads and factories they need through rising tax revenues and profitable industries.

The 'new growth' literature stresses economies of scale, especially in the returns to human capital. But before 'new growth' processes can get to work, there must be the institutions that permit the bright and innovative to obtain rewards. Without them, government can cram together as many of such people as it likes into a given space and nothing much will happen – the example of Sweden in recent times, full of brilliant and well-trained people directed by an all-wise government in such ways, illustrates how little indeed can be so achieved when taxation removes effective rewards.

So in what follows we take a look, one by one, at the key institutional developments of the post-war era. In the spirit of institutional analysis rather than history, the historical details will be blurred in a way that would not please a proper historian. My excuse must be that I am no historian and that I trust the rather different exercise I have in mind will be of interest.

After a short historical sketch, we proceed to analyse these developments under three main headings. Government spending is the first, and is the driving force of the second, taxation. Benefits could be considered under spending or under taxation; we will consider them under both. Finally, we will look at the paraphernalia of regulation and control, whether of labour and unions, credit and currency, housing, trade or industry.

A BRIEF HISTORICAL SKETCH OF POST-WAR RECOVERY

Britain's financial position after the second world war that it had fought in the twentieth century was ruinous. Having entered the First World War with net private overseas earnings (from property and other assets) equal to 9.4% of GDP, and the Second World War with them still equal to 3.9%, by 1945 they had dwindled to 1% and were dwarfed by the enormous (and largely unquantified) Lend-Lease debt to the United States. This was later generously written off except for $650 million of goods in the pipeline. In current terms, the position was one of large deficit, both in the public accounts and the external accounts. The public deficit in 1945, including the huge off-budget military programme, was 27% of GDP. The balance of payments deficit on current account was 10% of GDP.

To the Whitehall planners of the time, this state of essential bankruptcy, both internal and external, was the key problem to be dealt with. They had little time and gave little thought to issues of incentives; meanwhile, the Labour government's plans to construct a welfare state must have been a highly unwelcome distraction from the stabilisation problem. The economic history of 1945–51 therefore proceeds on two parallel tracks: the financial reconstruction allied to the physical redeployment of resources away from military use, and the building of the welfare state.

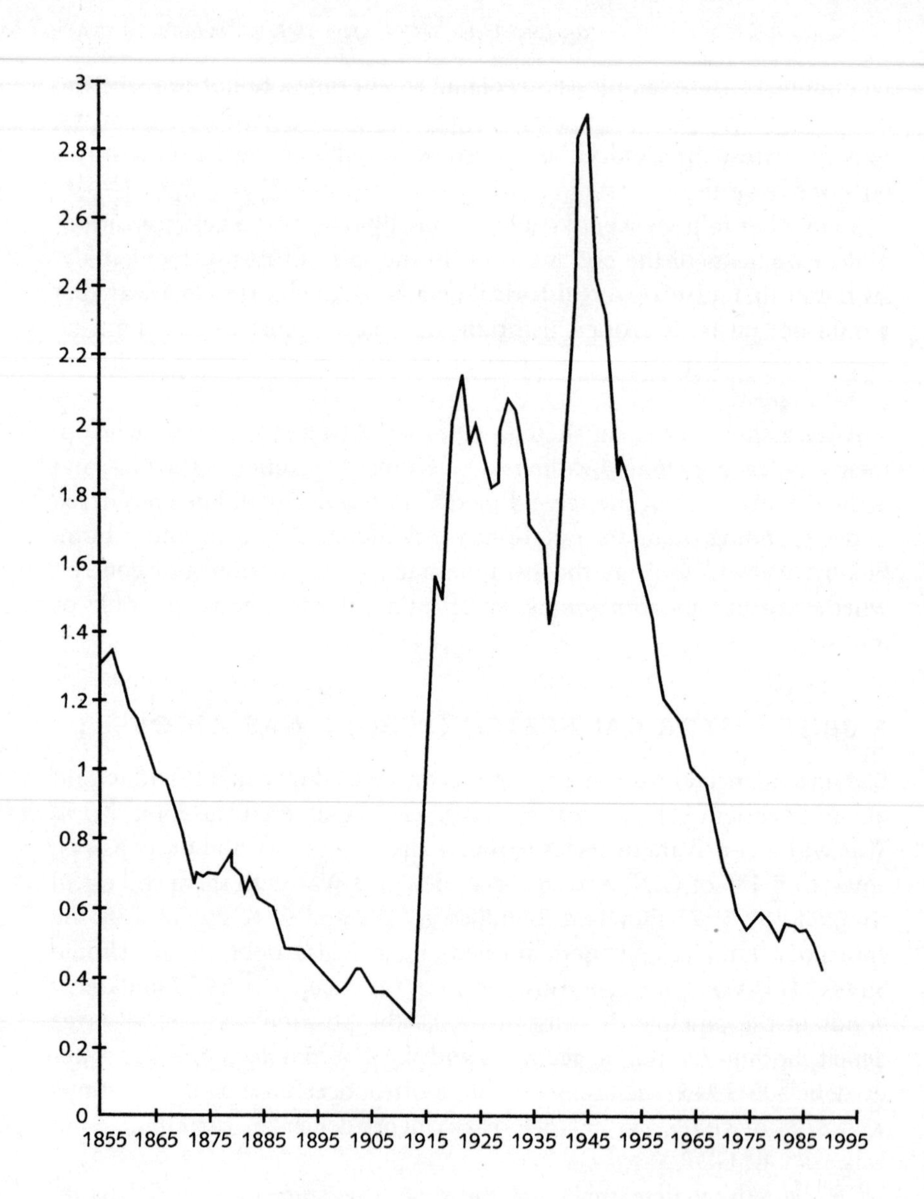

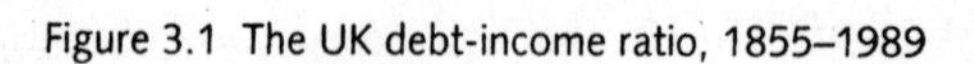
Figure 3.1 The UK debt-income ratio, 1855–1989

Source: *Public Debt Management: Theory and History*, ed. R. Dornbusch and M. Draghi, Cambridge, (1990).

On the financial side, the internal debt was partly dealt with by a rapid return to budget surplus through military rundown. Emergency military spending of 46% of GDP was rapidly eliminated – a record peace dividend. The overhang of debt, an extraordinary 300% of GDP, was brought down by inflation, none of it dramatic (the average rate in the six post-war years was 5%) but sufficiently different from the zero inflation at which pre-war long-term debt was issued and the similar terms on which war debt was compulsorily acquired as to cut its value by a quarter by 1951.

More intractable in the planners' eyes was the external debt. The government was expecting generous treatment from a grateful US. In the event, Congress returned rapidly and unsentimentally to business as usual: Lend-Lease was cut off in 1945, although as mentioned above the existing debt was also largely written off. A new loan was finally negotiated by 1947, on strict conditions that the UK adhere to free trade and full convertibility (which it failed to do).

Cheated of large grants or interest-free loans, the planners could see no market-led way to curb the balance of payments deficit, much of it with the US as the only unravaged supplier. The sterling–dollar rate was not felt to be a factor: the prevailing view was one of 'elasticity pessimism' (the view that there would be little trade response to any reduction in relative prices brought about by devaluation) and disillusion with inter-war exchange rate flexibility. Consequently, devaluation was ruled out. In its absence, import controls were kept on rigorously and a 'dollar gap' – the trade imbalance with the US – was proclaimed as the key problem for planners.

Other European countries were enlisted to help press this unfamiliar non-market concept on an impatient US. The result was the Marshall Plan. Although small in relation to GDP or the size of the peace dividend, this aid was large in terms of foreign exchange and the 'gap'. It therefore permitted the UK and other European countries to proceed with the dismantling of wartime controls, as desired by the Americans, without the excuse for delay provided by insuperable external liquidity problems (that is, the problems of finding enough dollars to pay the Americans for their trade surplus). Ultimately, these arrangements led to a general European devaluation in 1949, of which the UK's at 30% was one of the largest. But, arguably, in the intellectual atmosphere of the time (with its emphasis on controlling the economy and so, in effect, stifling its potential responses), such a devaluation would not have come in time to avert severe dislocation had there been no Marshall Aid.

By 1951, the external deficit was much reduced and the onset of the

Korean War, with renewed Allied co-operation, financial as well as military, pushed it into the background. The war over, the deficit had essentially disappeared. The stage was therefore clear by then for the elimination of the control economy. As we shall see, this opportunity was grasped by the new Conservative government of 1951 with but an uncertain and tremulous hand.

The parallel creation of the welfare state was, considering this background of financial crisis, a remarkable achievement whether one approves or disapproves of its objectives. Driven by the political forces of Aneurin Bevan, Minister of Health, and Ernest Bevin, the Transport and General Workers' boss, the programme went ahead at full steam, despite the occasional protest from Dalton and Cripps at the Treasury. By 1948, the welfare support system of pensions and other national insurance benefits (unemployment, sickness, disability, etc) and the National Health System (after a determined campaign of opposition from the doctors – who in the 1980s even more determinedly opposed its internal market reforms!) were all in place. The 1944 Education Act, under the war-time coalition, had already raised the school leaving age to 15 (to become 16 as soon as resources permitted), with universally free provision and streaming from 11. By 1951, the nationalisation programme had been completed.

Thus the reputedly pragmatic Clement Atlee had in six short years transformed a mostly private economy with a growing but spotty welfare system, essentially based on the Liberal theorising of Asquith and Lloyd George, into a mostly state-controlled economy with a private sector restricted to the less commanding heights of manufacturing and services and even there corralled by mighty unions, minimum wage-setting councils for the less strongly unionised industries, and other regulations.

The incoming 1951 Conservative government, which won the 1951 election after pushing Atlee to a bare majority in the 1950 election, was to enjoy power for 13 years. But the new generation of Tory leaders – Butler, Macmillan, Eden, as indeed Churchill himself – was in economic matters uncommitted to free-market ideas. True to time-honoured Tory principles, they regarded it as more important to govern than to pursue 'ideology' – that was for Liberals, Labour or Whigs. Nevertheless, among them were true liberals, such as Enoch Powell and Peter Thorneycroft. They had no chance, in the prevailing intellectual atmosphere, of achieving the sort of market freedom they espoused. Had the Labour government's programme collapsed in economic chaos, they might well have had; but Marshall Aid prevented that – like so much aid, it succeeded in propping up the government policies of the day. Labour had apparently succeeded and the Conservatives decided to keep the basic Labour inheritance, merely modifying it cautiously in a liberal direction.

From 1951 to the early 1960s, there was accordingly a discreet programme of liberalisation within the ground rules set out by Labour. Rationing gradually went, import controls were eased and had effectively gone by 1960, taxes were cut (but not on the rich; and the burden of income tax on the average earner steadily rose), steel was denationalised with much controversy, and there was an attempt at decontrol of private rented housing. The mixture in the 'mixed economy' moved only slightly in the direction of the private sector.

We now turn to the three themes of the post-war socialist revolution – spending, taxation and regulation.

GOVERNMENT SPENDING

Labour inherited a machine for war-time control and government spending in 1945, just as the Conservatives did in 1918. In 1918, it was assumed that this should be dismantled. In 1945, Labour assumed that it should be built upon.

The three key areas of building up were in health, education and welfare benefits. In education, there was a general commitment by all parties to public provision, as already put in place by the 1944 Education Act. Labour at this stage gave no priority to radical change in the system, contenting itself with substantially increased spending.

Health and welfare were another matter. The National Health Service 'nationalised' the doctors and hospitals, and provided their services free or at minimal charge to the populace. A national network of benefits and pensions, to be paid for out of National Insurance, was also introduced. The loss of wages due to such 'social' contingencies as illness, old age and unemployment was now 'socially insured' and refunded at least to some degree by the state.

Thus were proclaimed the three pillars of the welfare state. An explosion in civil state spending resulted between 1945 and 1951. Total real civil government spending, excluding debt interest, increased in this period at an average of 18% per year; as a percent of GDP it rose 8%. Of the overall increase in this spending, 12% was accounted for by education, 4% by pensions, and 40% by health and other insurance benefits.

Between 1951 and 1960, the Conservatives who regained power in 1951 and kept it for the next thirteen years pursued a policy of

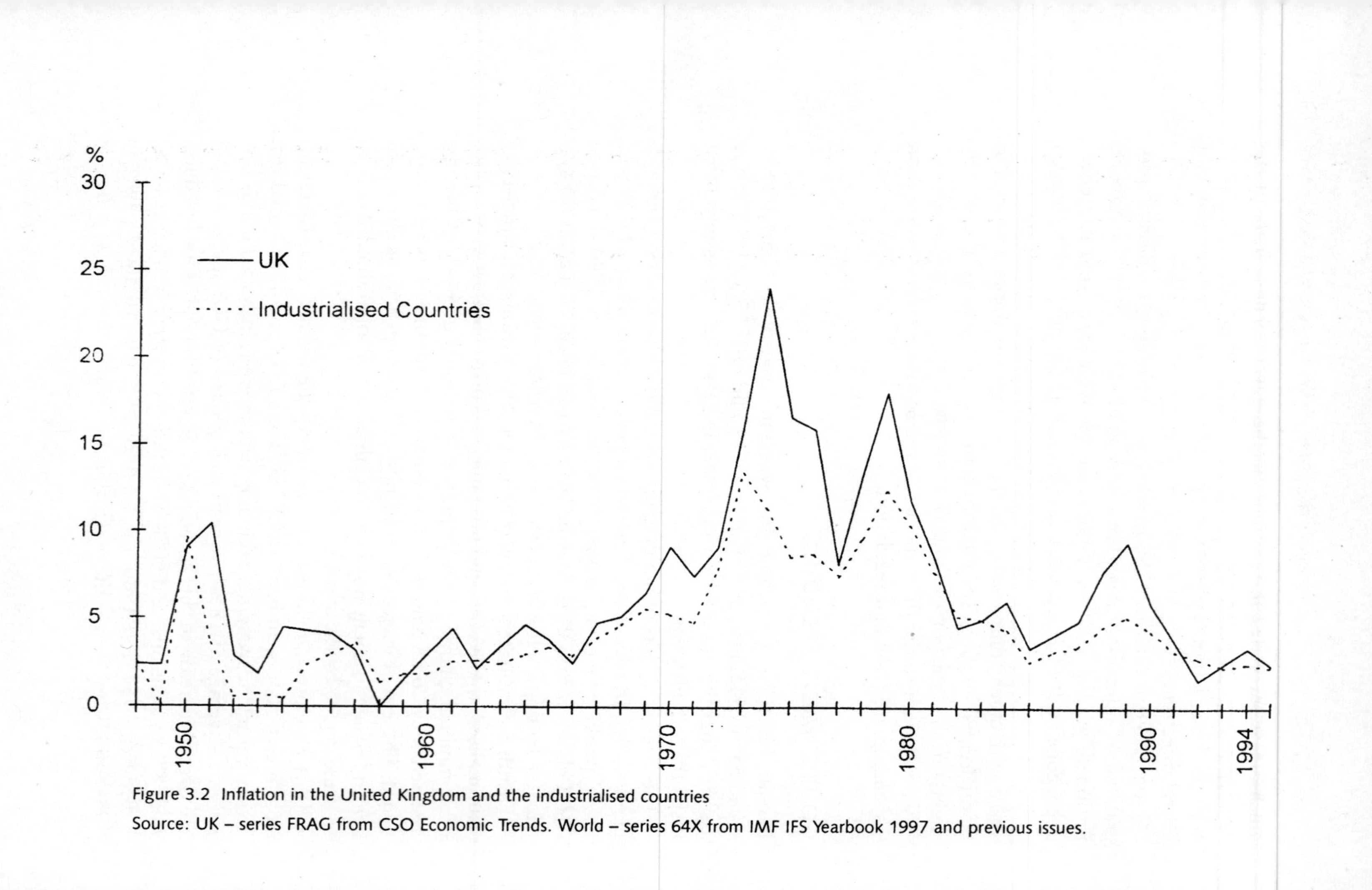

Figure 3.2 Inflation in the United Kingdom and the industrialised countries

Source: UK – series FRAG from CSO Economic Trends. World – series 64X from IMF IFS Yearbook 1997 and previous issues.

containment but acceptance of the welfare state that Labour had created. Indeed, in education they proved to be adept at spending, raising the school leaving age as scheduled and building up the 'grammar schools', grant-aided schools for the academically able children, while expanding the 'secondary moderns' which were to cater for the rest. There was a commitment to provide further technical schools, which were to have a less academic syllabus, but these barely materialised.

The net result of the Conservative continuation of Labour policies was that the growth of spending was held, at 1.9% per annum, only slightly below the growth of GDP for the decade. But then in this period of recovery GDP was itself growing at – for the UK – a rapid 2.4% per annum. Within this total, the growth in spending on health was held down, remarkably, to only 1.8% per annum, whereas education surged at 5.6% per annum and current grants, which were partly driven by demand and demography, grew only just less, at 5% per annum. The National Insurance benefits within this grew at 6.2% per annum, almost entirely accounted for by pensions and widows' benefits.

So Labour put in place an engine of welfare which the Conservatives unquestioningly fuelled throughout the 1950s. That they succeeded in holding health spending down as successfully as they did no doubt owes much to the ethos and old-fashioned administrative methods of the dedicated staff they inherited from the pre-NHS system. Later, when the NHS came to be 'reformed' in the early 1970s with a new administrative structure, much of this system was destroyed.

During the 1960s, there was little questioning at all of the new structure. Politicians assumed that this new framework was 'what the people wanted' and even those on the right therefore took it to be their democratic duty to deliver this in as efficient a manner as possible. For example, Enoch Powell, who was Minister of Health in the early 1960s, has stated as much publicly in respect of the NHS (speech to BIM/Civil Service annual conference, Cambridge 1989, author's recollection).

Although there were the usual complaints, and in particular Labour grumbled that secondary moderns and the associated '11-plus' selection exam at around 11 years old were 'divisive', the school system worked well in delivering good academic education for the able and in producing literacy elsewhere, while the NHS – in the undemanding spirit of the times – was perceived as doing an effective job. The people were pleased with the social insurance aspects too; in the aftermath of war, it seemed right to look after the old and sick, just as in war itself the wounded and disabled were cared for. There was negligible unemployment and so 'dole scrounging' was not an issue.

Had the welfare state been able to freeze itself in that condition, with dedicated medical staff and schoolteachers and an undemanding population grateful for release from the rigours of war, this chapter would have a different tone and history a different course.

But inevitably this would change, though it was not until the 1960s that this process began in a serious way; and even before then, it had to be financed, naturally by rising marginal tax rates, and it was accompanied by a philosophy of widespread control. Together, these inevitably ensured that the hopes of the war generation for the good life within a loving collective tribe would be frustrated.

TAXATION AND ITS INTERACTION WITH BENEFITS

Pre-war tax amounted to 22% of GDP. By 1945, this had risen to 34%, falling back a little by 1950 to 29%. There was only slight scope for tax cutting in this period. Even though military spending fell from 53% of GDP to only 7%, a deficit of 29% of GDP had to be eliminated (at the very least, given the huge debt burden, and in actual fact there was a shift to surplus of 4% of GDP). In addition, room had to be made for the large planned rise in the civil programme (by 8% of GDP).

During the 1950s, when the share of government spending in GDP fell modestly (from 24% to 22% of GDP), the tax share declined further as well, to 24%. This was assisted by a run-off in the budget surplus, from 4% to a borrowing requirement of 2% of GDP, under the Keynesian policies of the time. A further contributing factor was the fall in the debt interest burden by 0.6% of GDP. Nevertheless, up to the end of the 1960s it cannot be said – certainly by more recent standards – that the marginal tax rates paid by the average taxpayer were particularly high, even if, as Figure 5 shows, the income tax burden of the average person was steadily rising and marginal tax rates were significantly higher in 1960 than in 1938. One must look elsewhere for the principal incentive problems that beset the British economy.

Public debt had reached 300% of GDP by the end of the war. The Labour government felt it right to budget for a surplus to begin paying it off. Marshall Aid generated further capital resources between 1948 and 1951, totalling £696 billion, about 5% of 1950 GDP. However, the lion's share of debt liquidation was performed by inflation, which had written off nearly a half of the post-war debt's face value by 1960. By then the debt–GDP ratio had fallen to 160% of GDP.

The effectiveness of the inflation tax had diminished substantially by then, since long-term interest rates had risen to 5% to give some

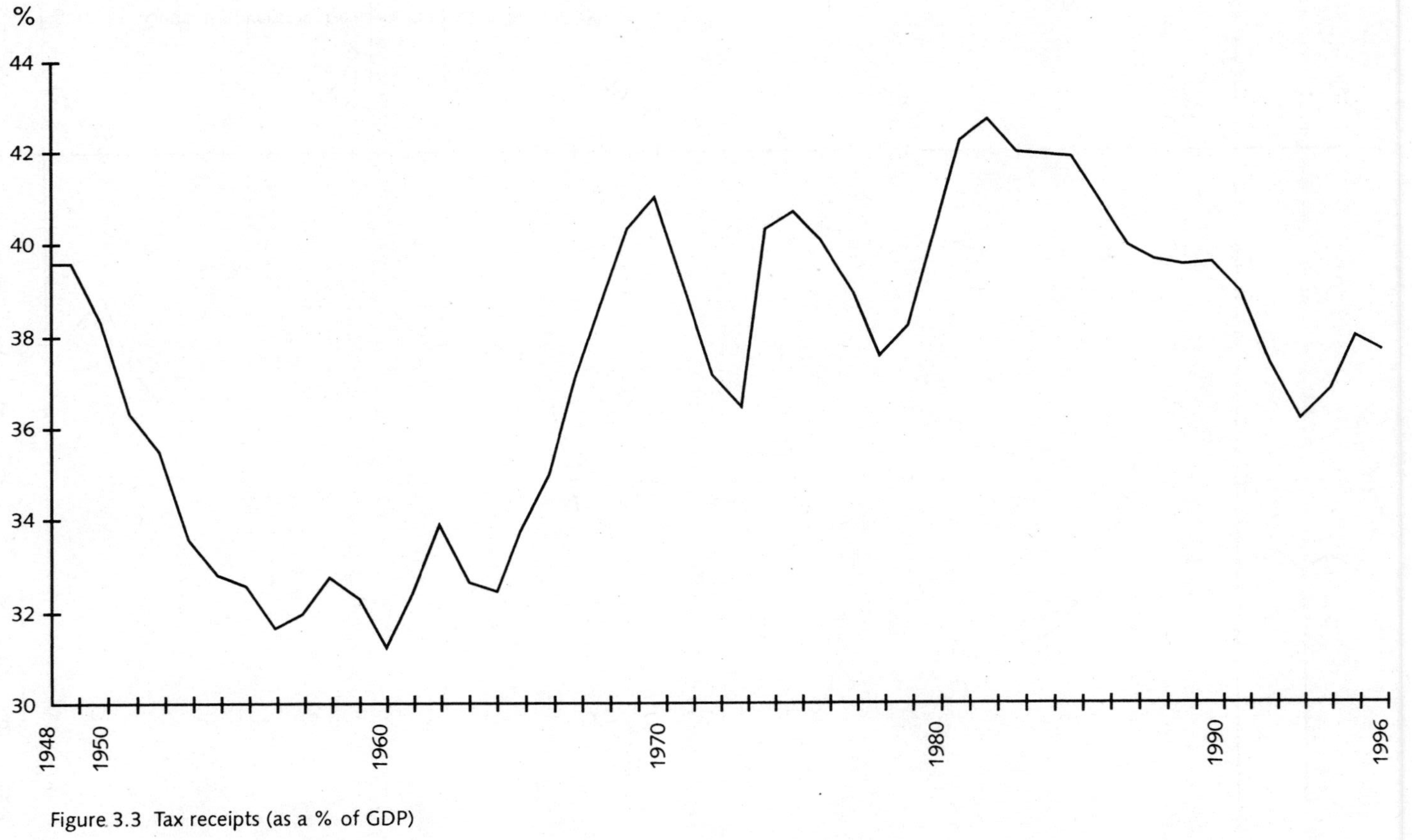

Figure 3.3 Tax receipts (as a % of GDP)

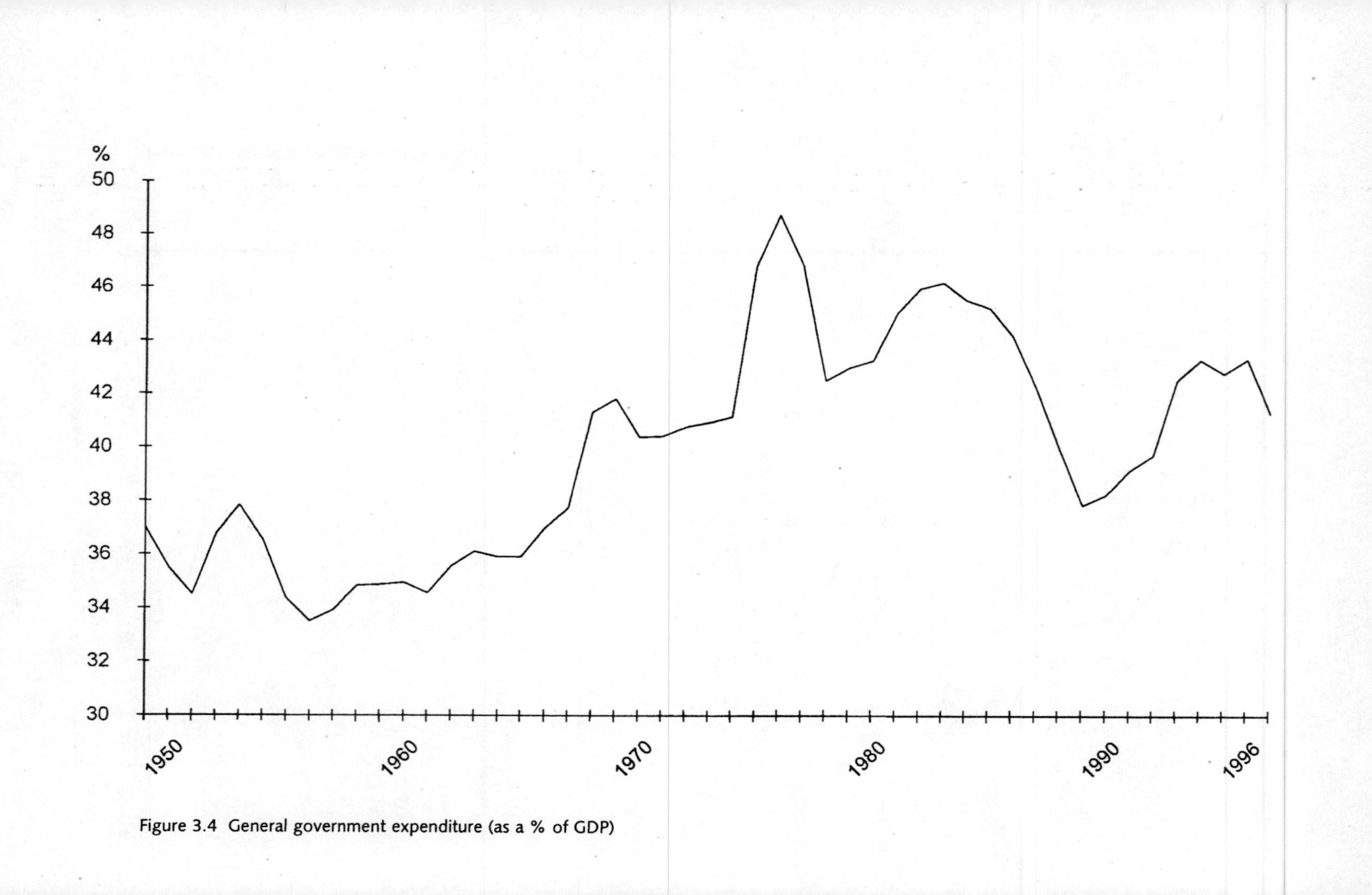

Figure 3.4 General government expenditure (as a % of GDP)

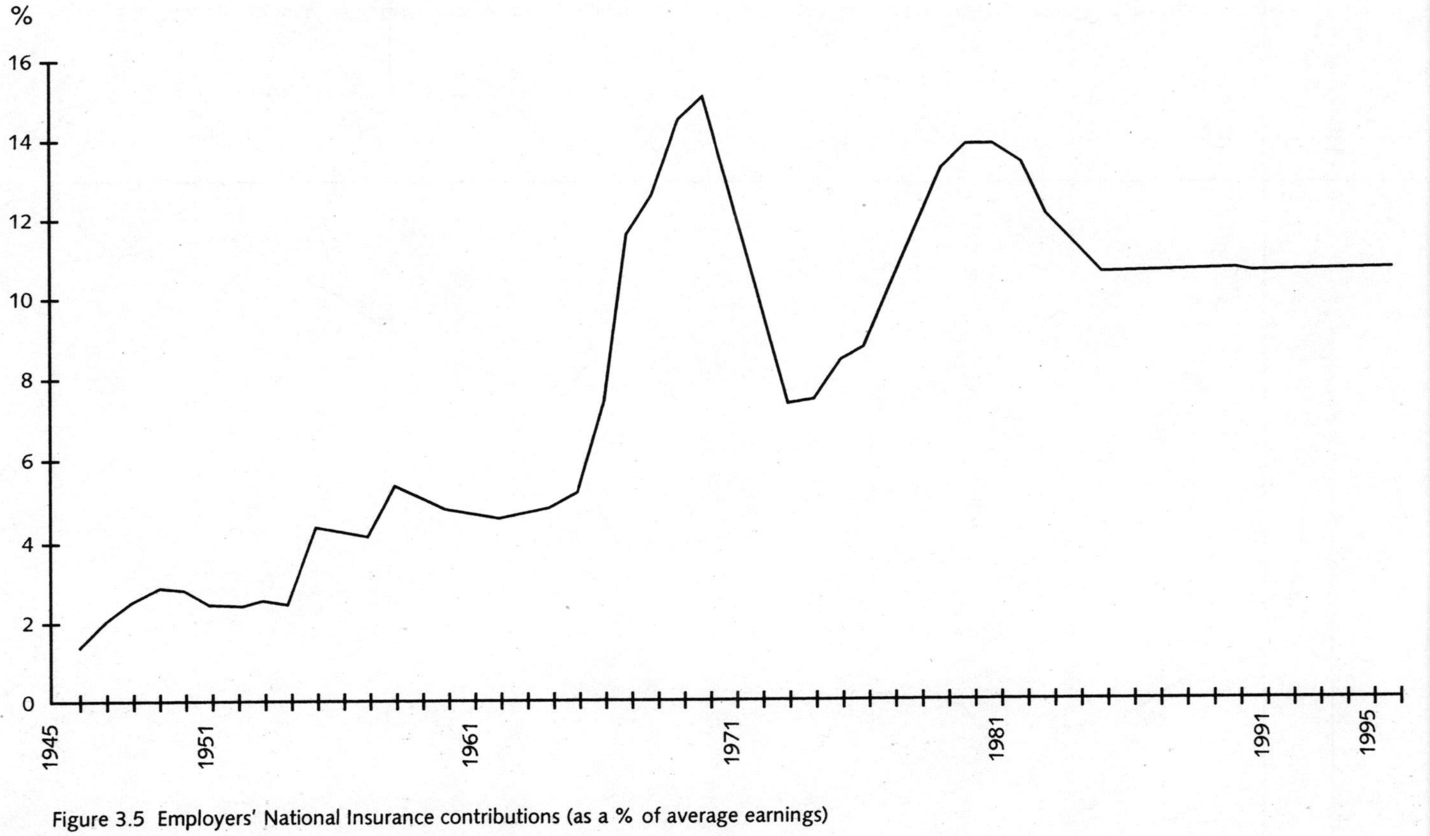

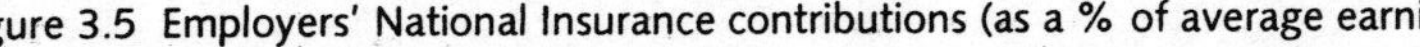
Figure 3.5 Employers' National Insurance contributions (as a % of average earnings)

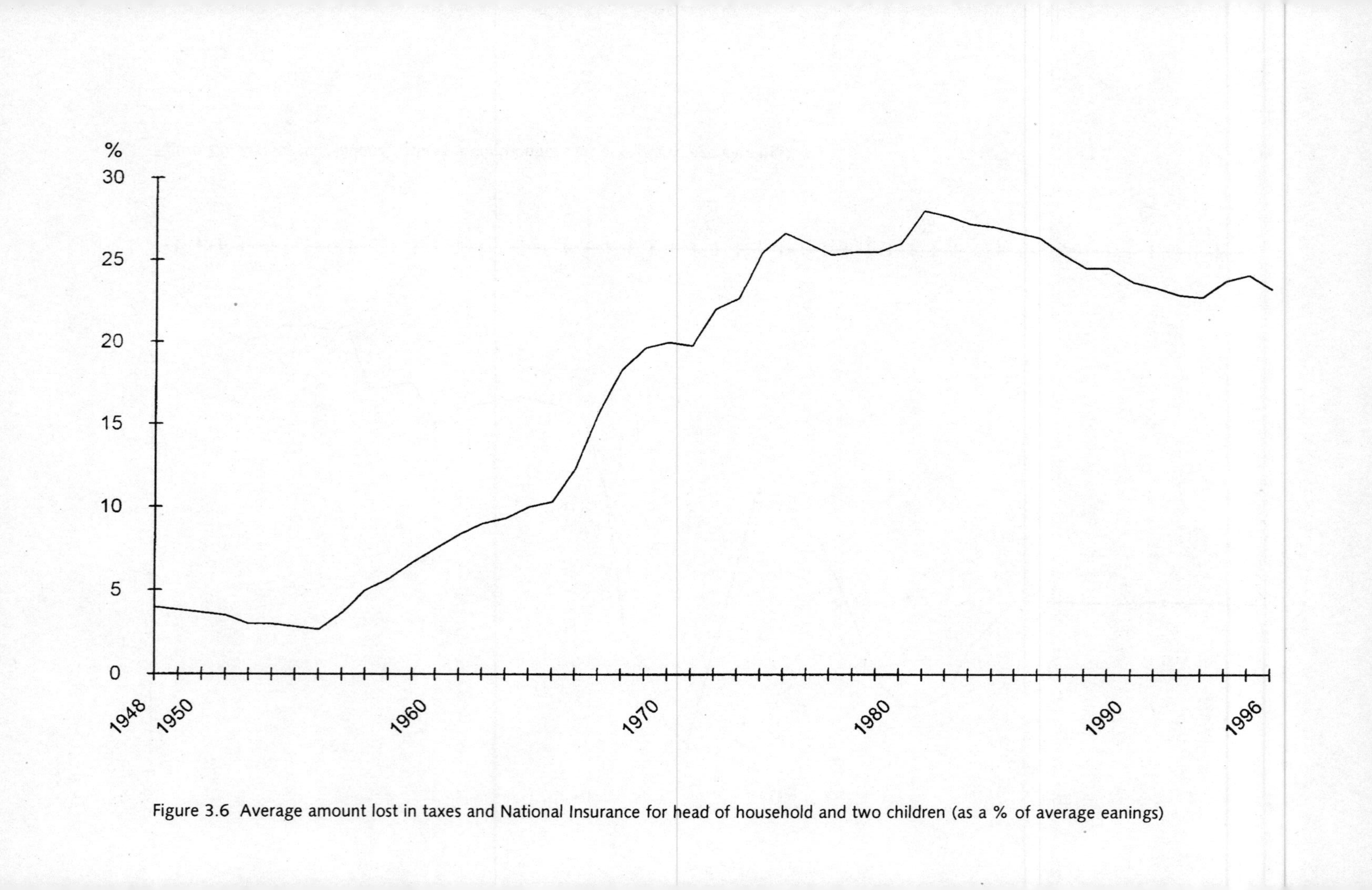

Figure 3.6 Average amount lost in taxes and National Insurance for head of household and two children (as a % of average eanings)

compensation for expected inflation (actual inflation had averaged 4% over the 1950s).

Another way of putting all this is that out of the enormous increase of the GDP available for civil use between 1945 and 1960, only one-third was put into private consumption; although civil-use GDP nearly tripled, growing by an average 7.1% per annum over the 15 years as a whole, consumption grew by only 2.4% per annum. Approximately 30% of the overall increase in civil GDP was devoted to public civil consumption, and another 30% to general investment (public and private). A tenth of the increased GDP flow was devoted to paying off foreign debt. This compression of private use was achieved by the capital levy of the inflation tax and by reducing tax rates only slowly. The enormous 'peace dividend' was largely appropriated by the state.

The burden of ordinary taxation was felt mainly in income tax, including the new National Insurance contributions, which chipped in a regular 4% of GDP from their inception. The share covered by income tax rose from 45% of the total in 1938 to 56% by 1950, and it was still at 53% in 1960. The standard rate rose from 27.5% in 1938 to 45% in 1945–50. By 1961, it had been cut back to 30%. However, the top rate on earned income, which had reached 97.5% in 1949, was still 80% in 1959 and 70% in 1961, after Selwyn Lloyd's supposedly reforming budget of that year.

Capital taxation also became confiscatory after the Second World War. The top rate of estate duty rose from 34% in 1938 to 70% in 1949–50. The rates were kept at these levels throughout the 1950s, and the yield of this and other capital taxes dropped from 2.3% in 1949 to around 1% by 1960. 'Unearned' income was treated worse than earned, in a similarly confiscatory spirit that did not change with the Conservatives, who maintained an unearned income surcharge of 19% after the Lloyd reforms.

Thus it was with higher earners and better-off savers that the culture of high marginal tax rates began in the post-war period. When one turns to the marginal tax rates produced by the tax–benefit interaction at the bottom end of the income scale, one finds that the seeds of today's poverty and unemployment traps were sown but had not grown much by 1960. Unemployment benefit was in principle generous at 70% of net wages for a lower quartile married man with 2 children. But it was fiercely 'work-tested' according to the Beveridge principles embodied in the law and there were few unemployed. In-work benefits ('National Assistance') were only available on a selective basis to those able-bodied workers in need, as established by National Assistance boards.

Later, work-testing was to fall into disuse and National Assistance became a means-tested right.

With the top rate of income tax and inheritance tax down to 40% today, it is hard to conjure up the nightmarish tax world for higher earners of the 1950s (in the 1960s it was to become still worse, as the peace dividend was not there to offset the new spending demands from the Labour programme after 1964). The Beatles discovered they 'would tax your feet' but economists, many of whom had been civil servants, few in any sort of business, made little fuss. Even such a robust and intelligent commentator as Ian Little dismissed routinely in 1961 the disincentive effects of high tax rates, remarking that 'the empirical evidence available strongly suggests that there is no significant connection between either marginal or average tax rates and the amount of effort on the part of wage earners and lower salaried workers. So far as higher-income earners are concerned, there is no quantitative evidence of any disincentive effect of marginal tax rates'. (Worswick and Ady, 1962, p 282).

In an earlier age when 'evidence' was less to hand and economists trusted their instincts more, Little had written more nervously, in 1950, after running through the potentially dangerous long-term consequences for effort, evasion and emigration: 'It can hardly be denied that a reduction in marginal tax rates might prove highly desirable.' (Worswick and Ady, 1952, p.182) In econometrics, as in all else, a little knowledge is a dangerous thing. Little mark-1 is the superior of Little mark-2 ten years later. Recent work of Lindsey (1987 a,b) and Feldstein (1995) for the US and Minford and Ashton (1991) for the UK suggests that high earners respond strongly to incentives. The last work mentioned, based on the 1980 General Household Survey, estimates the substitution elasticity for annual labour hours of high earners at around unity, and replication with the 1982 General Household Survey gives still higher elasticities.

In retrospect, it seems incredible that apparently responsible governments of both 'left' and 'right' took such risks with confiscatory marginal taxation. They did so with the connivance of the economics profession in the UK, which used the excuse of 'lack of evidence'. One might as well have said, before the arrival of carbon dating, that Schliemann's Troy showed no evidence of significant age. Economists had pathetically weak empirical tools and yet spoke pompously of evidence, forgetting their intellectual inheritance.

	1944/5	1950/1	1959/60
Gov't spending total	**6174**	**3417**	**5435**
Debt interest	435	515	869
Non-civil	5257	990	1771
Civil	482	1912	2795
Education	85	253	523
Pensions, health & other insurance benefits	301	928	1369
Taxes total	**3355**	**4157**	**5850**
Income & property	1390	1525	2488
Death duties	111	185	187
Profits	510	268	275
Indirect & other	1344	2179	2900
Balance	**-2819**	**740**	**415**
Memo items:	**1945**	**1951**	**1960**
Public debt (excl. floating)	21509	26125	27937
GDP	9831	14433	25522
GDP (civil use)	4574	13443	23761
Real GDP (1945=100)	100	109.7	139.8
Real civil GDP	100	204.0	279.9
GDP deflator (1945=100)	100	133.8	185.7

Source: Mitchell (1988) and Office of National Statistics

Table 3.1 Snapshots of central government finances, 1945–60 (£m.)

REGULATION AND CONTROLS

We turn last to the web of controls spun around economic activity by the Atlee government as it inherited the wartime panoply of interventionist powers. Given that government's plans to raise such high marginal tax rates, controls were a logical reinforcement. Disgruntled savers and entrepreneurs could take nothing out of the country, could obtain no credit for non-approved purposes that might deprive the taxman of his swag, could not pay workers in unusual ways without falling foul of the union–employer bodies, 'bargaining collectively' around them or the prices/incomes freezes (1948) or 'restraints' (1949), could find no lodgings for wandering workers because of rent controls, could obtain foreign exchange only by approval and so on.

Only the euphoria of recovery from war could explain the substantial resurgence of production in such a suffocating climate. As it was, even the muddled Conservatives of that time could not wriggle out of an attempt to loosen and occasionally eliminate controls. The spirit in which they did so was summed up by Sir Anthony Eden's ignorant disingenuousness in a note to his Chancellor over import controls:

> As to the question of imports, I should be most reluctant to contemplate any return to licensing and government controls. Is it not, however, possible to get something of the same results by other methods? Cannot the banks, for instance, be given some indication from time to time that such and such materials are those for the import of which we should be most reluctant to see money advanced? (Eden, 1960)

Labour not merely preserved but also built up the war-time control regime. Nationalisation was their most famous policy, taking in coal, all transport (road, rail and air), electricity boards, gas, iron and steel, all telecommunications, and the Bank of England. Some bodies, such as the General Post Office and British Overseas Airways Corporation, had already been nationalised in or before the war, in a spirit of 'pragmatic' control that later characterised the Conservative post-Labour approach.

The fact remains that this was a remarkable extension of government control over industry; it represented about one-fifth of British GDP. It was reinforced by Labour's links with a highly unionised labour force in private manufacturing (the 9.25 million union members in 1950 represented 53% of the employed labour force outside the armed forces, but public and private non-transport services with 35% of employment were barely unionised, implying 80% or higher unionisation in industry and transport). Where unionisation was negligible, Bevin introduced minimum wage laws (the Wage Council Acts of 1945 and 1948), which extended union-equivalent protection to 4.5 million workers.

One way or another, therefore, the government exercised controls, either through unions, management or direct labour market intervention, on virtually the whole of the economy's production. And control over production was buttressed by comprehensive financial controls – on bank credit, hire purchase, and foreign exchange – and controls on imports.

Finally, there was effective control over mobility by the government ownership of much rented accommodation and control over the private remainder of the rented sector. The market in rented housing was subsidised and distorted through these means so that a worker wishing to move would both lose his sitting tenant rights and have to rent expensive uncontrolled (furnished) accommodation in his chosen new location.

The Conservatives therefore confronted in 1951 a population and industry held in thrall by the government. The only concession towards decontrol that Labour had made was in the removal of much rationing, though food rationing was still in force. The Conservatives' reaction, however, when they came to power was considerably less radical in practice than the free-market rhetoric of their election campaign might have suggested. They retained all Labour's financial controls and union/minimum wage laws. Although they made no formal use of incomes or price controls during the 1950s, there was all the usual exhortation and joint TUC–industry–government consultation; and in 1961, Selwyn Lloyd was to reintroduce formal wage controls.

Apart from abolishing rationing, the only concessions the Conservatives made to free-market ideas were to abandon formal import controls (but as we have seen retaining informal controls through credit and foreign exchange controls) and to bring in a half-hearted Rent Decontrol Act in 1957 – and even this was soon to fall victim to popular outrage over the practices of one Mr Rachman. The pound also became convertible at the official fixed rate on the foreign exchanges, which meant that foreigners at least could use it freely at this rate (previously there was de facto a dual exchange rate, a freely floating one for foreigners and a fixed one for controlled residents). However, residents continued to be subject to exchange controls.

It is therefore in the controls, the politicised incentives of nationalised industry managers and the strong powers of government-encouraged unions, that one finds the factors most depressing to the incentives of

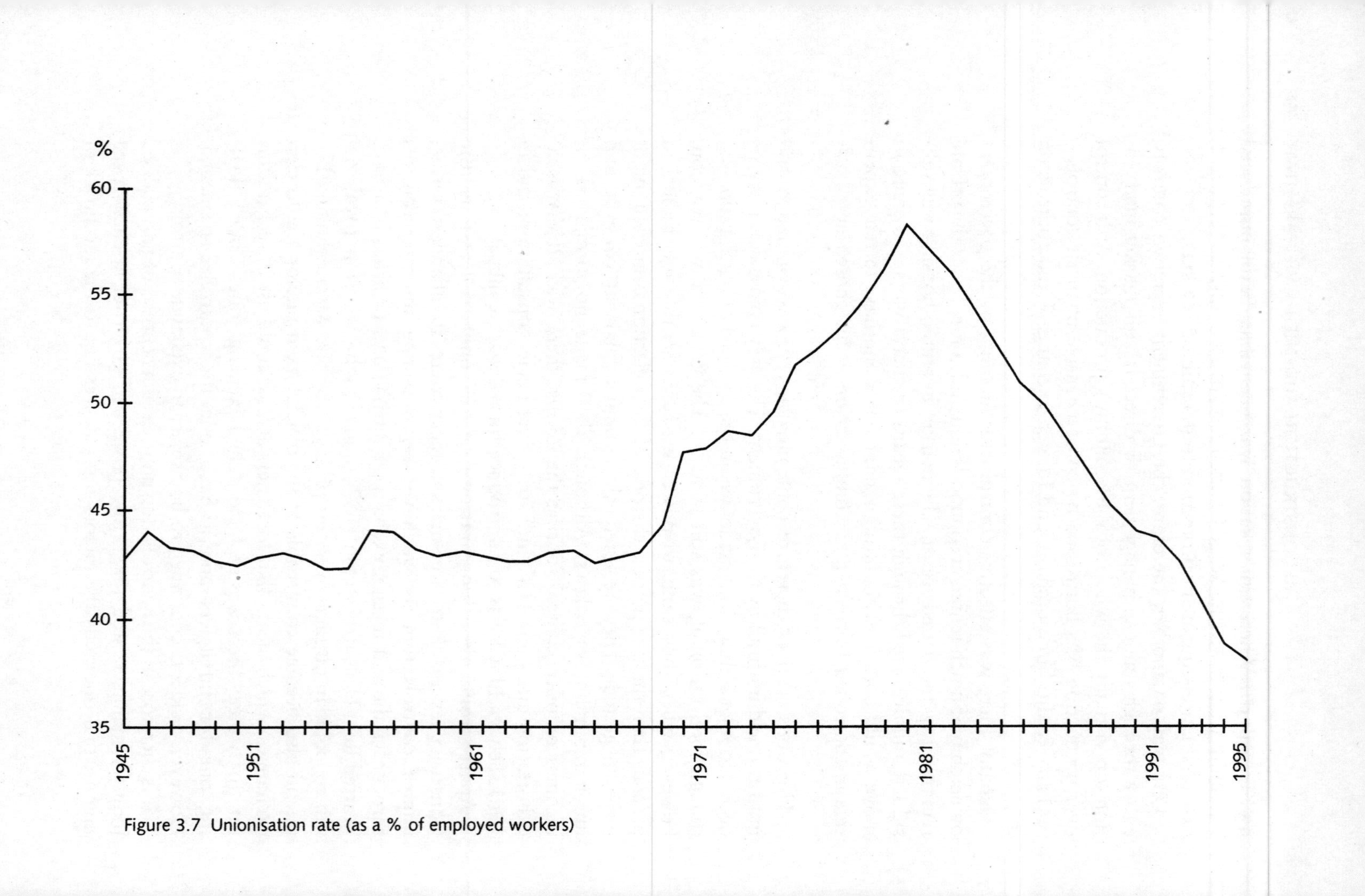

Figure 3.7 Unionisation rate (as a % of employed workers)

ordinary people during this time. The British working man became the character later immortalised by Peter Sellers in *I'm all right, Jack*, and the British manager was bound to feel – and did – that his main aim was to keep the workers happy so as to keep production running after a fashion and then go cap-in-hand to government if layoffs threatened.

BRINGING THE STORY UP TO DATE

This cursory account of the building of the post-war welfare state and its associated taxes and controls must suffice. We now briefly consider subsequent developments; full consideration is deferred to future chapters.

With minor interruption, the regime I have described for the end of the 1950s continued throughout the 1960s and 1970s. There were of course changes of detail, but apart from a brief interlude when Edward Heath's Conservative government came into office in 1970 and pledged to restore free markets, only to reverse direction within twelve months, nothing was done to alter the basic philosophy of intervention, high and rising government spending and taxation. The steady deterioration in the environment is well known. Mischief was afoot and it took its course.

The effects of these trends on the British economy were visible to the most casual observer by the end of the 1970s. Britain was 'the sick man of Europe', the butt of jokes at economic assessment conferences across the world. Its economy and even its social fabric had fallen into ruins in the final months of the Labour government in 1978-9, with the 'winter of discontent', the explosion of wages and pent-up inflation after the collapse of yet another incomes policy, and the descent into severe recession as corrective monetary policy was applied.

The causal connections between the policies described here and this ultimate collapse are essentially simple: the systemic suppression of incentives acted to erode proper economic behaviour. But the details are complex, and in the next few chapters we look at them carefully. Here, by way of an introductory review, we set out the broad evidence of the relative failure that emerges from the basic macroeconomic measures of performance.

THE RELATIVE PERFORMANCE OF THE UK ECONOMY – A PRELIMINARY OVERVIEW

At this preliminary stage, we examine two measures of UK performance: overall GDP per capita and productivity in manufacturing (where it can reliably be measured). Productivity measures the performance of those in work while total per capita GDP adds in the extent of labour participation.

For a comparison, we use Germany, because in the post-war period it pursued a very different, free ('social') market path of reconstruction. The history of that period cannot be pursued here but, in brief, under the leadership of Erhard and Adenauer, and somewhat in spite of Allied advice, West Germany decided to pursue policies of radical liberalisation in line with the ideas of the *Ordnungstheorie* school (Eucken, 1950), while conceding some 'social partnership' to unions that were in practice highly docile and co-operative for some two decades. Comparisons of growth over different time periods for the UK alone do not convey much because they do not allow for the differing circumstances of the times (inter-war depression and protection, post-war liberalisation and expanding world markets for example).

The comparisons are set out in Figures 3.8 and 3.9. The first set shows the trends in per capita income. In the period from 1913 to 1980, the post-war period up to 1979 stands out as one in which Germany massively outstripped the UK. This had not been true of the inter-war period, when the two countries had a rather similar performance. From 1979 also, the trend of relatively high German growth ceased.

It has been widely argued that Germany outperformed the UK in growth from around 1870 merely because it was able to catch up on a technological lead, the UK having been the home of the industrial revolution and Germany being late in achieving the necessary national identity and stability (Kennedy, 1988). It might be possible to extend this argument, whatever its merits, into the 1950s, but it seems implausible: the process would seem to have run its course by the 1930s, judging by the first portion of Figure 3.8. In any case, Germany's per capita income exceeded the UK's by 1958. It then continued to grow faster for nearly two decades. This seems to indicate clearly that deeper forces were at work, of the sort described in this paper.

As for the reversal from 1979, while it may be possible to point by now to the potential for the UK to catch up, the fact that the process began at all, let alone in 1979–82, points clearly to the causal role of the large-scale reforms of the Thatcher government.

We turn next to relative productivity, where only data since 1938 is available. Here the turn-round in relative performance is even more startling (see Figure 3.9). Between 1938 and 1979, German productivity growth was on average 3.9% p.a., the UK's 1.8% p.a. Between 1979 and 1990, Germany's was on average 1.5% p.a., the UK's 3.1% p.a. In

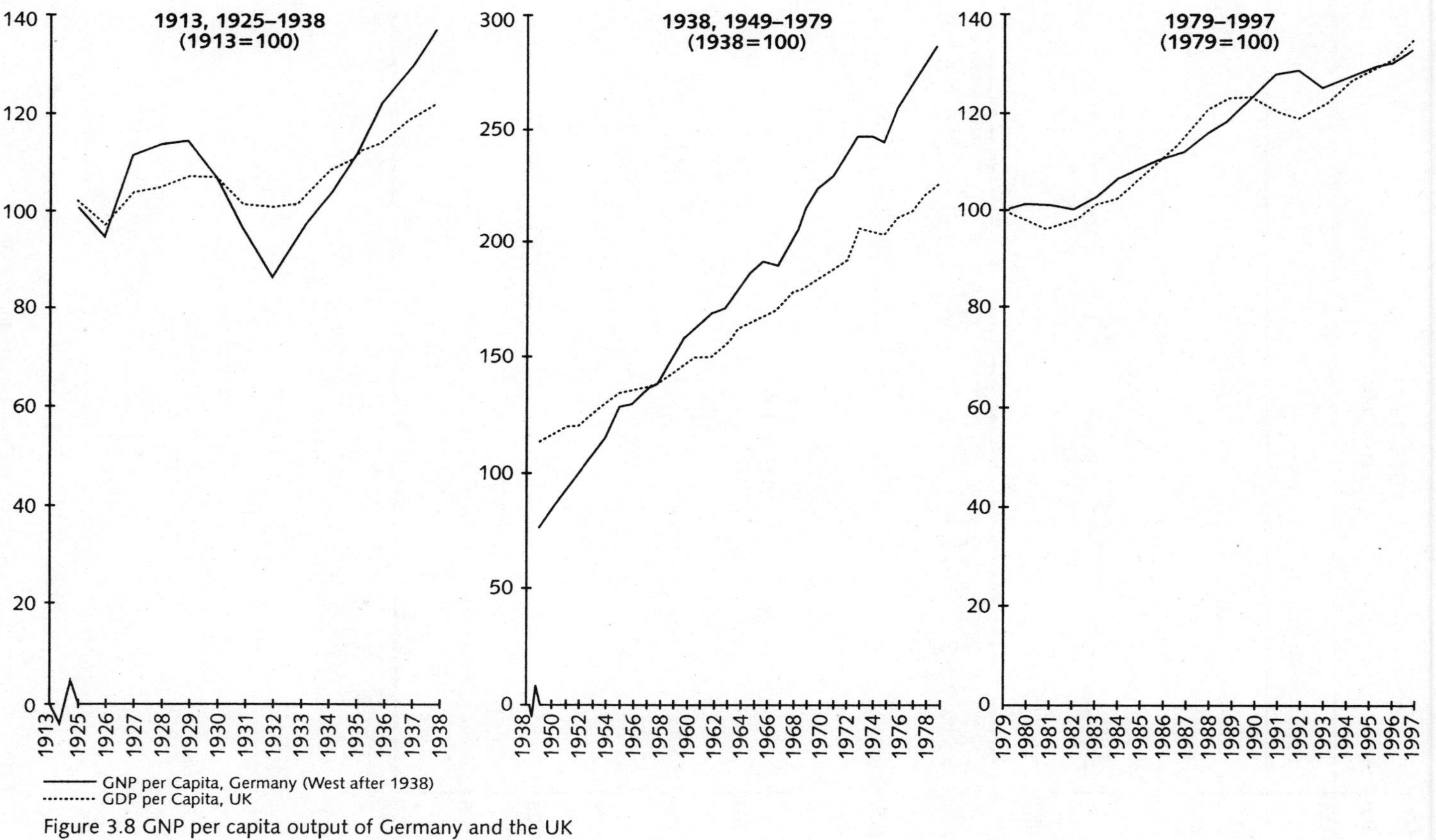

Figure 3.8 GNP per capita output of Germany and the UK

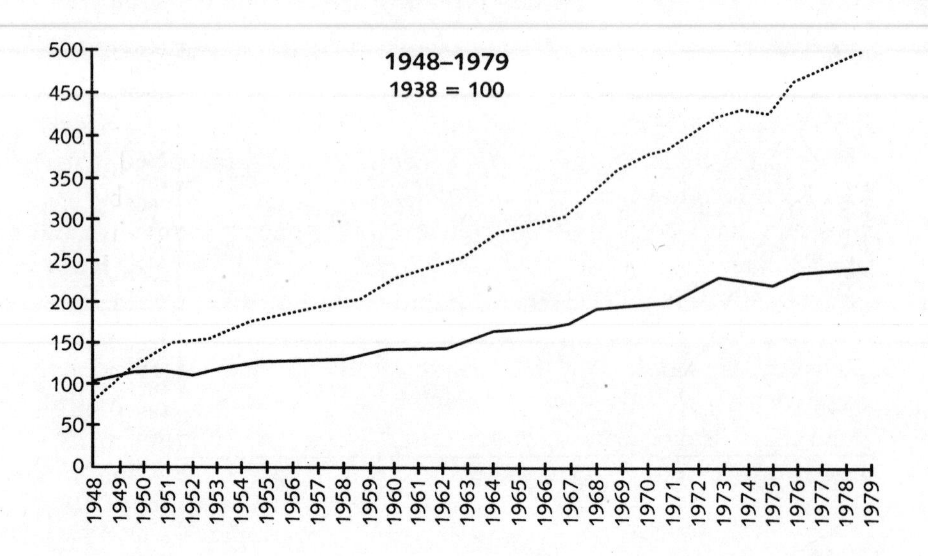

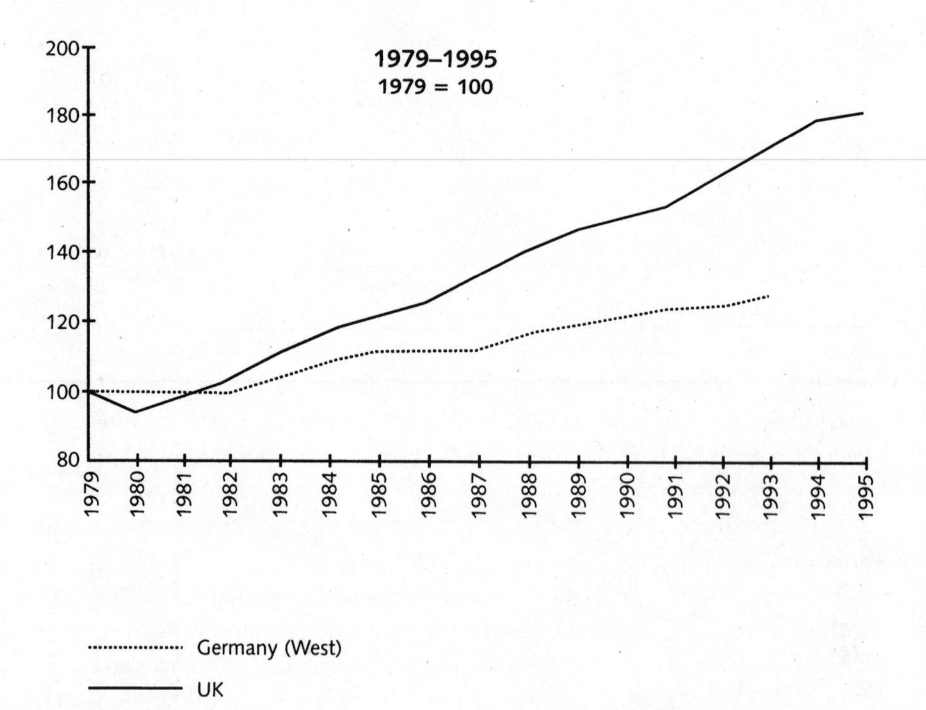

Figure 3.9 Manufacturing productivity in Germany and the UK

each period, growth of one is double the other's but the roles are reversed between periods.

These facts appear to support the conclusion that Germany set out on a free-market course after the Second World War and prospered, while the UK chose interventionism and underperformed, whatever absolute gains may have come its way from general post-war prosperity and rapidly expanding world trade. Belatedly, in 1979 the UK began (painfully) to copy the German free-market example and over the next decade ultimately reaped some (initial) rewards. An irony may well be (Davis and Minford, 1986) that by the late 1970s Germany was actually copying parts of the British 'social' model, and some of the turnround could be due to this negative factor. The point about the importance of relative incentive systems is thereby only further underlined.

CONCLUSIONS

Let me conclude by summarising the lessons of the experience reviewed here.

The first point is that of interactive complications. Medical people are familiar with the way a body, weakened by a serious disease, contracts numerous associated ailments, which cumulatively destroy it even when the original main disease has been tackled. So with economies. A serious and fundamental distortion, such as penal marginal tax rates on low- and high-paid workers, will cut back labour performance, with a series of knock-on effects – for example, on tax revenues, on the incentive to inflate, and on the propensity to introduce controls that further worsen microeconomic performance. Once unemployment takes hold, it will tend to become long-term; once long-term, it will produce deterioration in skills and motivation among the unemployed ('hysteresis' effects) and it will strengthen the defensive attitudes of 'insiders' (ie, those with jobs) who fear deeply for their own exposure to such risks. It is interesting to note the general absence of these effects in a well-functioning labour market such as that of the US.

The second point follows from the first. From a policy viewpoint, the path of corrective reform for such a weakened economy is hard to prescribe and depends crucially on the politics of the country and situation. Should everything be changed at once in a big bang (New Zealand, Poland)? Or should a step-by-step approach be followed (Thatcher's UK is the classic example, another is China)? No doctor would attempt a prescription without considering the patient's whole situation, and it seems that the same is true here. The account I gave in 1988 of Mrs

Thatcher's reform programme – though clearly her luck ran out in her third term for reasons that there is no space to go into here – can still stand for the achievement of a largely irreversible reform of British institutions (Minford, 1988). And at the time of writing (1997), the overwhelming evidence is in favour of step-by-step strategies and against any big bang.

Finally, it appears that monetary assistance is the least of the necessary inputs. Marshall Aid was as liberally available to the UK as to Germany; yet Germany forged ahead on the basis of a reconstructed free-market system while the UK wallowed in stultifying controls. Japan benefited little from monetary aid, yet after the MacArthur free-market reforms and destruction of the old cartelised, semi-feudal, restrictive networks, Japan built up a competitive industry so far without equal. One could go further, as argued by Kostrzewa, Nunnenkamp and Schmieding (1990), Marshall Aid to the UK may well have scuppered the chances of a free market policy by buttressing and subsidising the policies of the Atlee government. Disheartened that their prophecies of Labour collapse failed to come true, the Tories threw in the free-market towel and signed up to pragmatic interventionism.

What is certainly clear is that free markets must be the end, without compromise or ambiguity, even if they are deliberately not all freed overnight. The Soviet example seems to make that very clear: where people sense a lack of direction, they will not trust themselves to the risky business of business.

In the end, what the UK lacked was the excuse to have a General MacArthur sort us out. Instead, the UK got Marshall Aid and polite American's tut-tuts as they powerlessly watched us drift away on a flood of socialist emotion that set us back half a century.

References

Davis, J. and Minford, P.(1986) 'Germany and the European Disease', *Recherches Économiques de Louvain*, 52, pp 373–98.

Eden, Sir Anthony (1960) *Full Circle: the Memoirs of the Rt. Hon. Sir Anthony Eden*, Cassell, London.

Eucken, W. (1950) *The Foundations of Economics*, W. Hodge, London.

Feldstein, M. (1995) 'The Effect of Marginal Tax Rates on Taxable Income: A Panel Study of the 1986 Tax Reform Act', *Journal of Political Economy*, 103(3), June, 551–72.

Hayek, F.A. (1988) *The Fatal Conceit – the Errors of Socialism*, Collected Works of F.A. Hayek (Vol 1), Ed. W. W. Bartley III, Routledge, London and New York.

Howarth, T.E.B. (1985) *Prospect and Reality – Great Britain 1945–55*, Collins, London.

Kennedy, P. (1988) *The Rise and Fall of the Great Powers*, Fontana, London.

Kostrzewa, W., Nunnenkamp, P. and Schmieding, H. (1990) 'A Marshall Plan for Middle and Eastern Europe' *The World Economy*, March, pp 27–49.

Lindsey, L.B. (1987a) 'Capital gains rates, realizations and revenues', in *The Effects of Taxation on Capital Accumulation*, M. Feldstein (ed.), for NBER, Chicago University Press, Chicago.

Lindsey, L.B. (1987b) 'Individual taxpayer response to tax cuts, 1982-84; with implications for the revenue maximising tax rates', *Journal of Public Economics*, Vol. 33, July, pp. 173-206.

Minford, P. (1988) 'Mrs. Thatcher's Economic Reform Programme' in R. Skidelsky (ed.) *Thatcherism*, Chatto and Windus, London, pp 93–106.

Minford, P. and Ashton, P. (1991) 'The Poverty Trap and the Laffer Curve – what can the GHS tell us', *Oxford Economic Papers*, 43, pp. 245-279.

Mitchell, B.R. (1988) *British Historical Statistics*, Cambridge University Press, Cambridge.

Worswick, G.D.N. and Ady, P.H. (eds.) (1952) *The British Economy 1945–50*, Oxford University Press, Oxford.

Worswick, G.D.N. and Ady, P.H. (eds.) (1962) *The British Economy in the Nineteen-fifties*, Oxford University Press, Oxford.

CHAPTER FOUR

The remaking of the British economy 1979–97 – macroeconomics

THE LAST CHAPTER discussed the post-war drive towards socialism initiated by Atlee's Labour government and its consolidation under succeeding governments up to 1979. We briefly remarked on the reversal in the UK's relative performance resulting from the reforms started by Margaret Thatcher's governments from 1979. In this chapter we go into that story more thoroughly.[1]

The story falls into two parts: macroeconomic – the management of the economy, dealt with in this chapter – and microeconomic – the organisation of markets which I turn to in the next chapter.

On the macroeconomic side, policy in 1979 consisted of keeping the economy as close to full employment as possible by the use of interest rates and of the budget balance between spending and taxation – in other words, monetary and fiscal policy. Any consequential inflationary

[1] A number of authors have attempted an assessment of 'Thatcherism' and by implication its preceding opposite, for example Layard and Nickell (1989), Matthews and Minford (1987), Maynard (1988), Walters (1985). Then there is work on housing and labour mobility – Hughes and McCormick (1984), Minford et al (1987), Muellbauer and Murphy (1988). On privatisation, Veljanovski (1987) and Yarrow (1986) have made useful assessments. In the central labour market, there have been studies of classical and Keynesian wage-pressure effects (Layard and Nickell (1985), Minford (1983)), more recently studies of 'hysteretic' and 'insider' effects (Lindbeck and Snower (1986), Blanchard and Summers (1986)), and studies of union effects on performance (Blanchflower, Millward and Oswald (1991), Machin and Wadwhani (1991)).

pressure was dealt with by income and price controls. This 'Keynesian' approach (though whether Keynes himself would have approved is doubtful) would nowadays be regarded as absurd; but at that time it was conventional across Europe and even in the US – Nixon adopted such controls in the early 1970s and announced 'we are all Keynesians now', and Carter's policies were also Keynesian in this sense.

The Thatcher government was the first to adopt a primarily monetarist approach to economic management – with fiscal policy playing a supporting role, and income/price controls eliminated not merely because of their long-term ineffectiveness (in the end a market economy has to have wages and prices set by market forces) but essentially because of their damaging effect on economic behaviour through the mispricing of labour and output. The aim from 1979 onwards was to control inflation through limiting growth in the money supply. The policy was also intended to create stabilising tendencies for output because in booms interest rates would rise to hold down money supply expansion, and vice versa in slumps.

In order to support this policy, the government intended to bring its budget deficit down to a percentage of national income at which it would no longer be necessary to print money in order to hold down interest rates and the cost of the national debt. The argument here was a little convoluted. It begins with the notion of a 'sustainable' public-deficit-to-GDP ratio: this is the ratio at which public debt remains constant as a fraction of GDP.[2]

This sustainable ratio has two good properties. First, it implies that taxes can be held constant as a proportion of GDP indefinitely – a state of 'tax-smoothing' that is attractive from a business viewpoint as well as optimal in avoiding incentives to transfer activity artificially over time.

Secondly, it enables money supply growth to be kept constant at the rate that keeps inflation at that 2% target rate. Above this sustainable deficit, for example, a rising debt/GDP ratio puts pressure on the government to print money faster in order to reduce interest rates and raise inflation, both of which lower the real cost of debt and so slow the rise in debt. These possibilities undermine the monetary control of inflation

[2] Arithmetically, this depends on the growth of GDP at current prices and the debt/GDP ratio. For example, if inflation is 2% (the target rate) and growth 3%, and so GDP growth at current prices is 5%, then a debt/GDP fraction of 0.5 implies that the sustainable deficit is 2.5% of GDP. This is arrived at as follows: for the debt/GDP ratio to be constant, debt and GDP must be growing at the same rate, viz. here 0.05 p.a. Growth of debt=deficit/GDP=(deficit/GDP)(GDP/debt). Hence 0.05=(deficit/GDP)/ 0.5 so that deficit/GDP=(0.5)(0.05)=0.025 or 2.5%.

because people anticipate them – generating a lack of credibility for monetary policy. Their anticipations drive up wage settlements and long-term interest rates; inflation becomes more stubborn and people switch out of money into bonds and other financial instruments, so making an even tighter monetary policy necessary. The political strains may be too much for the policy to be kept up.

For these reasons, the Thatcher government set out a Medium Term Financial Strategy embracing targets for both the money supply and the budget deficit over the medium term. In the first section that follows, we detail the history of this policy, which has survived in one form or another since.

Microeconomic policy covered a broad spectrum of measures designed to increase the efficiency of the UK economy. They included not only the well known moves of 'privatisation' and associated deregulation – the withdrawal of government from controlling market outcomes as opposed to setting the framework within which free markets could operate – but also the programme to bring down marginal tax rates by reducing government expenditure and by reforming the tax structure towards greater 'neutrality', that is where marginal tax rates on different people and activities should be made as equal as possible. Within the two programmes, the tax and benefit disincentives and the state intervention (in support of union power and a miscellany of worker rights, such as minimum wages for some groups and controls on firing) in the labour market were of great importance. The labour market is the engine room of the economy; labour is the principal resource located in an economy, with no real chance to move away (land is another, but far less important for the modern economy). Its quantity and quality limit the economy's potential. Other inputs, such as capital and raw materials, can be hired in to fit with what labour can profitably produce.

The UK economy had performed badly in terms of productivity growth, as we saw in the last chapter; it was also beginning to perform badly in terms of unemployment by 1979. This was connected with the stranglehold on industry of many competing unions, whose demands were buttressed by rising benefits for those out of work and rising tax rates for those in work. The rest of the Thatcher microeconomic reforms produced undoubted gains, but it was the breaking-up of this labour market stranglehold that was the key to its success. Without it, the rest would have been of little value as union power would have frustrated management attempts to exploit liberalised output markets; and, where managements succeeded in achieving higher efficiency, those laid off from greater efficiency would have had poor prospects of finding fresh employment because of union and other regulative barriers, and so unemployment would have permanently worsened.

So in the chapter that follows, I focus generally on the microeconomic reforms but particularly intensively on these labour market reforms and their impact, which have not elsewhere been examined with as much attention as privatisation and the rest. But first we turn to monetary policy and inflation, which is where the reforms began.

MONETARY POLICY PRIOR TO MRS THATCHER

The monetarist policies pursued by Thatcher had their antecedents in those pursued by the Labour Chancellor, Denis Healey, from 1976 to 1979. It is also important to understand the evolution of monetary thinking in the post-war period, because Thatcher's programme was not merely a piece of modern conservative theorising but far more a reaction against the overt practical failures of pre-monetarist policy.

In fact, there is not a great deal to say about pre-monetarist policy, since basically it consisted in an absence of monetary policy. The post-war policy framework until the advent of floating exchange rates in 1972 was Bretton Woods where, under fixed rates, the money supply adjusted to demand via the balance of payments. Furthermore, apart from the brief experiment with bank deregulation between 1972 and 1974, the financial system was highly regulated so that broad and narrow money were well correlated.

In the immediate post-war period, with limited convertibility and tight exchange controls, money supply adjustment was slow and allowed substantial short-run monetary independence. Nevertheless the British government gave monetary policy a limited role, using fiscal policy and occasional devaluation as its principal instruments for controlling demand and the balance of payments. This subordination of monetary policy was given the academic imprimatur of the Radcliffe Committee in 1959 (Radcliffe Report, 1959); it and its principal author, Professor R.S. Sayers of the London School of Economics, argued that money could not be usefully defined because of the many assets that closely substituted in providing 'money services' and that, instead, 'liquidity' should be controlled in a discretionary way by interest rates and credit restrictions.

In practice, this meant that from time to time a credit squeeze – using both credit controls and higher interest rates – was implemented to help finance a current account deficit or as an emergency means of slowing demand when fiscal policy was not working fast enough. Unfortunately, such a hands-off approach to money creates problems when short-run monetary independence is as great as it was until the world capital market integration of the 1970s. Excessive money-supply growth, even with the exchange rate fixed, will drive up domestic prices, and the correction from falling reserves will only gradually occur, as the current balance goes into deficit with reduced competitiveness and capital flows respond slowly if at all. The UK had at this time a large if declining share in many overseas markets for manufactured goods, so that the response to higher prices was slow in coming.

Under this system, eventually the economy is forced either to reverse policies ('stop–go') in an attempt to force relative prices back down, or to devalue, validating the previous price shift. There was an enormous devaluation in 1949 (30%) and it is probable that this was not eroded until the middle 1960s. During most of the period 1949–67, money-supply growth was excessive and prices rose faster than those of competitors (Figure 4.1). By 1967, when the cumulative price shift had pushed the current account into permanent deficit at normal employment levels (see Figure 3.2), the case for another devaluation appeared overwhelming (Figure 4.9 shows how the real exchange rate had risen), given the difficulty of driving wages and prices down.

The devaluation of 1967 marked a change in attitudes to money. The problem of stabilising sterling after it required the help of the IMF, which insisted on the control of Domestic Credit Expansion (DCE) (see Figure 4.2).

DCE, the credit extended by the banking system (including both central bank and all commercial banks), is the analogue of money-supply control when the exchange rate is fixed. The change in the money supply equals DCE plus the change in foreign reserves, by the banking system's 'balance sheet identity'. Its assets are its lending (DCE) and its reserves, and these must be equal to its liabilities, the money supply (deposits and currency). At this time, the money supply was defined to include all the commercial banks' deposits, or M3 (later refined to £M3). According to the 'monetary approach to the balance of payments', it was argued that if bank lending (DCE) was set equal to a reasonable level of the money supply (ie, what was dictated by a stable demand for money), the change in reserves (the total balance of payments) would be controlled by implication.

This was probably the first time that monetary factors were taken seriously by the UK government in the post-war period. It was not of course monetarism, being merely a formalised monetary prop to the

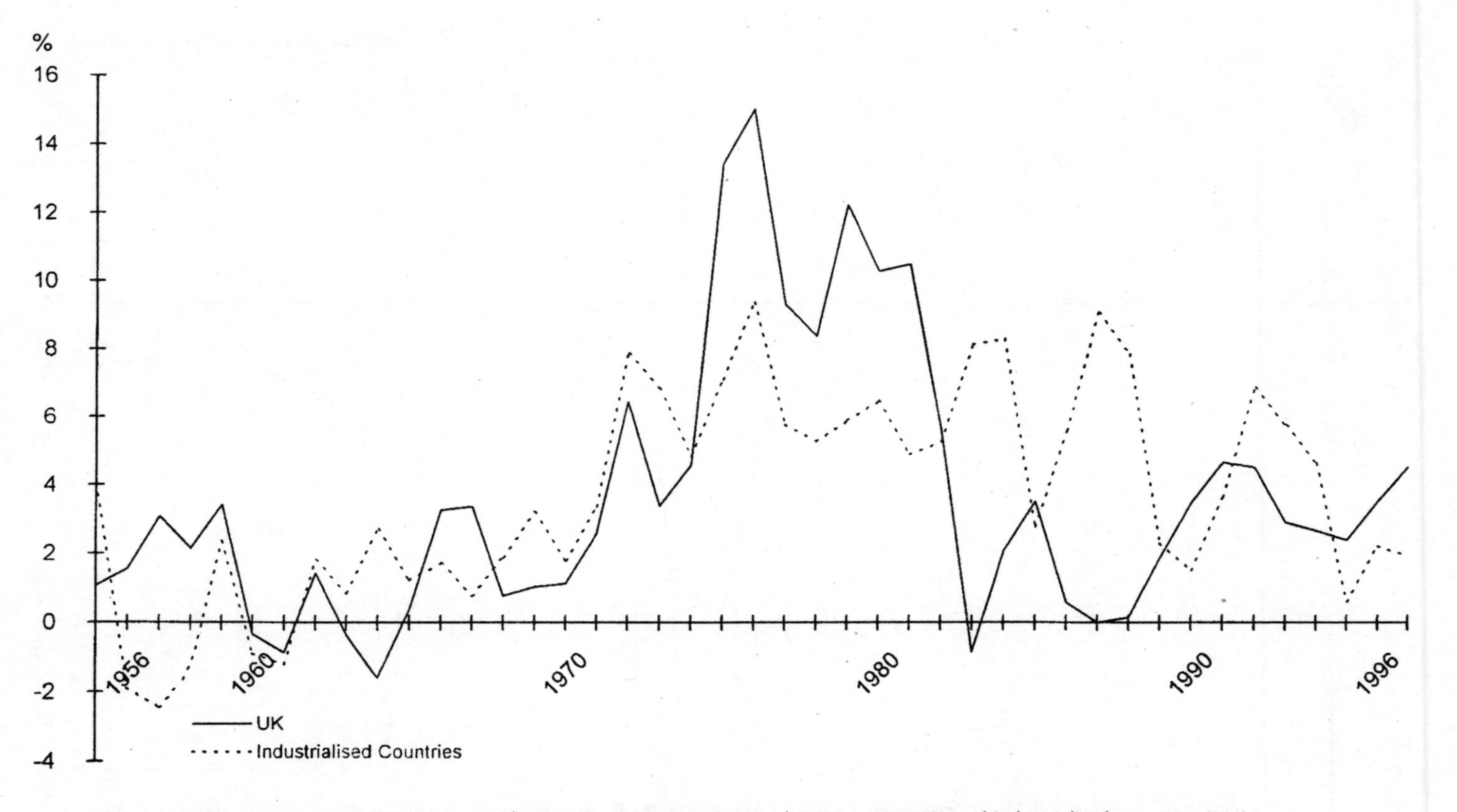

Figure 4.1 Excess money growth (money supply growth minus growth in real GDP) – UK (M0) and industrialised countries (M1)

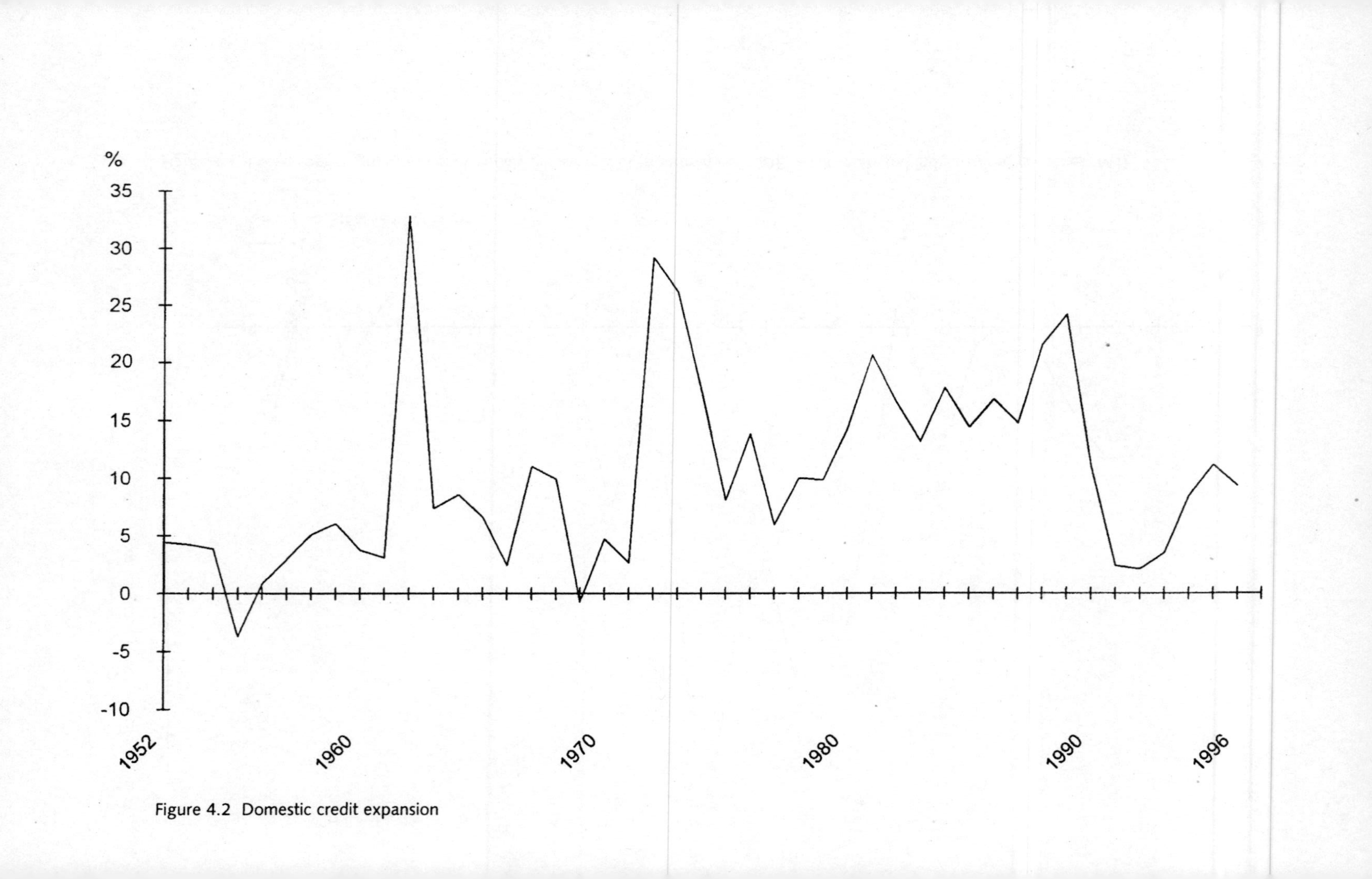

Figure 4.2 Domestic credit expansion

fixed exchange rate. But it created an effective control on the domestic creation of money, and was backed up by the most stringent fiscal policy since the war. By 1970, the budget deficit had been eliminated, DCE growth cut back to below 5%, and the balance of payments was in substantial surplus.

Had these attitudes persisted, the UK would have gone over to monetarist control when the world went onto floating rates in the early 1970s. However, the monetary approach went only skin deep in government circles. There had for a long time been a belief in incomes policies as the way to control inflation. These policies had been used intermittently from 1960. When the IMF's DCE approach was adopted, it was combined with a tough incomes policy from 1968 – the 'belt and braces' combination.

Once the balance of payments position was under control and the IMF team had returned to Washington, the government returned to its incomes policy approach. In 1971, the Prime Minister, Edward Heath, who had campaigned on a free-market platform, abandoned it in the face of rising unemployment and inflationary pressure to pursue, on the one hand, a highly expansionary Keynesian policy of rising budget deficits, falling interest rates, and a depreciating pound (the UK floated formally in spring 1972) and, on the other hand, a highly restrictive incomes policy. The absence of monetary control, especially in the context of bank deregulation, ensured that the incomes policy broke down by 1974 (with the miners' strike in the aftermath of the oil crisis) and that inflation surged in 1974–75 to rates of 25% and up to 50% annualised – rates unheard of in the UK, which had never had the continental European hyperinflations.

As policy veered around into fiscal contraction and credit squeeze, as well as further incomes restraint, the popular mood was one ripe for monetarism. Inflation was the major concern, and as it failed to be reduced in any permanent way over the succeeding years to 1979, especially after the breakdown of yet another incomes policy in 1978 in the 'winter of discontent', people were ready to try a totally different counter-inflationary policy.

In 1976, the Labour Chancellor, Denis Healey, did adopt monetary targets, again under pressure from the IMF, which was called in to help stabilise the balance of payments. However, again the main burden of policy was placed on incomes restraint, as the braces, with the monetary-control belt being mainly cosmetic. Indeed, control was mainly achieved by a tax on banks' interest-earning deposits (the corset), which did no more than divert such deposits into non-bank intermediaries acting in close competition. Samuel Brittan of the Financial Times dubbed this 'unbelieving monetarism'(Brittan, 1977, p 89).

By 1979, the whole framework was unravelling; inflation was rising through 13%, and it was to reach 18%, with 23% wage settlements, before it peaked. The public was eager to try Mrs Thatcher's monetarist experiment.

THE EVOLUTION AND SUCCESS OF UK MONETARY POLICY SINCE 1979

Monetary policy in the UK since 1979 was continuously styled by the governments of Margaret Thatcher and her successor, John Major, as 'monetarist'. Yet it is different in many ways from the monetarism to be found in the textbook. Some have even claimed that recent British monetary policy ceased to be monetarist at all, in its willingness at times to use the exchange rate as an indicator; however, this is a misunderstanding.

To understand a policy, it is necessary to know the implicit model being used by politicians and officials. The model that has dominated official thinking during recent years is one in which the government is dealing repeatedly with an intelligent and watchful private sector (who thus have 'rational expectations'). In such a context, it pays the government to be bound somehow into pre-commitments that prevent 'reflation', the use of monetary and fiscal instruments to stimulate the economy beyond its normal capacity to grow (its 'productive potential'). These pre-commitments create credibility and so greater effectiveness for counter-inflationary policy.

A similar implicit model has become influential in the late nineties on the continent too, especially among central bankers. In Switzerland and Germany, it has strengthened the tradition of constitutional restraint on monetary policy through an independent central bank. In France, Italy and the Benelux countries, it has prompted the switch to an increasingly hard exchange-rate link to the deutschmark, intended to exploit the German Bundesbank's reputation, and this has now evolved into the proposal for European Monetary Union and a European Central Bank modelled on the Bundesbank.

However, in the UK this latter approach was, at least throughout the 1980s, rejected in favour of domestic sources of credibility. The reasons for this rejection will be discussed below, but the search for domestic discipline was the origin of the Medium Term Financial Strategy, to which I now turn.

The Medium Term Financial Strategy

In 1979, as we have seen Mrs Thatcher inherited a monetary mess. Inflation was rising rapidly from an initial rate of over 10% (Fig 4.3). The policy of wage controls that had been used to hold it down in 1978 had crumbled in the 'winter of discontent' of that year, when graves went undug and rubbish piled up in the streets. Large public-sector pay increases were promised by a commission under Professor Hugh Clegg, which had been set up by the previous Labour government. The budget was in crisis; already the deficit was up to 5% of GDP and it would clearly rise sharply more with these pay awards on top of the usual spending pressures (Fig 4.4).

The advice from Professor Milton Friedman in 1980 was to reduce the money-supply growth rate gradually and to cut taxes in order to stimulate output. The first part was accepted but the second was not because the deficit was seen to be important in conditioning financial confidence, as explained above. Until the deficit could be reduced by other means, tax rates would have to stay up and perhaps even go higher. This was the view, not merely of the Treasury, but also of the financial markets; in Liverpool University we saw it as a rational-expectations effect, given the growing pressures for monetary financing of long-lasting budget deficits.

This was the background to the policies pursued at the start of the Thatcher government. As we shall see, little importance was attached to the operating method used by the central bank, whether by monetary base control or by interest-rate setting in pursuit of monetary targets. So what with this and the emphasis on fiscal policy support, the debate on monetary policy in the UK took a very different form from that in the US, for example, though it perhaps had a rather European character.

The Thatcher government's monetary plan

The key problem was seen to be lack of long-term credibility in counter-inflation policy. The previous government had instituted monetary targets, starting in 1976 in conjunction with the IMF support arrangement. It had also managed a substantial reduction in the budget deficit: the Public Sector Borrowing Requirement (PSBR), the usual measure of deficit in the UK including government net lending to the private sector, was reduced from 10% of GDP in 1975 to below 4% in 1977. Nevertheless, the policies lacked long-term durability. An incomes policy, which had been emphasised as the key bulwark against inflation, crumbled – as it was widely predicted that it must in a free economy. The money supply target for £M3, a wide aggregate, was generally 'achieved' by using a tax on

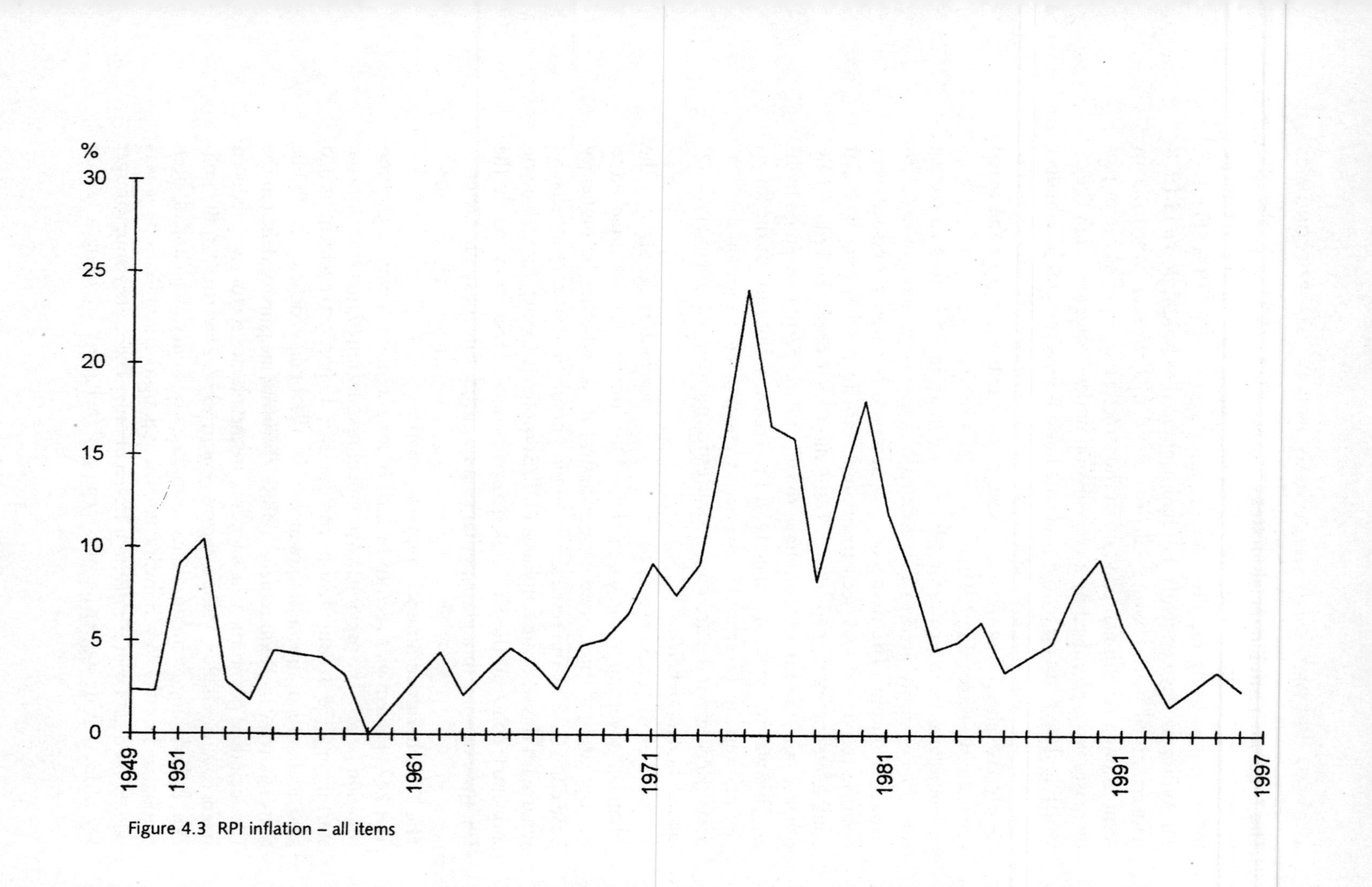

Figure 4.3 RPI inflation – all items

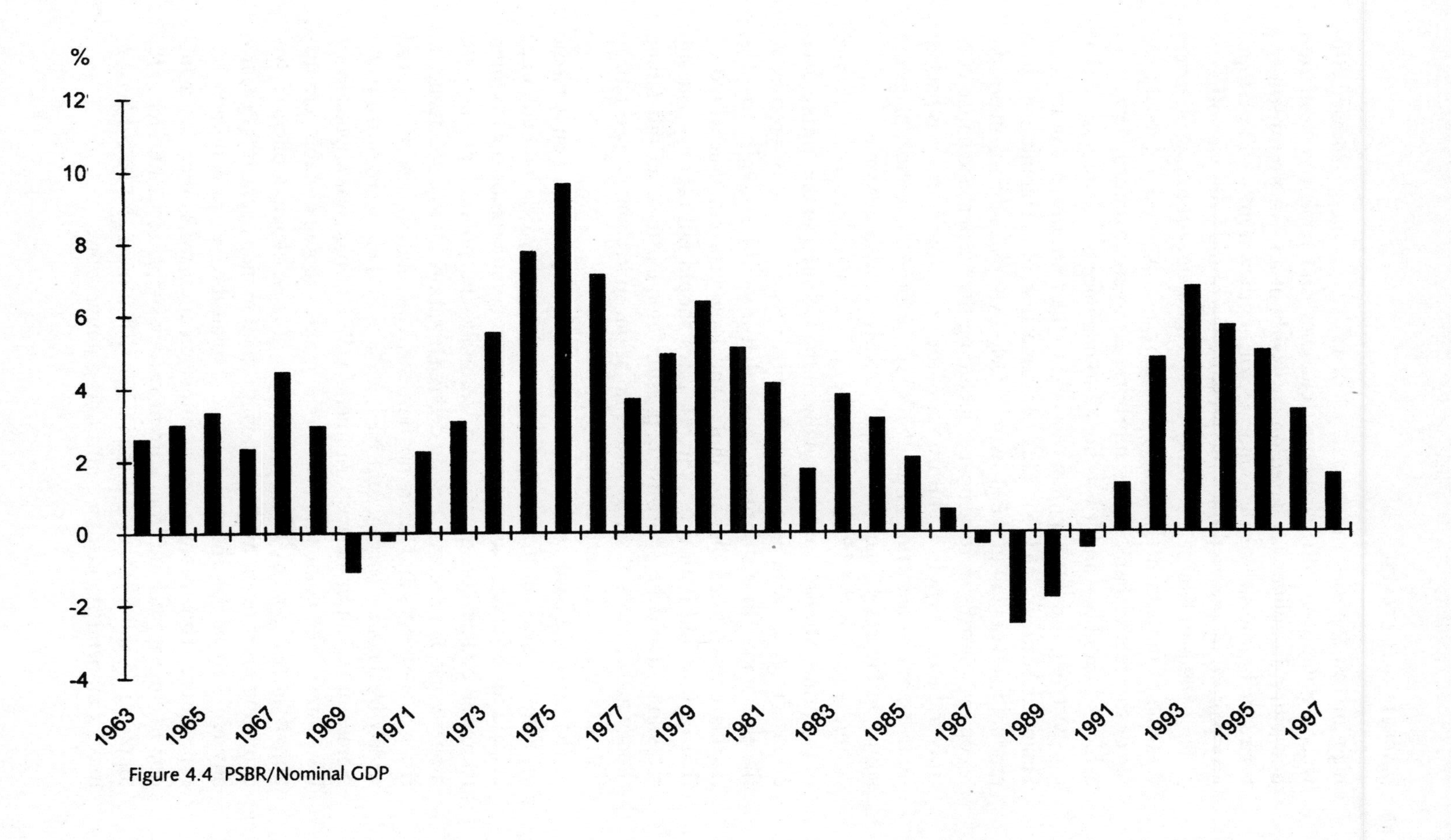

Figure 4.4 PSBR/Nominal GDP

high-interest deposits, the monetary 'corset'. Excess money showed elsewhere, notably in M0 (circulating currency and bank reserves). And budgetary discipline was based on cuts without any long-term strategy for reducing the size of the public sector; so they were seen as temporary pain to be reversed once the pressure (eg of the IMF) was off.

Thus the problem of a credibly durable monetary restraint on prices was one of fundamental political economy, not merely a technical matter of the central bank fixing appropriate targets (Minford, 1995). To achieve durability – and it was hoped to convince people rapidly of that prospective durability – policy was cast in the form of a Medium Term Financial Strategy (MTFS). This consisted first of a commitment to a gradual five-year fall in the growth of £M3 (M0 plus all bank deposits). Secondly, controls were removed, including the 'corset', exchange controls and incomes policy. Thirdly, the monetary commitment was backed up by a parallel reduction in the PSBR/GDP ratio – the original plans are shown in Figures 4.5 and 4.6, together with eventual outcomes.

Announced in the 1980 budget, the MTFS carried the full authority of the Prime Minister and notionally of the Cabinet, so that future deviations should be seen as a seriously embarrassing breach of promise to the electorate. On the optimistic view that it would be totally credible, market expectations of both short- and long-term inflation would be that they should both drop, interest rates should fall rapidly, and any recession should be short-lived, possibly non-existent, as the falling money growth was offset by falling inflation, so keeping up real money balances and consumer purchasing power.

The foregoing basic analysis could not be faulted. It rested on the logic of, first, the cash constraint on government whereby deficits today must be paid for by taxes, money expansion or economies tomorrow (its intertemporal budget constraint), and, secondly, the political pressure for money creation to relieve a rising debt/GDP ratio with its consequence in rising interest rates and future tax burdens. This analysis was later spread widely by Thomas Sargent and Neil Wallace in their well known paper 'Some unpleasant monetarist arithmetic' (1981), which was applied in the US context. The point was that if one assumes any reasonable termination of the rising debt/GDP ratio, whether because of a limit on incentive-damaging taxes or on available savings, then money financing is eventually required in the absence of quite implausibly severe cuts in public expenditure. This means a rise in future inflation worse than the reduction in current inflation from current money-supply restraint. Hence the 'unpleasant' policy lesson that the budget deficit must also be cut back to make a monetarist inflation-control programme work.

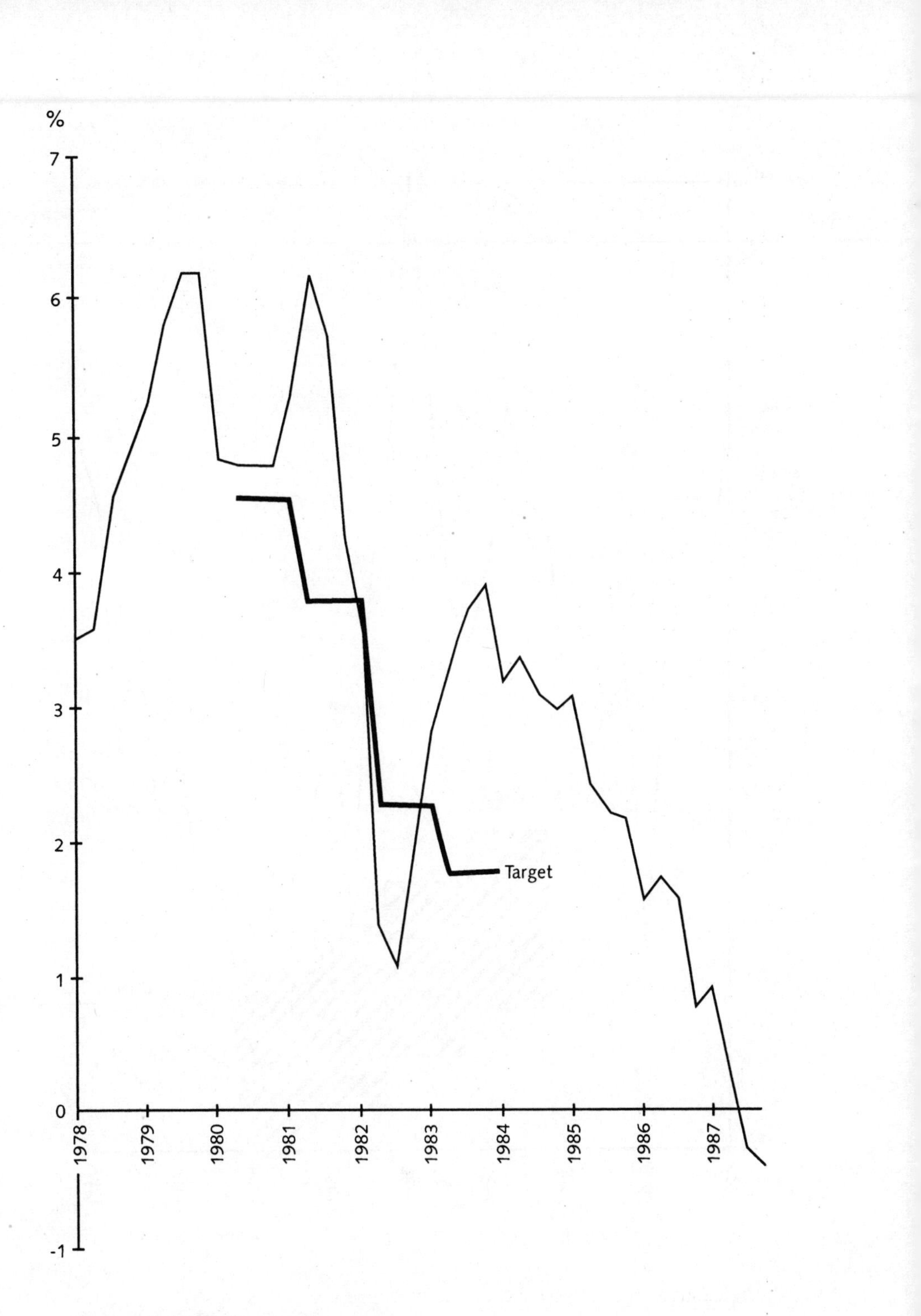

Figure 4.5 PSBR/GDP 4 quarter average

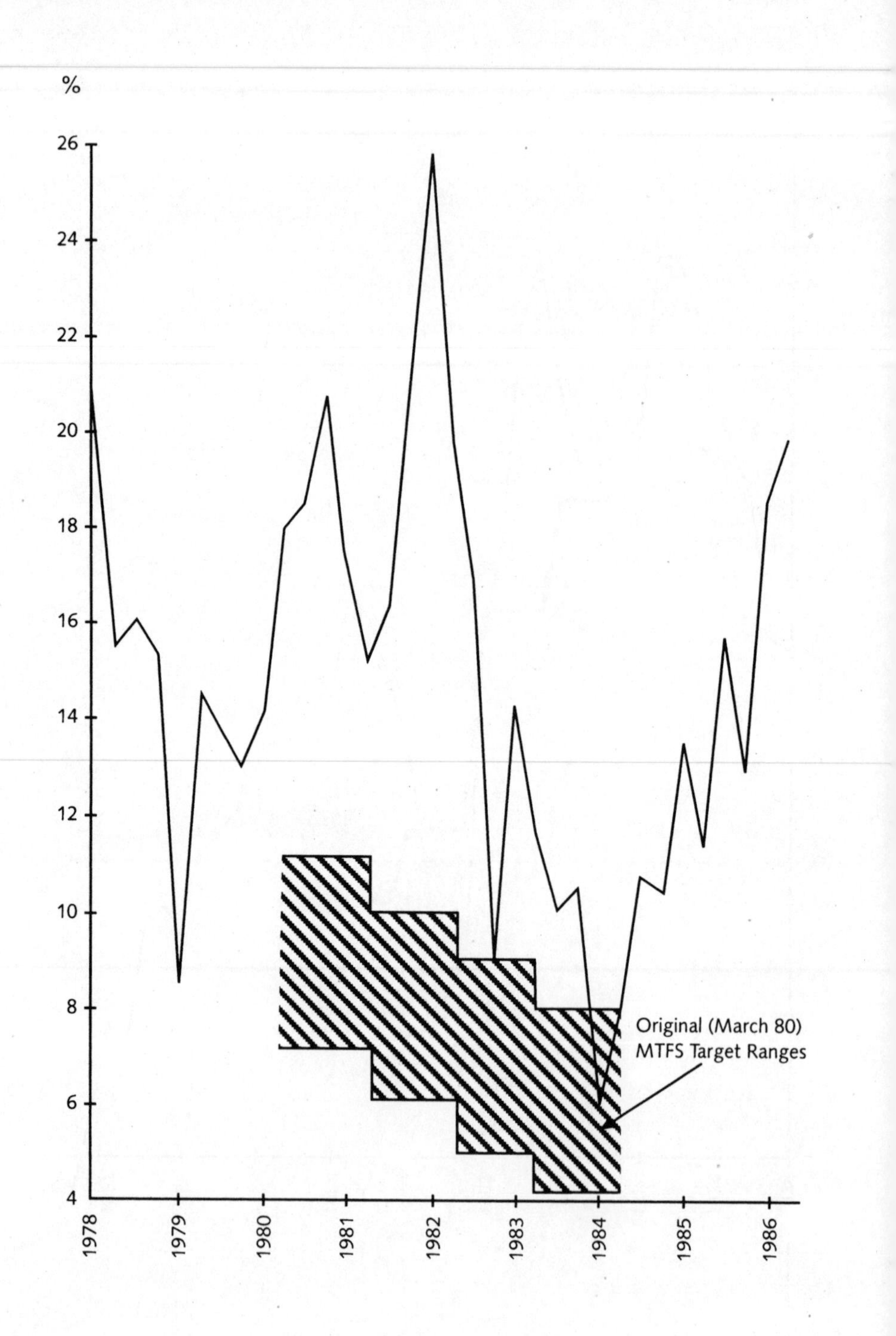

Figure 4.6 Annual percentage growth in £M3

Monetary Policy in Practice

Logic was not enough; the MTFS not only failed to command credibility, fully or even to a significant extent, but it also failed to be carried out in its own literal terms. Yet policy turned out to be more fiercely contractionary than intended – it was closer to shock tactics than gradualism, a paradox indeed! Tougher yet less credible; apparently the worst of both worlds. Severe recession resulted (Figure 4.7).

Trouble came from two directions: technical design and politics. Technically, the choice of £M3 was an error because after deregulating the banks (including those based offshore, with no exchange controls), high-interest deposits became the major weapon in the banks' battle for market share, and as the banks' fortunes ebbed and flowed, so did £M3. In 1980–81, £M3 overshot its targets massively – see Figure 4.6.

Yet M0 – the most narrowly defined monetary aggregate, consisting of currency in circulation and bank reserves – was unaffected by deregulation and told a quite different story, of sharply tightening monetary conditions (Figure 4.8). Its growth rate halved in the twelve months to mid-1980 and halved again in the next twelve. It is clear from data on the economy which story is the true one: the sharp recession in 1980-81, the rapid fall in inflation (Figure 4.3), and the strong exchange rate (Figure 4.9) all confirm M0 as the accurate indicator. M4, a broader aggregate than £M3 including building society (equivalent to US Savings and Loan institutions) deposits, told a similar story to £M3 (Figure 4.10). As I argue below, deregulation destabilises all of these wide monetary aggregates, and makes it difficult to read their implications.

Politically, the pain of recession, especially in the manufacturing sector, undermined the already insecure position of the monetarists in the Conservative party, and Mrs Thatcher faced substantial internal opposition. The days of the MTFS, and perhaps even of Mrs Thatcher herself, seemed numbered. So the MTFS was widely written off at this time as a failure because its targets had not been achieved and as a temporary interlude before traditional politics returned.

Meanwhile, the Chancellor of the Exchequer, Sir Geoffrey Howe, doggedly persevered through 1980 with the attempt to keep the MTFS 'on course'. Short-term interest rates (Figure 4.11) were kept up to reduce the money overshoot, and the PSBR was brought down on its track even though swollen by recession.

In early 1981, too, the technical problems were appreciated, with the arrival of Sir Alan Walters as Mrs Thatcher's personal economic advisor and his circulation of an influential paper by Professor Jurg Niehans of

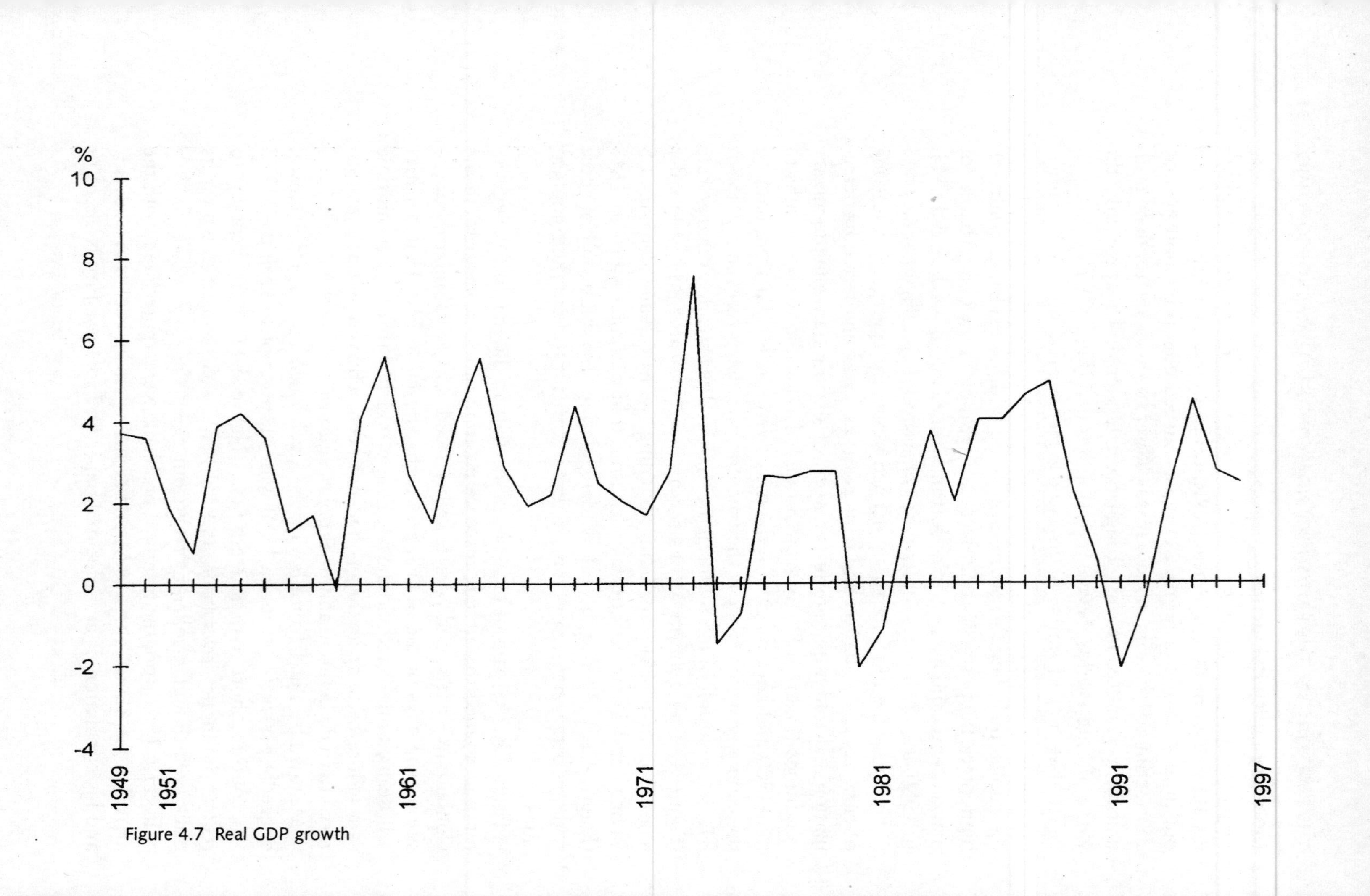

Figure 4.7 Real GDP growth

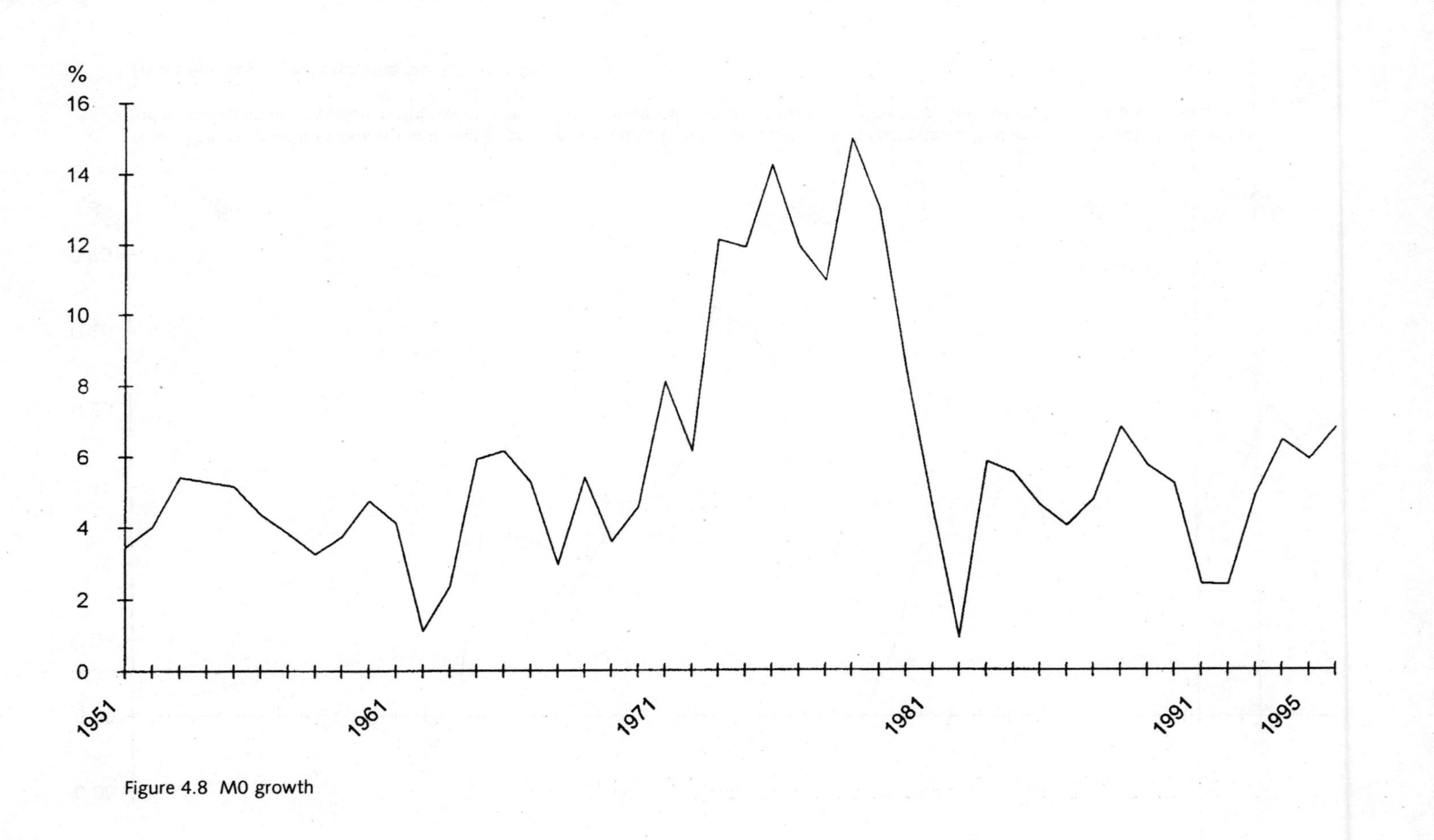

Figure 4.8 M0 growth

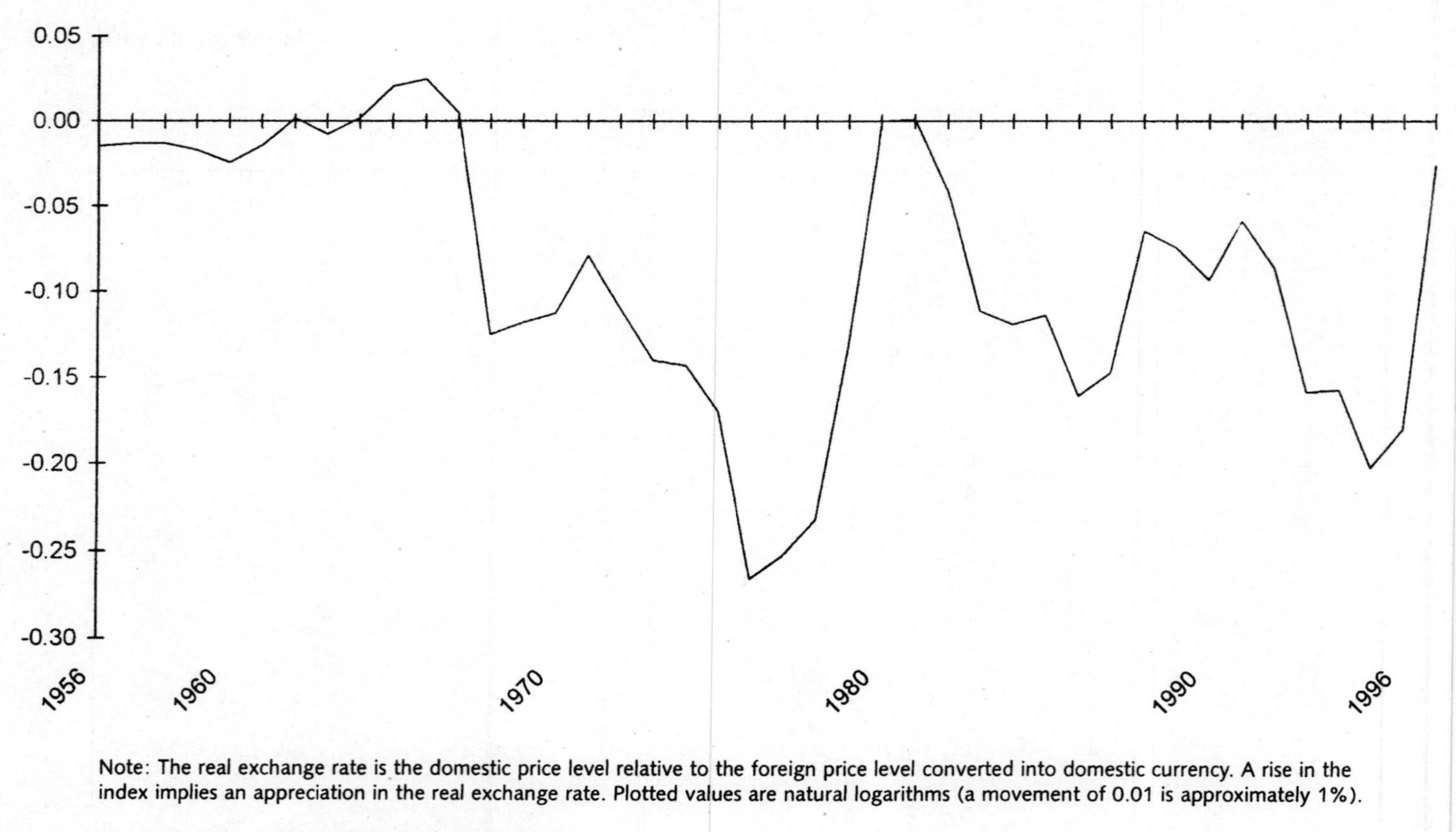

Note: The real exchange rate is the domestic price level relative to the foreign price level converted into domestic currency. A rise in the index implies an appreciation in the real exchange rate. Plotted values are natural logarithms (a movement of 0.01 is approximately 1%).

Figure 4.9 Log of real exchange rate (1980 = 0.0)

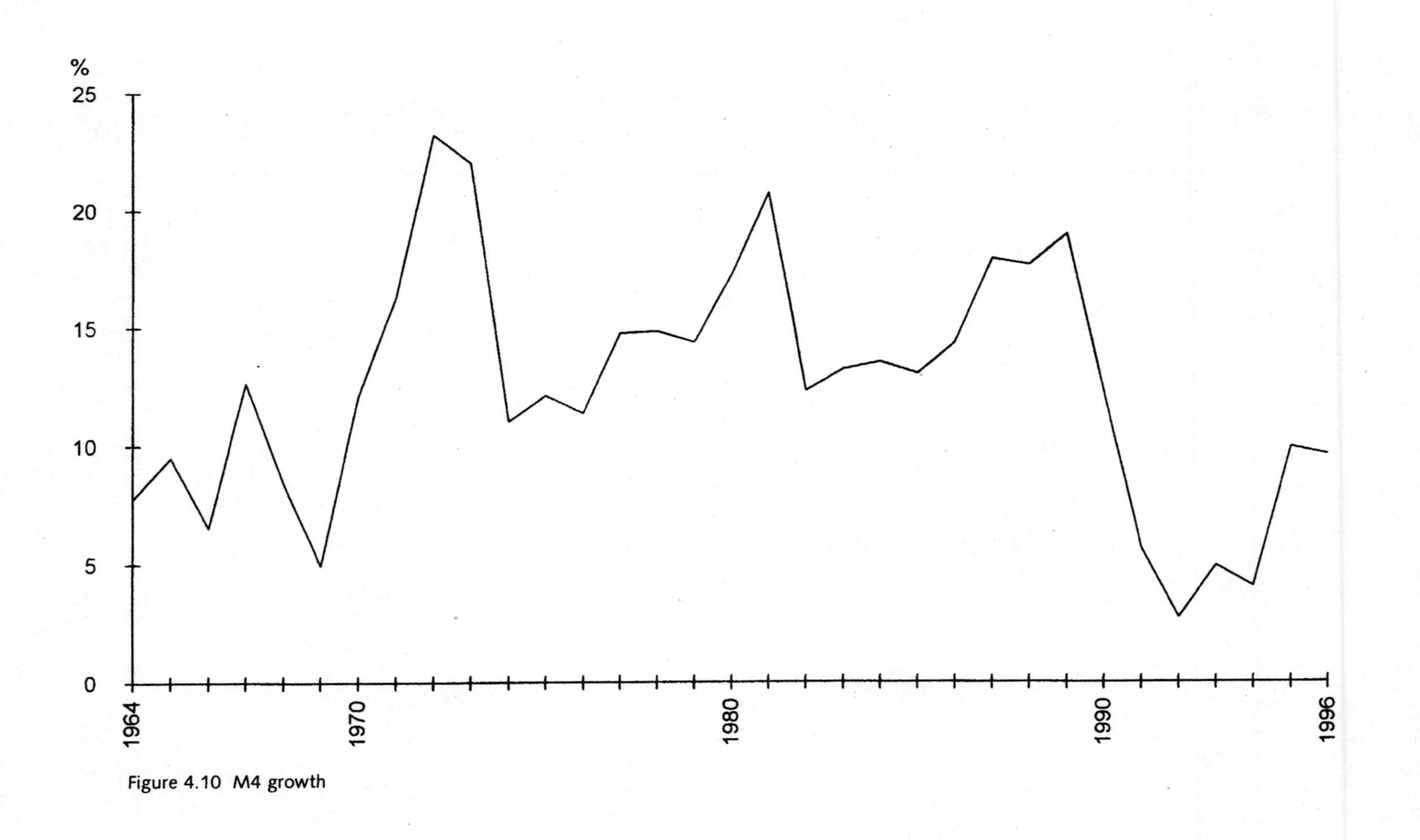

Figure 4.10 M4 growth

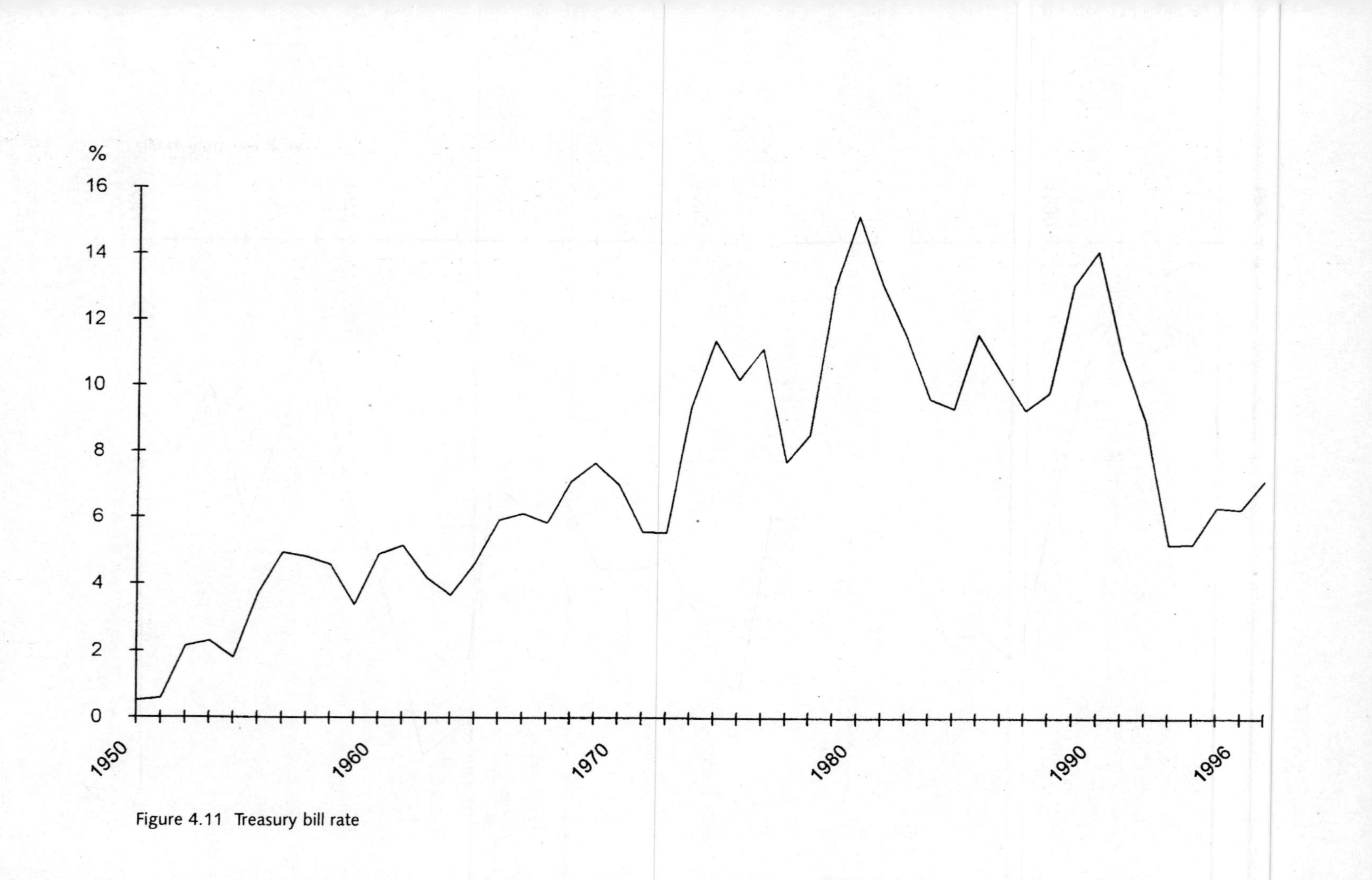

Figure 4.11 Treasury bill rate

Bern University (Niehans, 1981). The decision was taken to loosen monetary policy in order to weaken the exchange rate, to stabilise M0 at a growth rate around 5%, and permit output to recover. To enhance credibility, the budget of 1981 increased taxes by 2% of GDP so as to cut the PSBR even though the recession still had not ended. This cut was crucial in finally creating market confidence in the policy's durability: long-term interest rates, which had fluctuated around 14% for two years, began to fall at last during 1981; and output also started to recover in spring 1981. The policy emphasis thus switched towards fiscal, and away from monetary, tightness. But overall, policy remained extremely tight throughout.

As already stated, policies close to shock tactics were implemented by these means, perhaps mainly by accident but to some degree surely by intuitive survival instinct. Given that recession was connected in popular debate with the monetarist policies, it was vital to get results on inflation in short order as justification for the policy – better to be hung for a sheep as a lamb, if the sheep would produce much lower inflation and a possible reprieve. Later, Rastogi and I (1989) concluded that an explicit policy of shock tactics, with early, sharp cuts in the PSBR accompanying sharp early cuts within M0 growth, would have been best.

In the end, the rapid fall in inflation – down to 5% by end-1982 – did indeed restore the fortunes of Mrs Thatcher and her supporters.

This episode was the furnace in which the current monetary policy of the UK was forged (the ERM episode is now seen as an embarrassing deviation). Those now running that policy have fashioned it with that experience in mind. The key elements are:

1. The PSBR must be kept down to sustain market confidence.
2. M0 is a reliable indicator of monetary conditions (subject to interpretation of the effect of technological change, a matter discussed further below).
3. Rapid movements in the exchange rate may contain monetary signals, and will in general not be permitted, unless M0 supplemented by wider evidence from nominal indicators confirms systematically after the event that they should.
4. In controlling monetary conditions, what matters is that interest rates should be moved symmetrically as dictated by targets (without political intervention, for example, to hold interest rates down) and that market participants can understand the system's signals in forming their expectations. Monetary Base control – a method according to

which M0 should be kept rigorously to a fixed path – was rejected in favour of a system using M0 as the key monetary indicator to guide interest rate changes. This latter was an extension of familiar methods.

Though much ink has been spilt on such monetary control methods per se (Goodhart, 1989, has a useful account), from the modern perspective of rational expectations these key features of symmetry and efficient signalling attach to a wide variety of short-term control methods, and there is no reason in principle to prefer base control over the method currently used. The current method consists of setting the interest rates at which the Bank will lend to the money market on short-term instruments, with these interest rates then triggering immediate changes in the commercial banks' Base Rate (the equivalent of the US Prime Rate). Difficulties arise under the current method only when ambiguities creep into the practice, as occurred in 1987/8 (when Nigel Lawson as Chancellor shadowed the deutschmark, attempting to hold the pound down), with uncertainty arising about the exact status of exchange-rate targets. But these problems can arise in base control systems, as the Swiss have found in pursuing their policies, at times reacting to extreme buying of the Swiss franc.

Between 1982 and 1988, these principles were pursued with the objective of keeping inflation below 5%. No strong efforts were made to drive it to zero because of fears that such efforts might destabilise a smooth recovery with falling unemployment. The emphasis in policy innovation switched to the supply-side: deregulation, union laws, privatisation and tax cuts. Nevertheless, even the process of keeping inflation down implied occasional deflation. Over the whole period from 1979 to 1986, Matthews and I (1987) estimated that the cumulative effect of tight monetary and accompanying fiscal policy on unemployment was no less than one million, just over 4% of the labour force.

Since the experience of 1988–90, when inflation briefly rose towards 10% under the influence of a boom whose strength was widely underpredicted, the aim of policy has been tightened to an explicit target range of 1–4% with the bottom half of this range as the long-term objective. Most recently, this was updated in 1997 by Gordon Brown as Chancellor to a target of 2.5% for average inflation.

In all essentials, Brown and New Labour have maintained the MTFS framework. Their main innovation has been to put operational conduct of interest rate policy in the hands of a new Monetary Policy Committee within the Bank of England and under the Governor's chairmanship. Its job is to reach good technical judgements on interest-rate movements needed to reach the inflation target with minimum cost in fluctuations in output; it is accountable to Parliament in exactly the same way that the Chancellor would have been previously. The only difference is the element of delegation; responsibility for the objectives remain with government. But by isolating the interest-rate function in an executive agency, there should be efficiency gains in that those carrying it out are judged solely and continuously on this task, whereas previously the government would be judged on the whole range of their activities periodically in elections. However, the difference should not be exaggerated; the government remains responsible for the success of economic policy and it too will be continuously accountable over interest rates to Parliament. The change is therefore merely a logical evolution of the previous framework now that the aims of monetary policy are no longer politically controversial.

FUTURE DIRECTIONS: EUROPEAN EXCHANGE RATE LINKAGE?

We have argued that British monetary policy in its efforts to bring inflation under control has taken a form adapted to the institutions and political economy of the UK. It has emphasised the fiscal support needed, has put M0 in the role of key indicator with the exchange rate in a supplementary role, and has used a traditional indicator intervention system to guide interest rates rather than monetary base control. The policy evolved out of the experience of the 1979–82 inflation battle, and was later reinforced by poor experience of exchange-rate targeting, as well as difficulties in interpreting broad money behaviour under deregulation.

What lies ahead? The case for the UK joining the Exchange Rate Mechanism of the European Monetary System was urged on the continent and by those in the UK anxious for faster progress to monetary and political union. It was resisted until 1990 on the grounds that 'the time was not ripe', although the case in principle for eventual joining was not questioned. An attempt to delineate the precise conditions of ripeness was made at the EC Madrid Summit in autumn 1989. These conditions were that EC exchange controls should be abolished, that the 1992 programme of liberalisation should be operative for capital markets, and that the UK inflation rate should be close to the German rate. On the face of it, these conditions ruled out any early UK entry into the ERM, but by August 1990 there were strong rumours that for political reasons (namely the divisiveness of the issue both within the Tory party and the EC) Mrs Thatcher would soon be willing to treat them as met in the near future and join on wide exchange-rate margins, thus preserving some of the flexibility of floating.

Even though the UK did join the ERM for a difficult two years, it remained strongly opposed to a rigid link with the DM and to EMU (Economic and Monetary Union) as proposed by the Delors Committee (Delors, 1989). In the election of 1997, it became clear that both parties would oppose UK entry into EMU in any first wave, and this has been accepted on the continent. It is particularly unlikely that the UK will join any associated wider ERM to accompany EMU. Should EMU begin on time on 1 January 1999, this UK position will be a source of friction within the EC – a matter discussed in a later section.

Hughes-Hallett, Rastogi and I (1990) have evaluated the various design possibilities for the ERM and concluded that major evolution was necessary in order to avoid the potentially severe instability implied by adjustable parity systems. As such, the ERM is similar to the later stages of Bretton Woods and liable to repeated currency crises. To be controllable, monetary policy must veer sharply as a crisis occurs and probably exchange controls must be in place when currencies are devaluing; furthermore, the intervals between devaluations produce over-valuation for these currencies. In the face of repeated shocks, our work finds that these economic costs are high. By close monetary co-operation, however, implying the need to change parities only rarely, the ERM can achieve reasonable stability. This accounts for the attempt at rapid progress towards the Delors 'second stage', in which there was to be virtually no resort to parity change; EMU, the third stage, was thereby to be brought closer. This attempt took place in the absence of the necessary monetary co-operation and its demise, sooner or later, was inevitable.

There are two sets of difficulties for the UK in joining this ERM system. The first set is transitional. Even maintaining wide margins and national control over future parity change, the UK has the problem of reconciling appropriate domestic monetary control, as explained above, with the demands of the ERM. The resulting conflict, given initial inflation, can undermine current monetary disinflation by putting downward pressure on interest rates (to hold the parity down in the short term), while failing to increase long-term monetary credibility because of the lack of commitment to the parity in the long term. This point was made forcefully by Alan Walters (1990) and has come to be called the 'Walters Critique'. It was exemplified by the British experience noted earlier: of shadowing the deutschmark in 1987/8 when interest rates fell precipitately in early 1988 to prevent sterling's appreciation. Coming soon after the loosening of money in reaction to the October 1987 share price crash, this led to a worrying resurgence of inflation. This resurgence can therefore be directly ascribed to a temporary lapse in the pursuit of the monetarist approach.

The Walters Critique has been widely accepted among European economists following the experiences of both Spain and Italy. Its force can be limited by accepting greater rigidity in the ERM and close monetary co-operation (with Germany in practice). Both Spain and Italy attempted to move in this direction, in keeping with the general trend of the ERM's evolution; however, both countries were effectively forced out of the ERM, which collapsed totally in 1993.

For the UK in particular, moving into a more rigid ERM raises the second set of difficulties: that a rigid, co-operative ERM leading quickly to EMU is incompatible with UK monetary sovereignty, an all-party requirement. This requirement stems mainly from a political desire for control over the monetary instrument, and associated instruments of policy whose operation might be limited by outside monetary control. Usually, the surrender of monetary sovereignty accompanies the formation of a new state embracing the currency union, as for example with German reunification; the reason is that a state giving up the power over its currency is compensated within a federation by transfers from the central state budget. However, the UK totally rejects the idea of a federal European state on political grounds.

Economically, there is also a strong case against. The attractions of a common currency are obvious enough, as it permits the elimination of foreign exchange costs, including those of dealing with exchange-rate uncertainties (for example by covering forward), whatever these costs may be (and we have no good estimates). However, the disadvantages are also well understood. It takes away the power to use independent monetary and exchange-rate policy for economic adjustment (and for occasional emergencies such as wars, where the ability to print money defines the state's economic independence).

Such adjustment could be crucial for the UK economy, because its average productivity level is still below, its general economic structure is quite different from, and its rate and direction of supply-side reform is at variance with, the respective elements amongst the UK's continental neighbours. In other words, there may need to be sharp changes in the UK's relative price competitiveness (its 'real exchange rate') in the next decade, which would be more efficiently brought about by exchange-rate movement than by decentralised wage-price movements (which require costly changes in unemployment). In the new continental fashion for arrangements that deliver credibility in the absence of strong domestic leadership, this old-fashioned power over the currency has been widely overlooked. Hughes-Hallett, Rastogi and I found (1993), in extending our work referred to above (1990), that EMU, for this very reason, exhibits markedly less stability than floating exchange rates when dealing with the typical post-war environment.

There is a final point too, that a surrender of independent monetary policy would inevitably involve constraints on other policies, including taxes and regulations. These are all matters of great concern to a British government pursuing a programme of supply-side reform at odds with the prevailing corporatism of the continent.

One way or another, the issue of monetary union is clearly destined to create considerable tension between the UK and at least some other EC members.

DO INDEXED BONDS HELP?

Mrs Thatcher's government was the first and only one among the major industrial countries to issue indexed bonds. If one assumes that financial market participants make intelligent use of information (ie, have rational expectations), the issue of such bonds should not make any difference to either nominal or real (inflation-adjusted) interest rates. The reason is that it does not alter the expected present value of the government's future tax revenue or its distribution between ordinary tax and money creation; it merely adds an extra financial instrument.

Of course, it does enable the government to borrow at an explicit real interest rate instead of a nominal interest rate, but each of these rates reflects the risks on that particular instrument. Why should the government regard issuing this instrument as beneficial now when it was not for the preceding centuries?

Some commentators have argued that their issue reduces one obstacle to counter-inflation policy, namely the windfall gain to holders of long-dated nominal government bonds as inflation, and so interest rates come down. This gain arises because a long-term bond promises a series of fixed payments in money terms over its life; as interest rates fall, the discounted present value of these payments becomes higher. The gain is made at the expense of taxpayers, and since taxes damage incentives, it is preferable to bring taxes down rather than hand out this gain to bondholders. According to this argument, a complete replacement of nominal bonds by indexed ones would be desirable for a government contemplating anti-inflationary monetary policy.

The flaw in this argument is clear. If a government issues indexed bonds with the intention of curbing inflation less expensively, this intention will thereby be signalled to bondholders, even supposing it could have been kept secret without the issue. The result would be that the existing stock of nominal bonds being replaced would rise in value, reflecting the better real prospective returns on their nominal income stream. The bondholders would then reap at once the capital gain they would have reaped when the policy for reduced inflation would have otherwise been revealed.

So would the issue of indexed bonds fail to eliminate the transfer to bondholders? In the event, modest amounts of indexed bonds were issued in an experimental spirit. Apart from acting as a useful measuring rod for economists wanting to know the real rate of interest and encouraging private insurance and pension companies to offer indexed policies backed by indexed bonds, there is no evidence that they changed the behaviour of the economy.

DEREGULATION AND THE RISE OF THE CASHLESS ECONOMY

In a freely competitive banking and financial system, banks will drive the interest rate on their savings and current account ('sight') deposits up to the rate at which they can lend, minus the cost of intermediation (which is small in the UK, where there are virtually no formal reserve requirements). Devices like forgoing bank charges on current accounts in credit are equivalent to paying interest on them. As competition between the high street banks and building societies intensifies, they will probably largely give way to explicit interest payment.

The balance sheet items of firms, banks and other financial intermediaries – for example, whether firms finance themselves by credit from the banks or by issuing shares held by unit trusts – depends then on such things as the costs of different sorts of intermediation and the ability of different intermediaries to improve the risk-return combinations faced by savers, because they can deal in economic quantities of stock, for example. The structure goes on changing until no new intermediary opportunity is available. But the point is that all this reshuffling makes no difference to the overall return available in the market. Fama (1980 and 1983) discusses the behaviour of such a world.

In particular, if (as is surely the case) the high street banks are being driven by competition to make themselves more efficient, it is hardly surprising that they seek to expand their operations sharply, raising their interest rates to consumers, improving their loan services to firms. This shift in bank technology is just the sort of thing to cause an expansion on both sides of balance sheets.

It is therefore an implication of financial competition that money changes its form, and in particular the only 'pure' money left is currency. Hence the government's decision to target M0 in the MTFS, and the abandonment of the wider measures, described earlier. As for the school of thought that says 'exploding credit' threatens inflation, it is clearly wide of the mark, using concepts appropriate to a financial environment that has passed away.

The question arises whether currency itself will not ultimately be displaced by interest-bearing means of payment. Which transactions will continue to use cash, which credit cards and such like? It is presumably a matter of cost in interest forgone versus that of using computer technology (Switch cards, etc), yet the cost of currency technology remains negligible for small transactions – it is crime-free, requires no equipment, and is costless to print. It is only for large transactions that costs rise: because of physical transportation and the risk of robbery.

This suggests that, provided inflation is low, currency will continue to dominate small transactions. If inflation actually went negative, then the use of currency could even revive for larger transactions. Negative inflation is not in fact far-fetched: stability of measured prices implies falling prices after quality change.

The most recent behaviour of M0 has puzzled observers. It has been growing at 5–6% against growth in nominal GDP (national income measured in current prices) of some 6%. Hence the previous steady decline in its use relative to GDP (or, put another way, the steady rise in its 'velocity', the ratio of GDP to M0) seems to have been halted. Some have argued this represents a sign of inflationary pressure. However, a change in the trend of velocity is not unexpected in the context of an economy with inflation close to zero and interest rates likely to settle around 6% or even lower. Work of Hall and Henry, recently extended by the Bank of England (Hall, Henry and Wilcox, 1989; Breedon and Fisher, 1993) suggests that technological innovation in cash machines, credit technology, and so on may be related to the level of interest rates (the source of the return to innovation); and so, with interest rates low, innovation (and hence the rate of rise in velocity) may slow down too. It certainly appears from other evidence that the economy is experiencing, if anything, continued disinflation; this strengthens the case for a shift in M0's velocity trend.

The political instability of broad money, together with the current (presumably transitional) problems of interpreting M0, has implied that monetary aggregates have been relegated temporarily at least to a supporting role, with forecasts of inflation becoming central to the assessment of policy adjustment. However, monetary forces (the printing of money, M0) are still central to our understanding of inflation; it is simply that the appropriate supply of money is no longer so easy to judge, at least until M0 has re-established a new stable trend in behaviour.

CONCLUSION

The 1980s witnessed a prolonged experiment in monetarist policy for the control of inflation, after three decades culminating in high and persistent inflation in which monetary policy played at most a supporting role, whether to a fixed exchange rate, fiscal policy or incomes and price controls. Out of that experiment has emerged a strategy for the setting of long-term targets for inflation backed up by money and PSBR targets. The implementation of monetary policy has been through interest rate changes rather than by monetary base control, but given rational expectations this tactical issue is of little importance. The result of these policies was the reduction of inflation to around 5% from 1983 to 1987. The rise in inflation from 1987 to 1990 reflected a loosening of monetary policy connected with the October 1987 stock market crash and the shadowing of the deutschmark in the Exchange Rate Mechanism. This was followed by the equally unfortunate experience of substantive ERM membership in 1990–92, which severely destabilised monetary policy causing an excessive and prolonged squeeze.

Looking to the future, there are those who argue that the UK should permanently abandon domestic monetarism in favour of a common European currency. While this would deliver low inflation under certain EMU arrangements, it would also remove a key policy instrument from British hands, besides implying greater political union than is accepted in the UK. The alternative is to continue with current policies and a flexible currency relationship with the EC. The experience of the last two decades suggests such policies can control inflation without interfering with a vigorous supply-side reform programme. In short, after quite a bit of experimentation and a number of mistakes, it has proved possible to develop a successful policy for controlling inflation by domestic policy instruments and without recourse to direct controls on wages, prices or financial markets.

This is an important success for the policy programme initiated in

1979, a main element of which was to remove the market interventions supposedly needed to regulate the economy. Having removed these, the programme went on to remove other interventions in the market process; to this aspect we turn next.

References

Blanchard, O. and Summers, L. (1986) 'Hysteresis and the European Unemployment Problem', in S. Fischer, ed., *NBER Macroeconomics Annual*, MIT Press.

Blanchflower, D.G., Millward, N. and Oswald A.J. (1991) 'Unionism and Employment Behaviour' *Economic Journal*, 101, July, 815–34.

Breedon, F.J. & Fisher, P.G (1993) 'M0: Causes and Consequences', *Bank of England working paper* No. 20.

Delors, J. (1989) Delors Committee for the Study of Economic and Monetary Union, Report on Economic and Monetary Union in the European Community, Office for Official Publications of the EC, Luxembourg.

Fama, E. (1980) 'Banking in the Theory of Finance', *Journal of Monetary Economics*, 6, 39–57.

Fama, E. (1983) 'Financial Intermediation and Price Level Control', *Journal of Monetary Economics*, 12, 7–28.

Friedman, M. (1980) 'Memorandum on Monetary Policy', House of Commons Treasury and Civil Service Committee, *Memoranda on Monetary Policy*, HMSO, Norwich, pp 55–68.

Goodhart, C.A.E. (1989) *Money, Information and Uncertainty*, 2nd edn, Macmillan.

Hall, S.G., Henry S.G.B. and Wilcox J.B. *The Long-run Determination of the UK Monetary Aggregates*, Bank of England discussion paper No. 41.

Hughes, G. and McCormick, B. (1984) 'Do Council Housing Policies Reduce Migration Between Regions?', *Economic Journal*, 91, 919–32.

Hughes-Hallett, A., Minford, P. and Rastogi A. (1993) *The European Monetary System: Achievements and Survival*, in *Evaluating Policy Regimes - new research in empirical macroeconomics,* R.C. Bryant, P. Hooper and C. L. Mann eds., Brookings Institutions, Washington DC, pp 617-671.

Layard, R. and Nickell, S. (1985) 'The Causes of British Unemployment', *National Institute Economic Review*,3, Feb., 62–85.

Layard, R. and Nickell, S. (1989) 'The Thatcher Miracle?', LSE Centre for Labour Economics discussion paper No. 343; shorter version in *American Economic Review*, 79(2), 215–19.

Lindbeck, A. and Snower, D.J. (1986) 'Wage Setting, Unemployment and Insider–Outsider Relations', *American Economic Review*, papers and proceedings.

Machin, S. and Wadwhani, S. (1991) 'The Effects of Unions on Organisational Change and Employment', *Economic Journal*, 101, July, 835–54.

Matthews, K.G.P. and Minford, P. (1987) 'Mrs. Thatcher's Economic Policies, 1979–87', *Economic Policy*, 5, October, 57-101.

Maynard, G. (1988) *The Economy Under Mrs. Thatcher*, Blackwell, Oxford.

Minford, P. (1983) 'Labour Market Equilibrium in an Open Economy' in *Oxford Economic Papers*, 35 (supp.), 207–44.

Minford, P., Peel, M. and Ashton, P. (1987) *The Housing Morass – Regulation, Immobility and Unemployment*, Hobart Paperback 25, Institute of Economic Affairs.

Minford, P. and Rastogi, A. (1989) 'A New Classical Policy Programme' in *Policymaking with Macroeconomic Models*, ed. A. Britton, Gower, London, pp 83–97.

Minford, P., Rastogi, A. and Hughes Hallett, A. (1993) 'The Price of EMU Revisited', *Greek Economic Review*, Vol. 15, No. 1, pp 191–226.

Minford, P. (1995) 'Time-inconsistency, Democracy and Optimal Contingent Rules', *Oxford Economic Papers*, 47, pp 195–210.

Muellbauer, J. and Murphy, A. (1988) 'House Prices and Migration: Economic and Investment Implications', Shearson, Lehman and Hutton Securities research report.

Niehans, J. (1981) 'The Appreciation of Sterling - Causes, Effects and Policies', ESRC Money Study Group discussion paper, ESRC, London.

Radcliffe Committee on the Working of the Monetary System: Report, 1959, Cmnd. 827, HMSO, London.

Sargent, T. and Wallace, N. (1981) 'Some Unpleasant Monetarist Arithmetic', *Quarterly Review*, fall 1981, Federal Reserve Bank of Minneapolis, 1–17.

Veljanovski, C. with M. Bentley (1987) *Selling the State*, Weidenfeld and Nicolson, London.

Walters, A.A. (1985) *Britain's Economic Renaissance: Margaret Thatcher's Economic Reforms, 1979–84*, Oxford University Press, Oxford, for the American Enterprise Institute.

Walters, A.A.(1990) *Sterling in Danger: The Economic Consequences of Pegged Exchange Rates*, Collins (Fontana) with the Institute of Economic Affairs, London.

Yarrow, G. (1986) 'Privatisation in theory and practice', *Economic Policy*, 2, 323.64.

CHAPTER FIVE

Remaking the British economy 1979–97 – The supply-side programme

IN THIS CHAPTER, we turn from macroeconomic to microeconomic reform: policies to improve the workings of markets, the so-called 'supply-side' policies designed to increase the economy's supply of goods and services.

The Thatcher government's supply-side programme had as its main objective the raising of the economy's potential growth rate per head, and as a further objective the increase of consumer sovereignty and related improvement in the use of the economy's output. If the national statistics of the quality of output are to be believed, then the value of output at constant prices should reflect improvements in the use of output, ie, in the benefits each unit of output provides. The only omission would be any gains in consumer welfare due to the reduction in distortions such as taxes; unfortunately, we have no general direct measures of this and so will have to ignore it here in favour of straight output measures.

Arithmetically, we can split potential growth-per-head gains into gains in:

output per worker (productivity)

X

working age population as a share of total population
(demographic and retirement trends)

X

worker supply as a share of the working age population
(work participation)

X

employment as a share of worker supply
(one minus the unemployment rate).

Government policy has an effect on all of these; and the Thatcher programme was intended to raise each of them.

PRODUCTIVITY

If we begin with productivity, we can see a considerable effect in behaviour after 1979 on a wide variety of measures benchmarked against major competitor countries. This benchmarking is necessary because it allows for the opportunities available to all countries from the general environment of technology change.

We saw a clear improvement for manufacturing productivity in the comparison with Germany in chapter 3 (Figs 3.8 and 3.9). Here we present comparisons with other industrial countries. Table 5.1 shows the general relative improvement in labour productivity in manufacturing; Table 5.2 shows 'total factor productivity' in the business (ie, the non-governmental sector): this is an estimate of the productivity of the average of all inputs (labour, capital and land) in producing the sector's added value (output net of any use of output from other sectors). What all these comparisons show is the unambiguous and significant improvement in the UK's relative performance since 1979 on what went before.

Attributing this improvement to the different changes in the environment is not easy. An attempt has been made by Bean and Crafts (1996) in a statistical analysis of 137 industries' behaviour from 1954 to 1986. Their results are shown in Table 5.3. They find that the power of multiple unions is the major factor responsible for poor productivity, and that the Thatcher government's union laws and related developments reduced this power virtually to zero.

Another element they identify is the shock effect of the 1980-81 recession and the accompanying shift of government and company attitudes towards cushioning labour redundancies. Whereas previously the government had often become involved in efforts to contain redundancies (a famous example being the intervention in state-owned British Steel during the late 1970s), the new government refused any involvement, preferring to give help instead for relocation and retraining in particu-

	1960–73	1973–79	1979–89	1989–94
UK	4.14	1.01	4.13	3.95
USA	3.28	1.41	2.34	2.47
Japan	9.59	5.15	4.58	4.18
France	6.55	4.39	3.28	3.04
Italy	6.14	5.60	3.86	3.91
Germany	5.71	4.21	1.83	2.22

Table 5.1 Labour productivity in manufacturing – growth of output per hour worked (% per annum)

Sources: Broadberry (1996) and Oulton (1995) cited in Crafts (1997)

larly badly hit regions such as South Wales and towns such as Corby. This signalled clearly that efficiency rather than job-preservation would guide employment behaviour; unions accordingly lost influence and power to hold up changes to working practices.

Other factors were found by Bean and Crafts not to be of much significance: in effect it was union power and government labour market policy that were the key determinants of productivity growth.

These factors seem to increase the growth rate of productivity, not just its level. Hence we should expect to see this higher growth maintained. This supports the view that not merely static but also dynamic efficiency was reduced by the UK's overwhelming union power to obstruct.

WORKING AGE AND RETIREMENT PATTERNS

Demographic trends over which governments have little obvious influence are reducing the share of normal-working-age people within the total population across the OECD countries generally.

	1960–73	%		1979–94	%
1	Japan	5.5	1	Ireland	2.6
2	Portugal	5.4	2	Finland	2.5
3	Ireland	4.6	3	Spain	1.7
4	Italy	4.4	4	Portugal	1.6
5	Finland	4.0	5	UK	1.5
6	Belgium	3.8	6	Denmark	1.3
7	France	3.7	7	France	1.3
8	Netherlands	3.4	8	Belgium	1.2
9	Spain	3.2	9	Japan	1.1
10	Austria	3.1	10	Netherlands	1.1
11	Germany	2.6	11	Sweden	1.0
12	UK	2.6	12	Austria	0.9
13	Greece	2.5	13	Italy	0.9
14	USA	2.5	14	Australia	0.8
15	Denmark	2.3	15	USA	0.5
16	Australia	2.2	16	Germany	0.4
17	Switzerland	2.1	17	Canada	-0.1
18	Norway	2.0	18	Norway	-0.1
19	Sweden	2.0	19	Switzerland	-0.2
20	Canada	1.9	20	Greece	-0.3

Table 5.2 Total Factor Productivity (TFP) growth in the business sector (% per annum)

Source: OECD (1996) as cited in Crafts (1997)

	With Order dummies	No Order dummies
Capital growth	0.153	0.141
	(1.49)	(2.11)
Union recognition	-0.086	0.055
	(0.25)	(0.17)
Multiple unions	-0.754	-1.112
	(2.06)	(3.38)
Multiple union dummy	0.689	0.668
for Thatcher policies	(1.33)	(1.28)
Employment shock	-0.130	-0.134
– Thatcher period	(3.36)	(3.62)
Concentration ratio	0.703	0.388
	(1.22)	(0.96)
Import share	-0.301	0.561
	(0.47)	(1.07)
Standard error	2.391	2.689
R^2	0.210	0.196
Durbin-Watson	2.042	1.959
No. of observations	794	794

Notes: t-statistics in parenthesis; coefficients on time and Order dummies omitted for brevity. The regression related TFP growth, in seven different periods (1954–8, 1958–63, 1963–8, 1973–6, 1976–9, 1979–82, 1982–6) for 137 different industries, to the factors listed in the table: the 15 standard industrial Classification Order dummies allow for the effect of different broad types of industry.

Table 5.3 Panel regression of Total Factor Productivity (TFP) growth in British industry (dependent variable Total Factor Productivity growth)

In the absence of changes in retirement age, this must imply a steady fall in productive workers per head of population. However, in the UK some mitigation of this is under way through pressures to raise retirement age. The first was the straightforward decision to equalise the official (state pension) retirement ages of men and women at 65 by raising that of women from 60 to 65. This equalisation was mandated by EC regulation but it created an opportunity both to reduce the financial burden on the state of pension provision and to increase the incentive for women to stay longer at work. Figure 5.1 shows the effect of official retirement age policies.

The second set of measures concerned the treatment of state pensions and the incentive to make private additional provision. The basic state pension was indexed to prices rather than wages from 1979 and the State Earnings-Related Pension Scheme (SERPS) was reduced in value in the mid-1980s review and turned, by the ability to opt out, into the equivalent of a private pension. Both these measures increased the incentive to stay longer at work because less pension was available at age 65 (so inducing longer work to provide more – an 'income effect'), and privatisation for most introduced a tighter relationship between

	Both sexes	Male	Female
USA	57.2	66.0	49.2
Japan	66.2	84.8	48.5
UK	51.5	62.5	40.9
Germany	42.6	54.5	31.3
France	36.1	41.5	30.9
Italy	28.3	44.1	13.8

Table 5.4 Labour force participation rates among 55–64 year olds, 1995 (%)

Source: OECD Labour Force Statistics

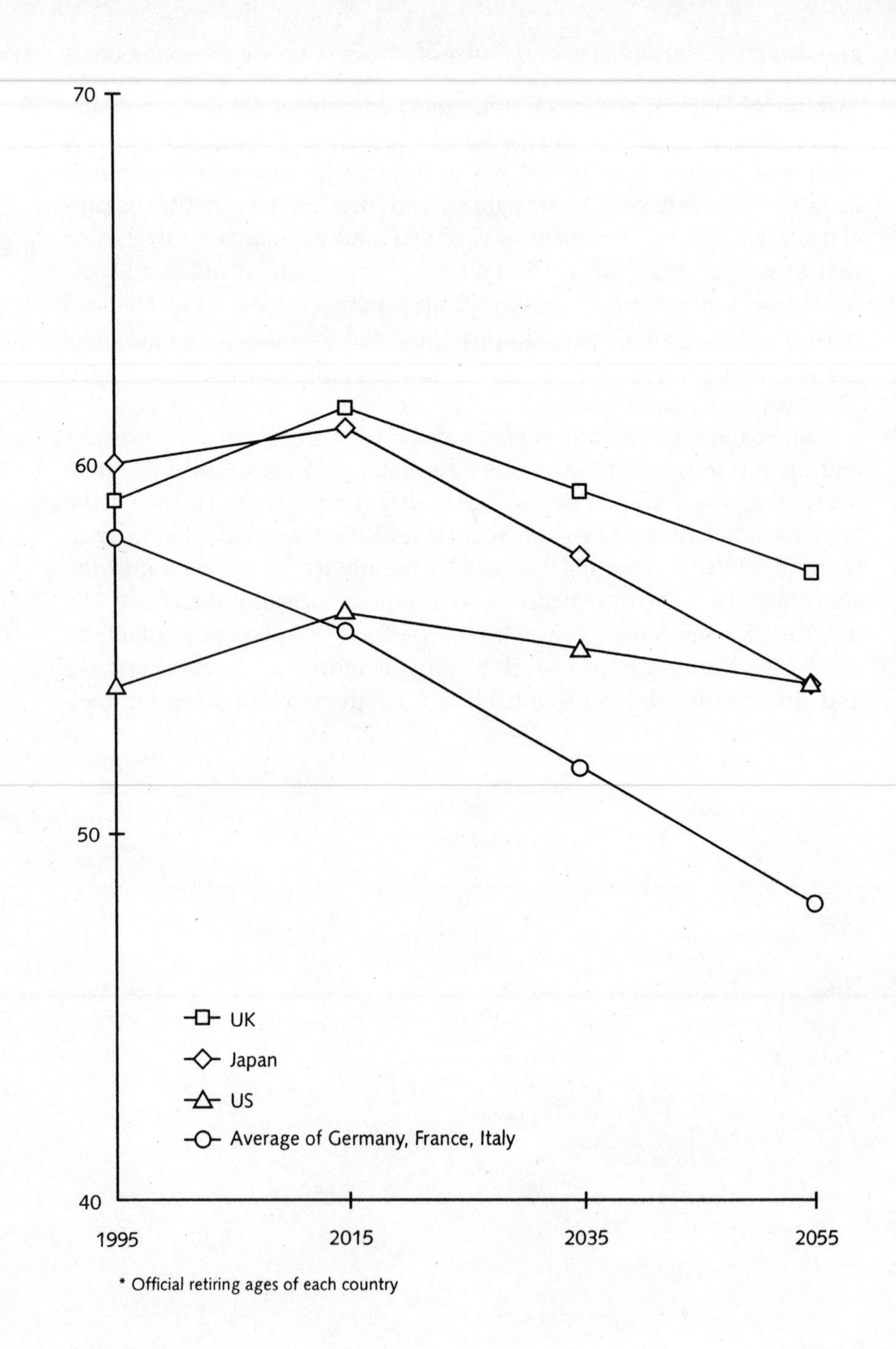

Figure 5.1 Working age population (% of total)*

Source: OECD 1995

contributions and pension entitlement (so inducing a substitution between earlier retirement and additional work and saving).

The effect of these changes can be seen in the comparison of actual working-age shares in the UK and the continent. Table 5.4 shows participation among 55–64-year-olds: one sees that among the countries where private pensions are important and labour markets relatively flexible (including the UK), there is substantially greater participation.

WORK PARTICIPATION

The UK has for a long time been liberal in its approach to part-time work and female participation, and has never encouraged the 'work-sharing' that has been an increasing feature of continental labour markets (the latest example being the proposed 35-hour working weeks in France and Italy). In this respect, the Thatcher government's reforms did not so much change the UK environment as prevent a change for the worse towards work-sharing that was associated on the continent with rising unemployment.

Work-sharing on the continent has taken the form partly of restricting female participation, discouraging part-time work and stretching out youth training, so concentrating work as far as possible on male workers of prime working age. Table 5.5 shows the comparisons of participation across the whole labour force.

Another aspect of work-sharing is the restriction of working hours: Table 5.6 compares hours in manufacturing and the whole economy among the same group of countries. We can see that the hours worked in the UK are markedly higher, as in others of the flexible-labour-market economies, than those on the continent. The limiting of hours there has thus been encouraged not merely on grounds of health and safety but also in order to share work between workers.

UNEMPLOYMENT

We turn lastly to unemployment – last, but not least. Table 5.7 compares current UK unemployment with rates elsewhere, notably the European continent with its stakeholder approach. In early 1993, UK unemployment once again all but reached the notorious 3 million mark, equivalent to a rate of 10.6%. A number of economists suggested at the time that it would not fall much below that rate in the foreseeable future. The implication of such a view was that the UK 'equilibrium' or 'natural' rate of unemployment (the rate at which the economy could

	Both sexes	Male	Female
USA	66.6	75.0	58.9
UK	62.2	73.0+	52.9+
Japan	62.9	77.5	49.6
France	55.3	64.3	47.3
Germany	53.1	64.1+	44.1+
Italy	47.6	62.7+	33.6+

+1994

Table 5.5 Participation rates (share of working age population wishing to work), 1995 (%)

Source: Bureau of Labor Statistics, Washington D.C. Working age is 16 and over. Figures are provisional other than USA and Japan

	Manufacturing (1993)*	Total (1995)+
USA	1943	1952
Japan	2014	1898 (1994)
UK	1826	1735
Germany	1557	1559
France	1612	1631
Italy	1790	n.a.

Table 5.6 Hours worked per annum

Sources: * Bureau of Labor Statistics, Washington D.C. + OECD comparisons of levels for total economy must be carried out with caution because of differences of definition

settle without inflationary pressure developing) was of this order. Even in May 1994, when unemployment had fallen to 9.4%, a number of economists (for example, Metcalf (1994) and Barrell et al (1994)) continued to take a pessimistic view of the natural rate.

By autumn 1997, unemployment had fallen to just under 1.5 million (5.2%) and the sceptical economists of that time have had to abandon such views. Nevertheless, few believe unemployment can fall much further without triggering higher inflation. In this section, we argue that the evidence suggests strongly that not only have reform policies been responsible for the fall so far but also that this fall has substantially further to go.

This alternative view is based on the work of my research group based in Cardiff and Liverpool, the results of which are embodied in the Liverpool model of the UK. We have used this model for regular forecasts, policy analysis and other exercises since 1980: a full account of it in its early annual form was given by Minford et al in 1984, and a fresh account in its latest quarterly version by Minford et al in 1990.

In brief, we would argue that the economic reforms of the 1980s created a new flexibility in the labour market, which has pushed the

'Anglo Saxon' approach	%	Month
USA	4.9	August
Japan	3.4	July
UK	5.5	July
European		
Germany	11.6	August
France	12.5	July
Italy	12.4	April
Belgium	14.1	August
Spain	20.9	2nd qtr.

Table 5.7 Unemployment rates around the world, 1997 (%)

Source: *The Economist*

natural rate down sharply from the peak of 12% that it reached early in that decade to an astonishing 2.5% today.

Before we go on to discuss our estimates of the natural rate, we give a more detailed account of the labour market reforms that were responsible for the changes here (and also, as we have seen above, for the raising of productivity growth).

THE LABOUR MARKET REFORMS

The most important reform was the curbing of union powers through a series of union laws. The right to strike in the UK is now heavily qualified: a strike cannot be for 'secondary' action, it must be strictly about wages and work conditions, and it must be backed by a ballot. Action beyond the law carries, on conviction, serious financial penalties and these are massively compounded if the courts are defied, by sequestration provisions. Picketing is strictly limited so that other workers hired to strike-break can gain easy access to the place of work.

Combined with the fall in traditional manufacturing employment, which has anyway greatly reduced union membership, these reduced rights have eliminated union power as it was known in Britain during the turbulent 1970s. During that period, a coal strike brought down a government and the car industry was frequently paralysed by strike action. By contrast, strike action in the UK is now virtually non-existent (Fig. 5.2).

If we turn to work incentives changes in taxation have not succeeded in bringing down the average tax rate (measured by tax revenues as a percentage of GDP). Indeed, if one adjusts for the business cycle, this has risen since 1979, approximately from 37% to 39%, in order to help eliminate the 5% of GDP public borrowing of 1978–9, while public spending (again adjusted for the cycle) has fallen by some 4% of GDP, from 43% to 39% approximately (see Figs 3.3 and 3.4 in Chapter 3). However, the marginal income tax rate (a key measure of tax pressure) has been reduced at certain important points in the income distribution. The top rate of income tax has come down from 83% to 40% and the 'standard' rate from 33% to 23% (this rate is the marginal rate for the majority of taxpayers; otherwise there is now only the single top rate and a lower-rate band of 20%).

When all tax rates, direct (including National Insurance) and indirect, are taken into account, the marginal tax rate on the average worker has in approximate terms come down from 49% to 47% and on the top earner from 86% to 51% (Matthews and Minford, 1987, my updating).

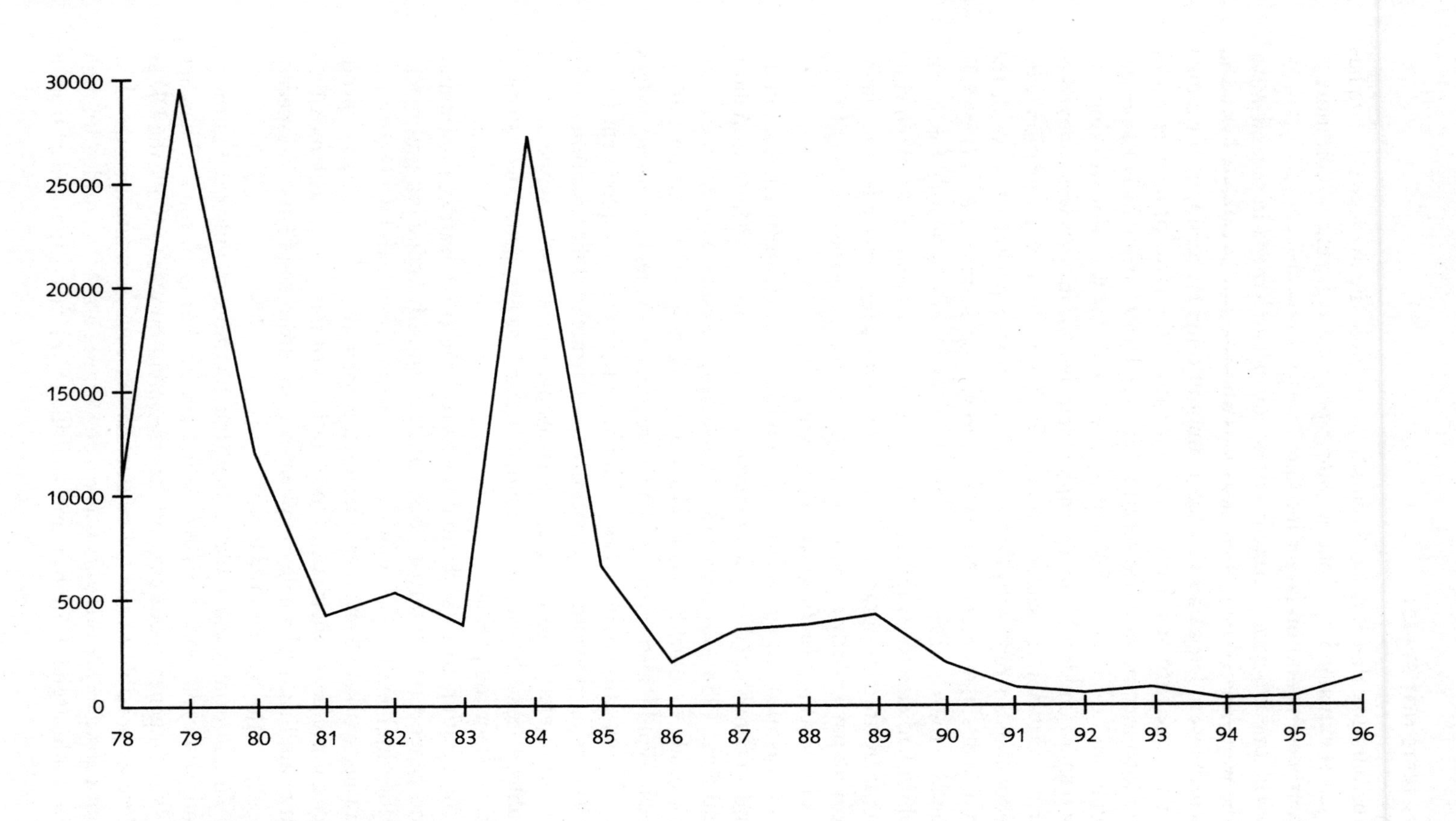

Figure 5.2 Working days lost in strikes

The paradox that this has been achieved while the average tax rate has risen is explained by rising incomes: people are paying tax on more of their income and on larger incomes.

The unemployment benefit system has been changed in several ways. The wage-related benefit element was abolished in December 1981 and benefits were left as a subsistence amount only: for example, for a man on average earnings the replacement ratio – the ratio of income out of work to income in work – ranged in April 1993 from 22% (if he was single and over 25) to 54% (if married, with his wife not working and two small children). His unemployment benefit in turn was indexed to prices and not to wages. Though the interaction of indexation with reductions in rent subsidies caused the benefit package to rise in the mid-1980s, the overall effect was to lower replacement ratios (Fig. 5.3). Finally, the conditionality of benefits on a serious search for work, which had effectively disappeared by 1979, was eventually tightened up in the 'Restart' programme of 1986 (a counselling service for the unemployed, particularly the long-term unemployed, who risked loss of benefits in the case of refusal to co-operate).

It was also recognised that the housing market obstructed mobility and so contributed to unemployment black spots (see Minford, Ashton and Peel, 1988: the mover loses subsidised housing, which he/she cannot easily or quickly regain elsewhere). Such inequality of unemployment would also increase aggregate unemployment: regional wages would not fall flexibly so as to eliminate regional unemployment black spots, being prevented by nationally-set benefits. Liberalisation of the private rented housing sector was brought in in 1988, while sales of publicly rented housing ('council house' sales) proceeded steadily throughout the period.

In addition to these formal measures, the privatisation programme and general policy thrust (towards both subsidy reduction and macro tightening) made both industry and government careful about costs, causing workers to be dismissed on a large scale if their marginal product did not cover their cost. One can think of this change as removing a large implicit, and smaller explicit, subsidy from employment, especially within the nationalised sector.

This brief account must suffice (but for more details see Matthews and Minford, 1987; Lawson, 1991; and the *locus classicus*, Thatcher, 1993). In general, one can say that the intention was to move the UK as close as possible to the US labour market environment. It seems clear that considerable progress was made in quite a short period. Although one could argue (Calmfors and Driffill, 1988) that a movement from a

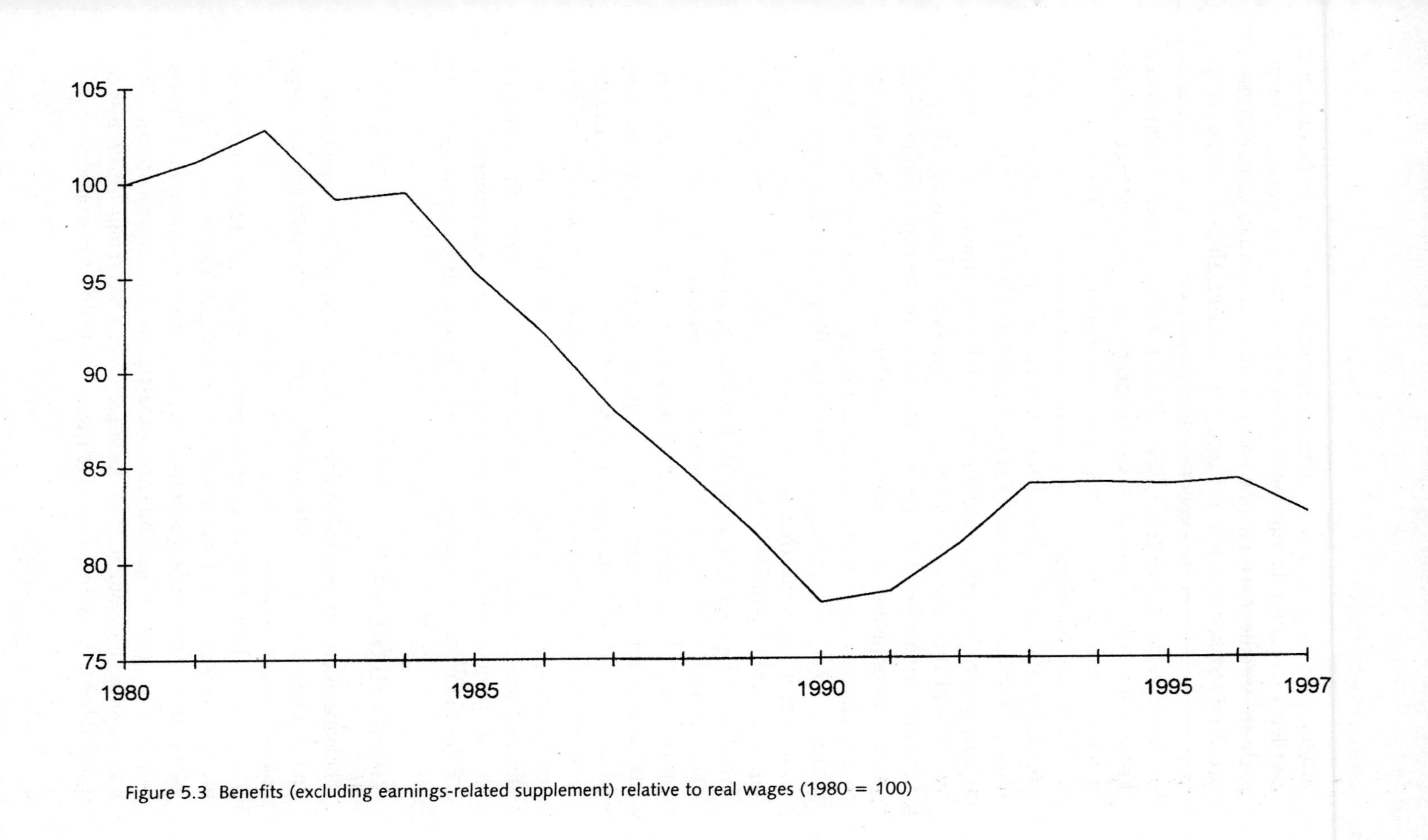

Figure 5.3 Benefits (excluding earnings-related supplement) relative to real wages (1980 = 100)

heavily centralised union-dominated environment such as Austria and Sweden to a US-style environment might not reduce unemployment, such an argument would not apply to the UK, which started from a decentralised but union-dominated environment, the worst-case situation. Instead, one might expect an unambiguous improvement in unemployment performance from such a determined movement towards the liberal end of the spectrum – a movement consisting not merely in the wholesale reduction of union power throughout the economy but also in further decentralisation towards firm-level bargaining. These changes should have resulted in both higher productivity (and, as we saw above, they indeed have) and greater wage flexibility (Calmfors, 1993).

I now turn to formal econometric analysis of the issue. But before doing so, I should make a point about the data: I am using UK unemployment as measured by the benefit count (ie, the raw national count, seasonally adjusted, of people to whom benefits are paid because they are unemployed). It is often suggested in popular debate that frequent changes to the benefit eligibility rules have distorted this series. However, it turns out that the resulting series tracks fairly closely the one generated by the UK Labour Force Survey (LFS a large sample of working age people), a series that conforms to the ILO definition of those actively seeking work according to survey questions. The LFS measure for the autumn of 1997 was 6.6%, some 1.5% above the claimant count. This gap is the widest it has been in recent years, possibly because of the introduction of the Job Seekers' Allowance in place of unemployment benefit - this may have encouraged some switching to other benefits. Over the past five years the gap has mostly been less than this and often negligible. The advantage of the claimant count series is that it is timely, totally accurate in its own terms, and extends back to 1950. It also mirrors approximately the movements in the LFS measure.

THE NATURAL RATE

The natural rate of unemployment is calculated in the Liverpool model as the interaction between pressures driving up wage demands and the wages that employers can offer while still remaining profitable. Both wage amounts are defined in terms of purchasing power (ie, adjusted for inflation) since that is what matters to both parties. At the point where these two forces equate (supply=demand), we obtain an 'equilibrium' inflation-adjusted (or 'real') wage and employment (also unemployment) rate. This can therefore be thought of as the situation in which employment is (just) profitable for firms and wages are (just) worthwhile for workers.

The idea is illustrated in a supply-and-demand diagram in Fig. 5.4. In this diagram, demand corresponds to what firms would want when the economy is in its normal state (that is, in practice, where the balance of payments on current account is not in deficit and where inflation is not unexpectedly high or low); and supply is defined similarly for normal circumstances. A further important point is that we allow firms to invest as much as they wish in computing their demand, so that what we are estimating is their 'long-run' demand once they have been able to invest as much as would be profitable given the wages they are faced with.

On the demand side, the factors involved are familiar: productivity, taxes on employers (including National Insurance contributions), indirect taxes, and the level of world trade (which means how much more can be sold abroad profitably).

On the supply side, the factors are less obvious. Unemployment benefits in particular have a direct effect in raising demands in so far as they compete with wages of low-paid workers (why work if wages do not pay at least as much as benefits and no doubt more?). But there is a further subtle effect: they act as a floor on wage demands, creating a rigidity downwards in wages. This prevents adjustment (or 'flexibility') in

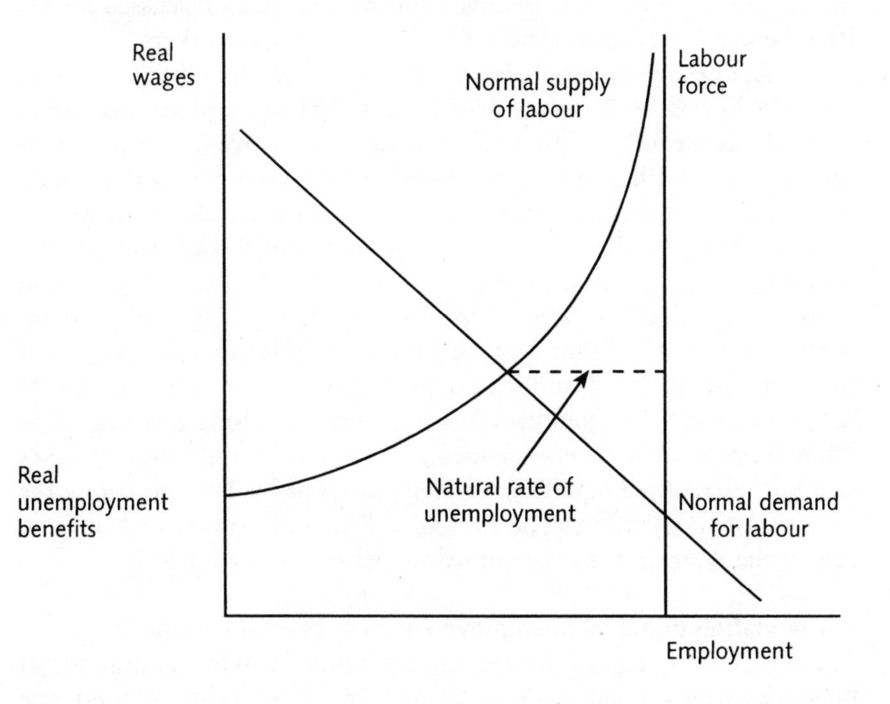

Figure 5.4 The natural rate of unemployment

wages, and so the labour market – in response to new shocks requiring wage falls – instead generates falling employment and rising unemployment.

Other factors on the supply side include the effect of union power in raising wage demands, and the direct and indirect taxes on workers (which mean that more has to be earned to compete with benefits).

Figure 5.5 shows the overall natural rate of unemployment my research group and I have obtained from our model for the last two decades as a result of the interaction of all these factors. It rose to a peak of 12% in 1981–83 and since then has fallen to around 2.5% today.

What were the constituent contributions from the factors that we have enumerated to this natural rate estimate? Figure 5.6 shows the effect variable by variable.

Interestingly the flat profile of benefits during the 1970s rules them out as having contributed to changes of the natural rate in that decade. However, in the 1980s the sharp rises in council house rents, fully compensated in unemployment benefits but only partially by in-work benefits, substantially raised the benefits package. Besides this contributory role, the key role of benefits is in giving wage demands (along the supply curve of labour) their relative rigidity, arising, as discussed above, from benefits creating a 'benefit floor' for low-wage workers.

The main elements producing change have been found to be unionisation, followed by taxes of various sorts. The former rises steadily to 1980 before steadily falling back. The tax rates move in largely offsetting ways until 1983, when their net effect is to lower unemployment, led by falling employer taxes on labour. Besides these elements, we can see that the trend elements (productivity and world trade trends) produce a tendency to improvement, which is reversed by the serious world recession of the early 1980s. Thereafter, the ground is gradually recaptured over the 1980s. One way to summarise this story is to say that trends in productivity and world markets managed after the world recession of 1982 to dominate (just) the effect of rising benefits, while 1980s supply-side influences reducing union power and lowering taxes had further reduced equilibrium unemployment by 1991 to below the level of 1970, restoring it (at around 2.5%) well towards the natural rate of the 1950s (put by the annual model at about 1%).

The deviation of actual unemployment from the natural rate

There are two sources of deviation of the actual from the natural rate of unemployment, or the 'unemployment gap'. First, as the natural rate changes it takes time – about three years – before actual unemployment

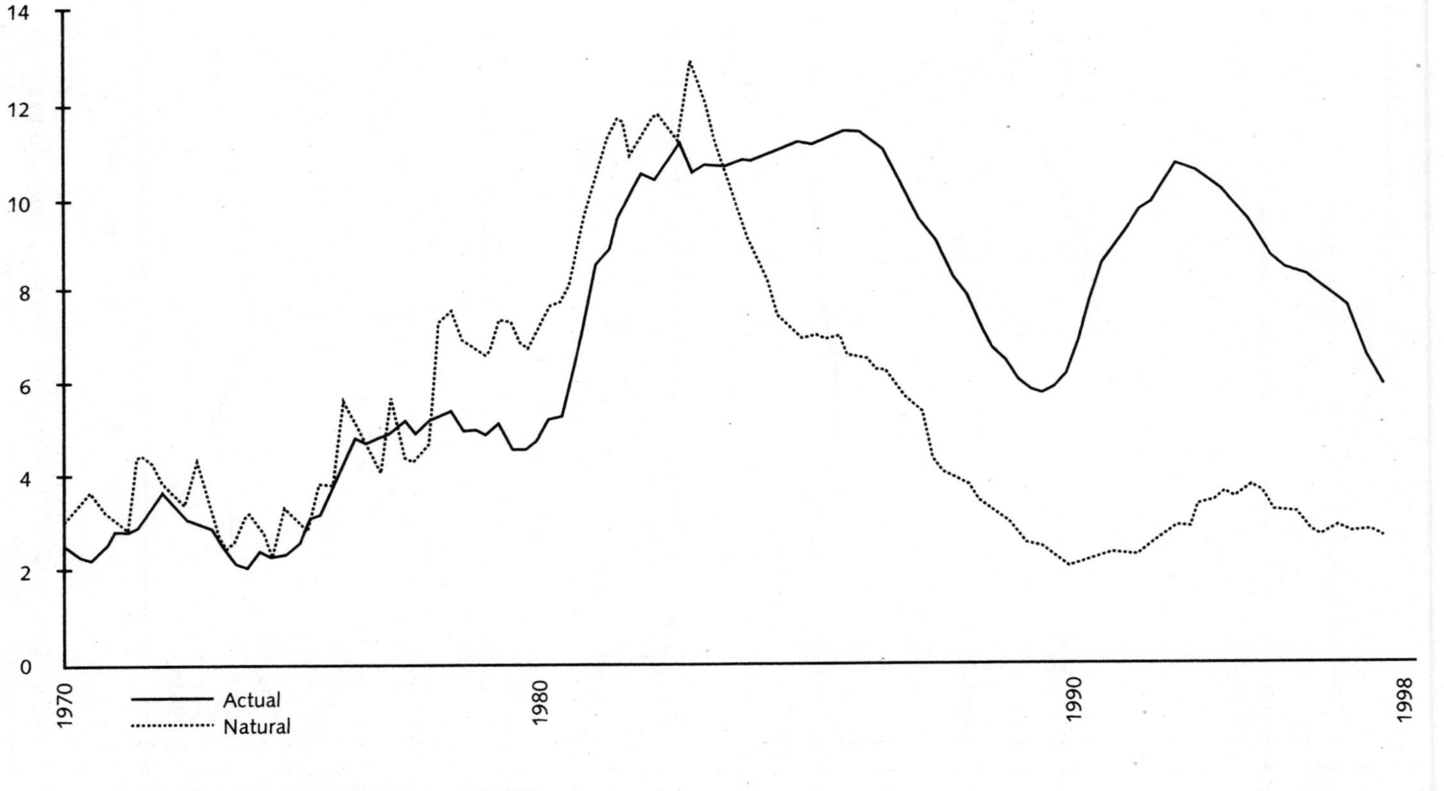

Figure 5.5 Actual and natural rates of unemployment

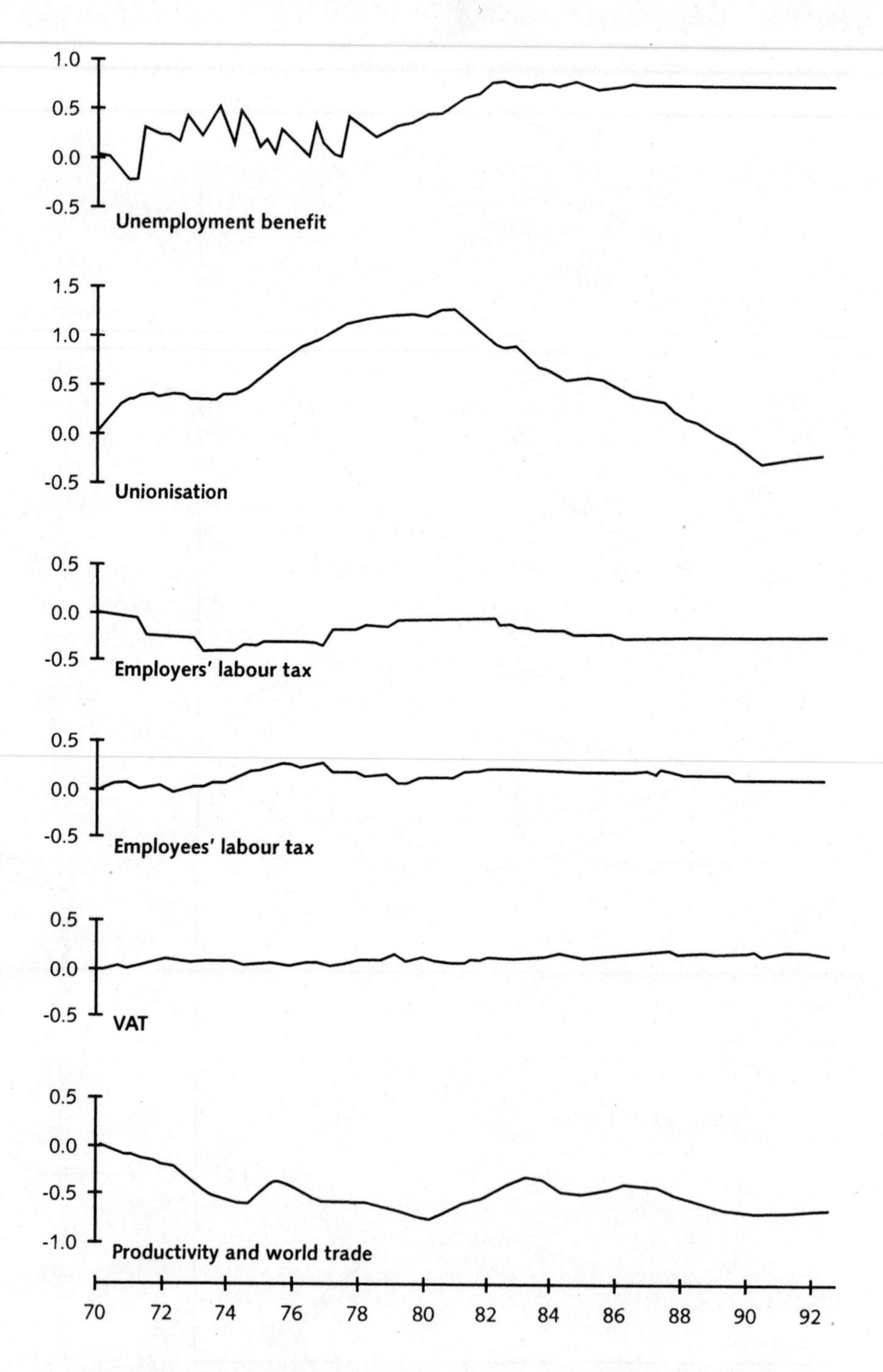

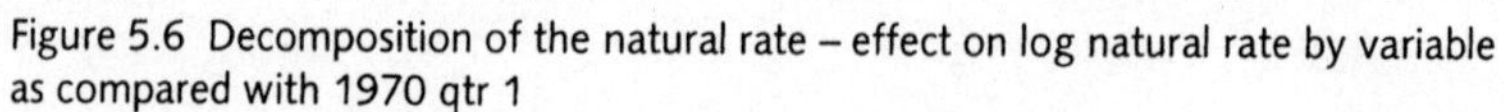

Figure 5.6 Decomposition of the natural rate – effect on log natural rate by variable as compared with 1970 qtr 1

is fully affected. This lag can be thought of as the delay in investment taking advantage of new profit opportunities or the capital stock being run down as losses are realised. It follows that changes in the natural rate affect the unemployment gap in a manner illustrated in Fig. 5.7: a falling natural rate raises the gap while a rising one lowers it.

The net effect on the gap of the estimated changes in the natural rate is shown in Fig. 5.8 up to 1993 (thereafter the natural rate has been roughly constant and so the net effect has been close to zero). In the early 1970s, this factor generated a fluctuating but on average small gap. But by the late 1970s and early 1980s, as the natural rate grew steadily, this had become substantially negative, peaking in 1981 at -2.6%. From 1981, as the natural rate levelled off, the gap dropped to zero and then from 1983 as the natural rate fell the unemployment gap rose, to a peak of 2.6% in 1984. It then fluctuated before falling away as the natural rate levelled off in the late 1980s.

The rest of the gap is the effect of shocks to demand, the 'demand element' (estimated here by subtraction of the first element, just discussed, from the total gap), although we do not attempt to decompose this element here. In Matthews and Minford (1987), we did attempt such a decomposition (using the earlier annual Liverpool model) for a purely floating period from 1980–86. On this occasion, we are faced with a much longer period and a regime change – the shadow ERM 1987–88 and the ERM proper 1990–92 – which upset this floating transmission in a manner that is not easy to model. Instead of formal decomposition, we make some informal comments about the demand pressures revealed by this demand element.

Figure 5.9 shows this element. During most of the 1970s, fluctuations in it were fairly modest. There was a peak of demand-induced unemployment of 1.1% in 1976 against a trough of -1.6% in 1973, a not-implausible net swing of 2.7% from the Barber boom to the recession after the first oil price rise. Thereafter the swings become larger. In the 1979 expansion, it falls to -2.3% in 1979 before emerging into the trauma of the 1980s.

During the early 1980s demand-led unemployment fluctuates between 0.7% and -0.7% before the lagged effects of persistent deflation come through from 1984 onwards. The peak of demand-induced unemployment is 4.3% in 1986 (much in line with Matthews and Minford, 1987). From then, the recovery begins to reduce the total, bringing it down to 2.5% in 1990.

At this point, we run into the phase of deflation associated with the aftermath of the 1988 boom and the entry into the ERM. According to

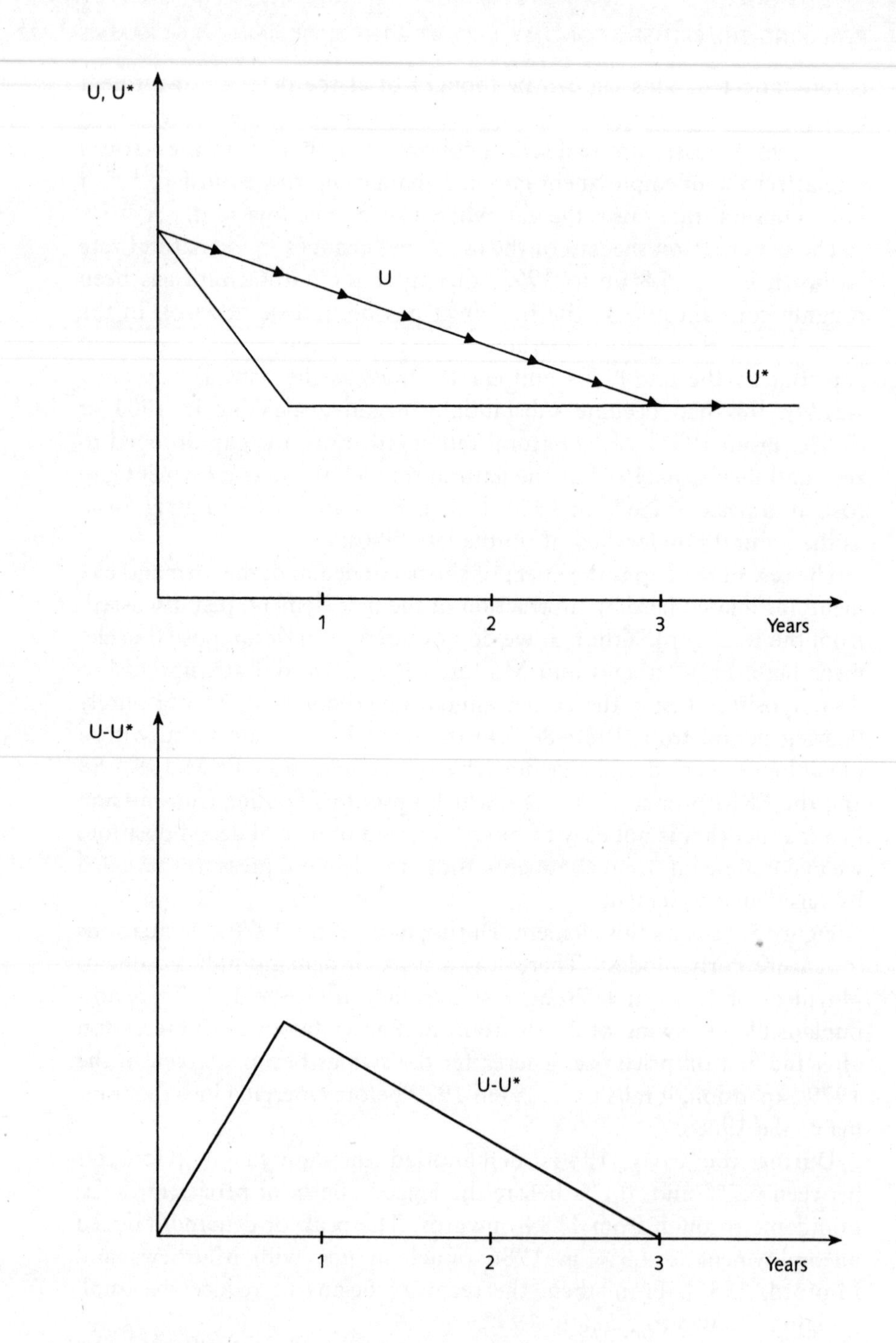

Figure 5.7 Effect of natural rate (U*) on the deviation of the actual from the natural rate (U-U*)

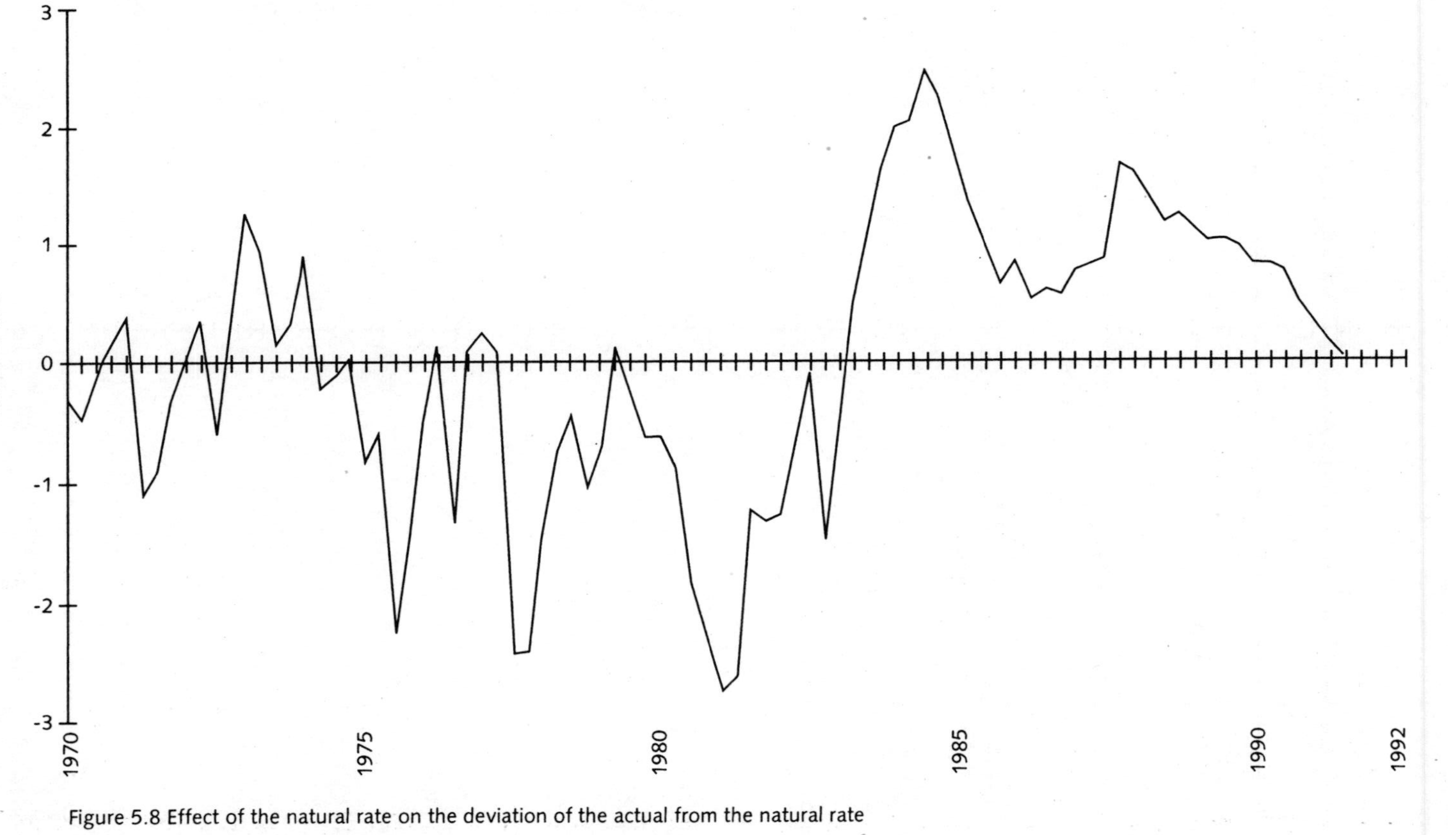

Figure 5.8 Effect of the natural rate on the deviation of the actual from the natural rate

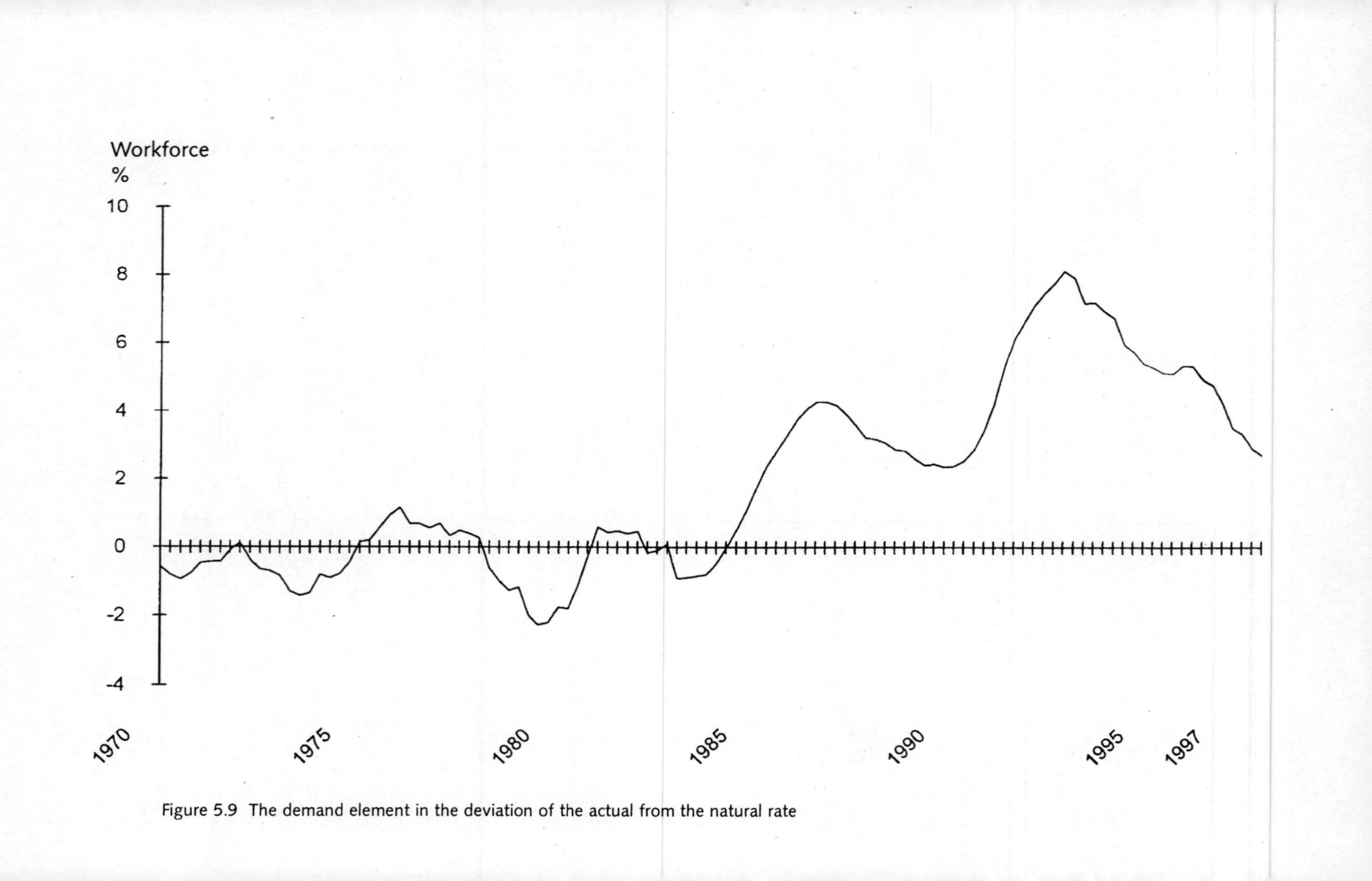

Figure 5.9 The demand element in the deviation of the actual from the natural rate

these figures, demand-led unemployment had reached no less than 8% by the end of 1992. They clearly indicate that the 1989–92 deflation was of an extraordinary magnitude.

The natural rate, although inevitably something which can only be pinned down with quite wide margins of error, is an important concept for policy makers, crucial to gauging the pay-offs to supply-side and demand-side policies. The direction and size of these movements in the natural rate and their broad decomposition into supply-driven and demand-driven components does in my view indicate four main things: first, that there was a large rise in the natural rate between the 1960s and the early 1980s; secondly, that this rise was probably more than reversed by the somewhat draconian labour market reforms of the 1980s; thirdly, that there have been two major deflationary episodes with sharp effects on unemployment in the 1980s; and, fourthly, that the second of these, associated with ERM entry, was the more deflationary and had the sharper unemployment effect, on a scale comparable with that of the 1930s.

Interpretation and contrast

The picture drawn in these pages could not be in greater contrast to the generality of comment one has read about the UK economy from 1993 to date. True, most commentators by now have had perforce to admit that the natural rate of unemployment must have dropped to some 5%, given that it is now at that rate and that wages are growing at a mere 3.0–4.5% depending on which survey one believes. Nevertheless, the view is widespread that the UK has little excess capacity and that in the labour market wage pressures will restart at unemployment rates much below where they currently are (5.2%).

However, I see no reason to believe such prejudices against the evidence of our model, which has rather remarkably defied the gloomy consensus of the early 1990s that unemployment could not fall much below 10% without inducing rising inflation. Indeed, although I have not dwelt on this aspect here, quite apart from this, our forecasting experience and what formal exercises we have done on the model's forecasting capacity have been reasonably encouraging (eg Matthews and Minford, 1987; Matthews et al, 1986; and Andrews et al, 1996).

There is little need to expatiate at great length on the weakness of this pessimistic position; the evidence so far that the labour market reforms have had a sharp effect is clear enough. But if we review in addition the state of current indicators, they suggest that the model is indeed correct that unemployment has much further to fall before it triggers inflationary pressure. What sort of evidence is adduced against our position? There are four main pieces of which I am aware.

First, it is often argued that wage behaviour became aggressive again as unemployment fell towards the end of the 1980s (Metcalf, 1994). Wages grew by 10% by 1990, after averaging 8% through the mid-1980s. Downward pressure on wage increases from the unemployed is muted because they are 'outsiders' who have no real access to jobs owing to being long-term unemployed and hence deskilled and demotivated.

Secondly, unemployment itself is argued to be on a rising ratchet-like trend. In the last boom, it fell only to 5.6% (in mid-1990), against 4.9% in the last cyclical upturn of 1979.

Thirdly, on the matter of capacity it is said that there is limited excess capacity because of accelerated write-offs of plant during the 1990–92 recession. As evidence, we are pointed to CBI survey data in 1993 showing that, in the upturn, an unusually low proportion of firms was working below capacity (Fig. 5.10). It is argued that this shortage of capacity has continued to get in the way of any theoretical fall in unemployment.

Fourthly, it is said that, since 1990, labour supply has shrunk because of adverse shocks, namely 'downsizing', the effect of benefits in creating 'two-jobless' households, and the rising desire for part-time work.

Let us take each of these four arguments in turn.

Why did the rate of increase in average earnings rise from 8% to 10% between the mid-1980s and 1989? According to my story, this reflected rising inflationary expectations in the context of the excessive monetary expansion of 1987–88, which caused GDP to grow by over 9% in those two years after five years of expansion, and produced bottlenecks in goods markets. It is actually remarkable (Fig. 5.11) how little wage settlements reacted to the sharp rise in inflation over the same period (from 5% to 10% on the retail price index and to around 8% on 'underlying' measures). My research group and I explain this by our view that unemployment was *above* not below the natural rate. For the second half of the 1980s (Fig. 5.12), real wages were growing by substantially less than the productivity growth rate in manufacturing and even below the (probably understated) rate in the whole economy.

Then we must query the lack of pressure from 'outsiders', in the form of the long-term unemployed. Those unemployed more than a year had dropped by end-1990 to 1.8% of the workforce, from 4.6% in 1987. Furthermore, the turnover rate in the labour market had risen by 1992 to around 14% of the labour force per year, against 9% in 1988. Hence,

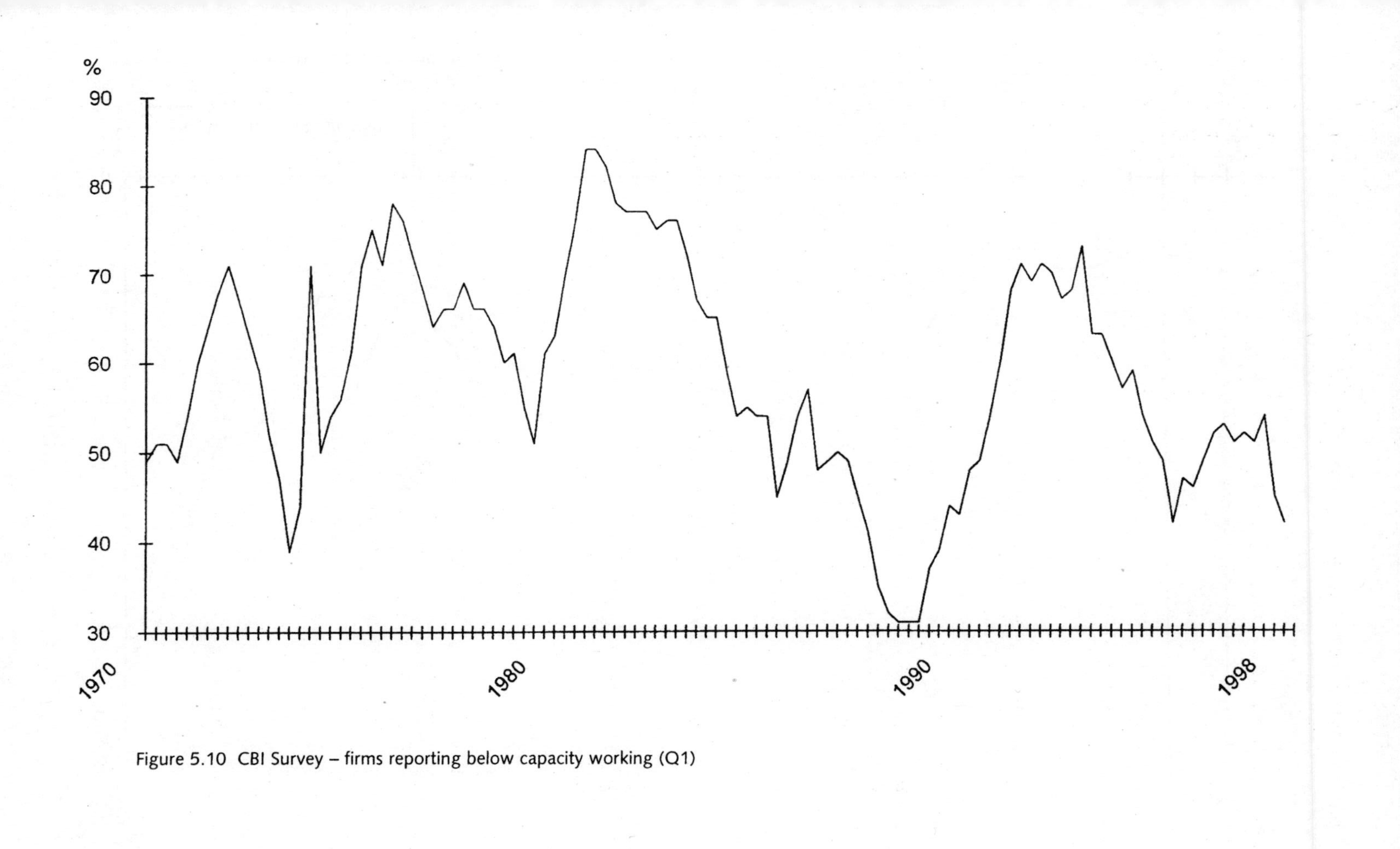

Figure 5.10 CBI Survey – firms reporting below capacity working (Q1)

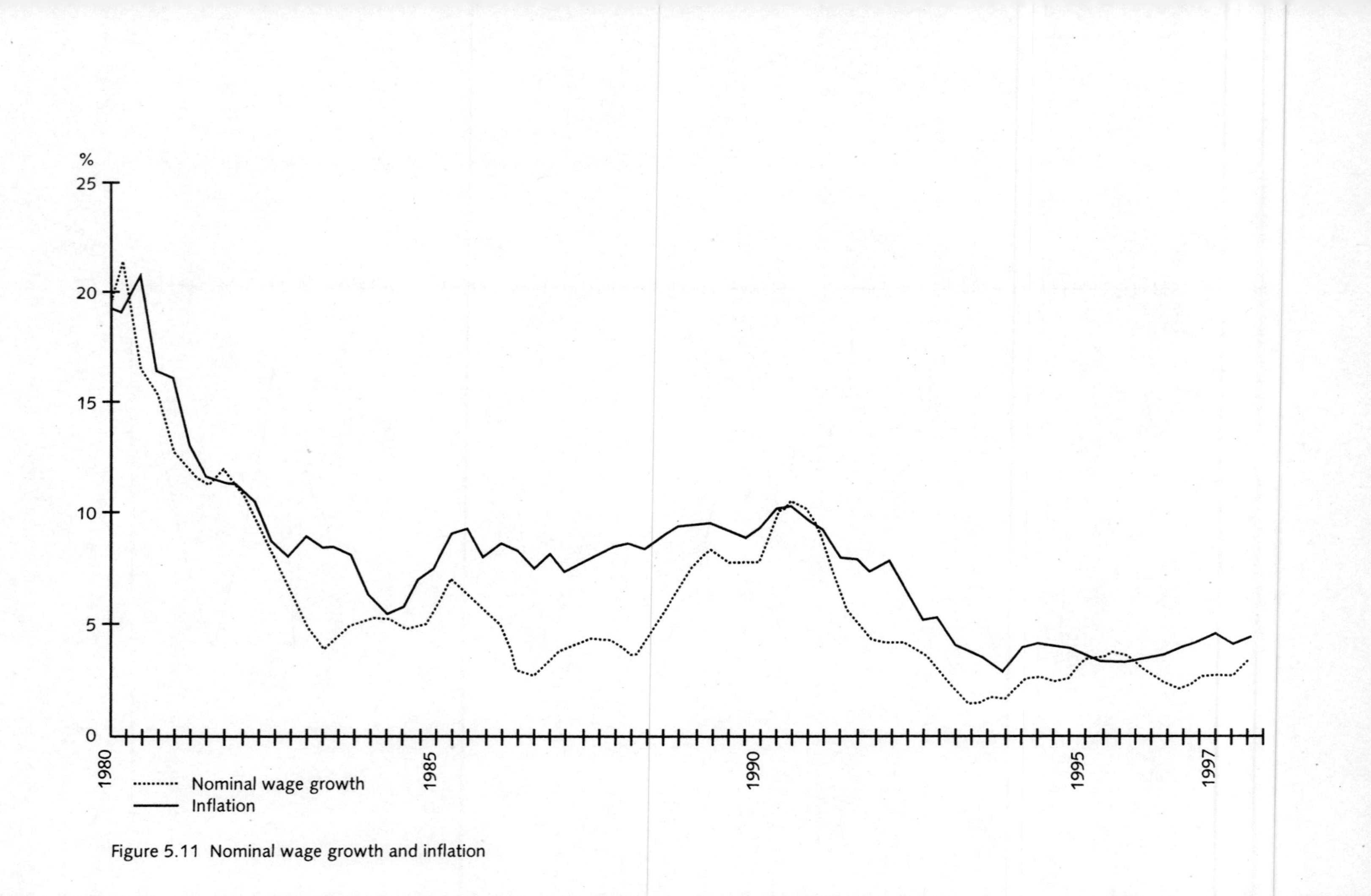

Figure 5.11 Nominal wage growth and inflation

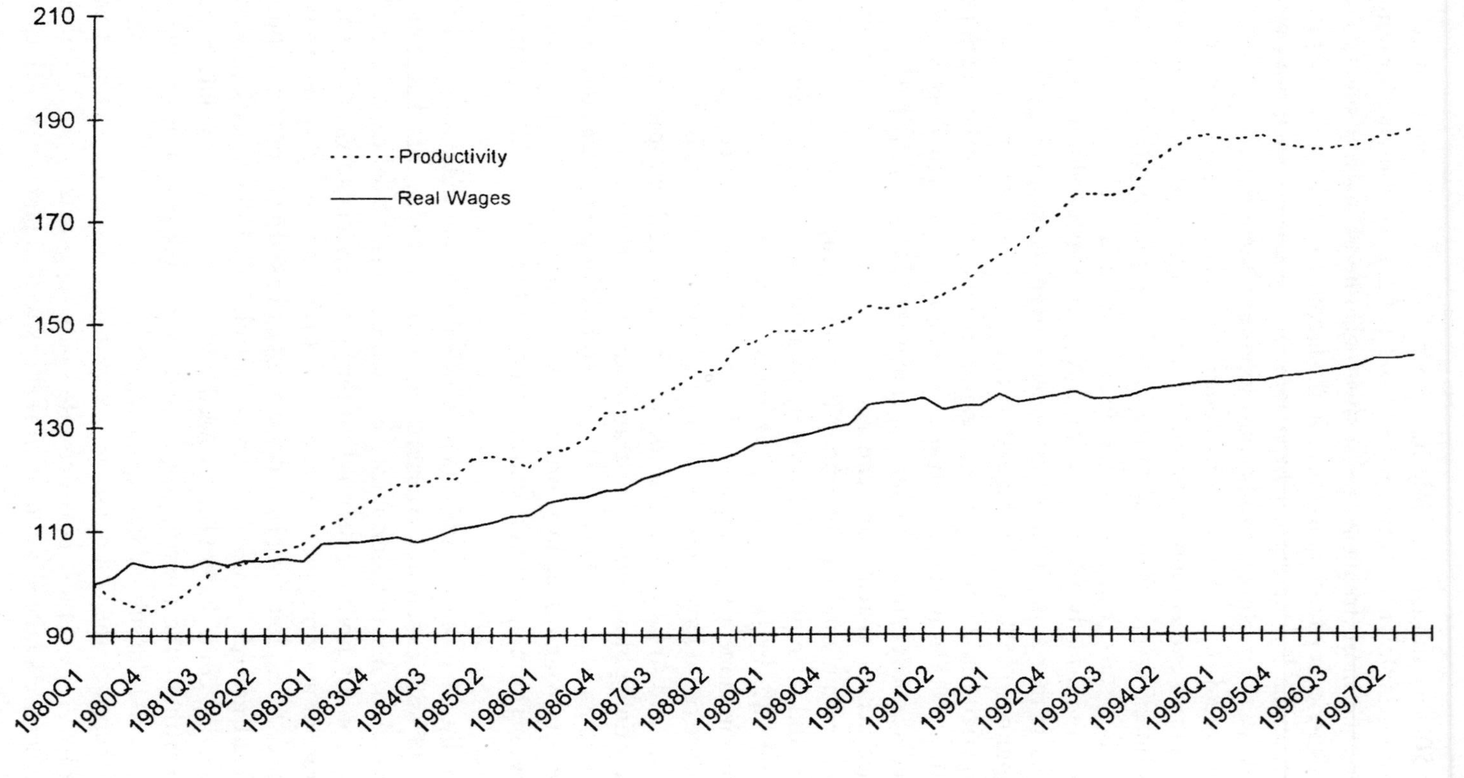

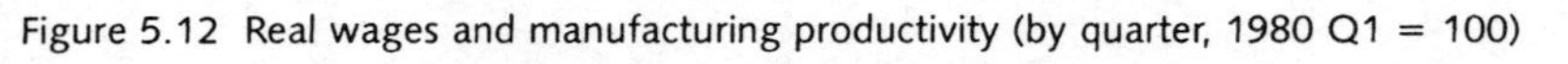

Figure 5.12 Real wages and manufacturing productivity (by quarter, 1980 Q1 = 100)

some 50% of the labour force may have quit jobs and experienced a spell of unemployment between 1988 and 1992. Even allowing for double or even more frequent spells, this high rate of activity suggests a wide experience of unemployment in the labour force. This is not a picture of supine labour market behaviour by the unemployed, not even those with the misfortune to become long-term unemployed.

Nor would supineness be consistent with other evidence we have on benefits (now exceedingly low relative to the wages of all but the lowest paid), on the greater vigour with which work-testing (together with job-start and re-start programmes) is being applied, and finally the weakness of the traditionally militant unions. A particularly relevant fact on benefits is that some 50% of the unemployed at its 1993 peak were non-manual (25% in the highest occupational groups: professional, managerial and administrative), against around 25% in the previous recession (12.5% in the highest occupational groups). For these workers, replacement ratios are nugatory under the UK's flat-rate, basic-subsistence benefit system. One can assume desperate efforts were being made to regain employment among this large group.

Why did unemployment drop only to 5.6% in 1990 and why did it rise to 10.6% by January 1993? Our answer is that owing to our tragic errors in monetary policy, we had to hit on the head an economy that otherwise could have remained on a sustained growth path of some 3%. After we had so hit it on the head, we joined the ERM proper and continued raining blows on its prostrate body. The resulting deep recession produced an unemployment 'gap' (due to lack of demand, as discussed above) of around 8%. In short, it was recession, not the trends of a poorly performing labour market, that delivered us this apparent ratchet.

Thirdly, what of capacity? There is little doubt that the sheer speed of the 1987–88 expansion overtook available capacity at that time. Nevertheless, a distinction must be made between actual capacity and the potential output (or 'natural output' rate) associated with the natural rate of unemployment. It takes time for the necessary capital to be installed, to exploit the profit opportunities linked with potential output. Had growth been steady and controlled in 1988, goods market overheating could have been avoided and unemployment would have fallen without the interruption caused by the temporary inflationary pressure and the subsequent squeeze.

Furthermore, the CBI question on capacity is qualitative and must be treated with caution. It has been informally suggested by the CBI that survey answers take account of workers as well as plant, in which case under the UK's permissive hire-fire regulations it is an elastic concept. In addition, capacity, even when written off, does not thereby cease to exist. It is merely discounted by managers or even sold off. Interestingly, total private gross fixed investment fell only 20% from its peak during the last long and severe recession, suggesting that there was likely to be large-scale spare (physical) capacity as it ended in 1992. This is confirmed by the relative inertia of manufacturing investment in the upturn – up to mid-1997.

A supposed lack of excess capacity is also difficult to reconcile with the answers to the CBI's pricing questions (which systematically since 1990 have shown that virtually no respondents plan price rises), especially given the large rise in imported material costs after exit from the ERM. There has been a clear unwillingness to raise prices and margins, which can only be explained by an extreme desire to raise sales and capacity.

The fourth argument is that labour supply has shrunk since 1990. First, 'downsizing' in big companies has been concentrated on older workers, who have taken early retirement on a reasonable pension. Secondly, among low-paid workers the benefit system stops one partner working when the other is out of work; so we have the rise in double-jobless households. (This is not to be confused with 'jobless households', the overwhelming majority of which are single or single-parent households; single people face no special incentive problem in getting work because their benefits are low, while the difficulties of single parents are very particular and most of them may well return to work once their children reach school age.) Thirdly, the rise of part-time working has gathered pace, and reflected the preferences of those (mainly women) doing it.

Consider these in turn. Yes, it is true that some who have experienced their firm's downsizing will retire. Others, though, will come back as self-employed consultants and part-time directors. And do not forget the 'cohort effect': every year the working age population loses one year's cohort of retirees but also gains a cohort of school and university leavers. Since 1990, six cohorts have changed places. This changing of cohorts will have removed many of the early retired, and more will be removed by the year 2000. The preferences of the working-age population are therefore only temporarily affected by early retirement, as we saw plainly in the 1980s.

Secondly, the two-jobless households are indeed a serious benefit-induced problem. But they are not new, nor are there that many. They constituted 9.3% of all households in the spring of 1996 and their unemployment rate was 12.4%; with some 2% growth in employment since then, it is now likely to be in single figures. These same households were being sucked back into work in 1986–90; the reason is that if both adult members can get jobs, it is thoroughly worthwhile. But this possibility depends on generalised recovery.

The part-time trend is indeed longstanding and, of course, is largely based on women's increasing participation in work and their desire for limited flexible hours. However, recent part-time work has grown above this trend, suggesting an element of making do by those who would like to work longer hours.

Ultimately the test of these views is the emerging evidence of the UK economy's behaviour. This has not fitted well with such general pessimism about the natural rate. Wage settlements remain moderate, averaging a little over 3%; full-time earnings in summer 1997 were 4% up on a year before, according to the Labour Force Survey (based on individual workers' replies), 4.5% up according to the regular monthly survey of employers, having fallen from 7.5% at the beginning of 1992; part-time earnings rose only 2.1%, so that the LFS average earnings growth overall was 3.7%. These figures do not suggest the overheating of the labour market that has been so widely and wrongly anticipated every year since 1992.

Furthermore, if one compares present hours of employment with those at their peak of the last employment cycle of 1984-90, they are down by 3%, and this is even though we estimate that, at the peak, there was still additional scope for employment of the order of 3%. All this fits well with our model estimates of the natural rate of unemployment. We conclude that the labour market reforms have indeed had a dramatic effect on the UK economy's ability to create jobs and reduce unemployment – a crucial element in the UK's supply-side performance.

In the end, a low natural rate of unemployment depends on policies that permit wages to find a level equal to productivity, especially at the bottom of the pay scale where benefits and ideas of social justice put an artificial floor below them. These policies are politically hard to implement in Europe because of its tradition of Christian and Social Democracy; in the United States with its tradition of decentralised liberalism there has never, except during the Great Depression, been much pressure to pursue such policies. Furthermore, the downward pressure of low wage costs in 'emerging markets' makes the policy dilemma of European governments the more acute, as we will argue in Chapter 7. However, there seems to be no escape from the horns of this dilemma. EC governments will have to acquire toughness on these matters if they are to bring down high natural rates of unemployment. It is to that issue that we turn next.

CONCLUSIONS

What we have seen in this chapter is that the UK, gradually liberated after 1979 from its version of the stakeholder (or in some aspects crudely socialist) economy, managed to transform its performance in the creation of wealth. This transformation reached across all dimensions of that creation process: productivity growth, working-age population, participation, and unemployment.

The contrast with the continent of Europe, where the stakeholder approach if anything has become more intense over the past few decades, is marked. We shall consider the continent's difficulties further in chapters 7 and 8. Here we conclude by underlining the wider lesson of, and evidence provided by, the UK experience: that freeing markets has a powerful effect in enhancing economic performance.

References

Andrews, M. J., Minford P. and Riley J. (1996) 'On Comparing Macroeconomic Models Using Forecast Encompassing Tests', *Oxford Bulletin of Economics and Statistics*, Vol. 58, No. 2, pp. 279-305.

Barrell, R. (1994), ed., *The UK Labour Market – Comparative Aspects and Institutional Developments*, Cambridge University Press, Cambridge.

Barrell R., Pain, N. and Young, G. (1994) 'Structural Differences in European Labour Markets', in Barrell (1994), ch.7, pp 214–57.

Bean, C. and Crafts, N. (1996) 'British Economic Growth Since 1945: Relative Economic Decline ... and Renaissance?' in N. Crafts and G. Toniolo (eds.) *Economic Growth in Europe Since 1945*, 131–72, for the Centre for Economic Policy Research, Cambridge University Press, Cambridge.

Broadberry, S.N. (1996) 'Convergence: what the historical record shows?' in B. van Ark and N.F.R. Crafts (eds.) *Quantitative Aspects of Post-war European Economic Growth*, Cambridge University Press, Cambridge.

Calmfors, L. (1993) 'Centralisation of Wage Bargaining and Macroeconomic Performance – a Survey' in *OECD Economic Studies*, No. 21.

Calmfors, L. and Driffill, J. (1988) 'Centralisation of Wage Bargaining and Macroeconomic Performance', *Economic Policy*, 6, 13–61.

Crafts, N. (1997) *Britain's Relative Economic Decline 1870-1995: a Quantitative Perspective*, The Social Market Foundation, London.

Lawson, N. (1991) *The View from No.11*, Bantam Press, London.

Matthews, K.G.P., and Minford, P. (1987) 'Mrs. Thatcher's Economic Policies 1979–86', *Economic Policy*, Cambridge University Press, Vol. 5, October, pp. 57-101.

Matthews, K.G.P., Minford, P. and Riley, J. (1986) 'The Forecast Performance of the Liverpool Group: the Record Straightened', *Quarterly Economic Bulletin*, Liverpool Research Group in Macroeconomics, 7(1).

Metcalf, D. (1994), 'Transformation of British Industrial Relations?', in Barrell (1994), Ch. 4, pp 126–57.

Minford, P., Ashton, P. and Peel, M. (1988), 'The Effects of Housing Distortions on Unemployment', *Oxford Economic Papers*, 40, pp 322–45.

Minford, P., Matthews, K.G.P. and Rastogi, A. (1990) *A Quarterly Version of the Liverpool Model of the UK*, working paper 90/06, Liverpool Research Group in Macroeconomics, University of Liverpool.

Minford, P., Sprague, A., Matthews, K.G.P. and Marwaha, S. (1984) 'The Liverpool Macroeconomic Model of the United Kingdom', *Economic Modelling*, 1, Jan.

OECD (1996) *Economic Outlook*, OECD, Paris.

Oulton, N. (1995) 'Supply side reform and UK economic growth: what happened to the miracle?', *National Institute Economic Review*, 154, pp. 53–70.

Thatcher, M. (1993) *The Downing Street Years*, HarperCollins, London.

CHAPTER SIX

The triumph of global capitalism – The death of inflation

I HAVE GONE into some detail on the experience of the UK because it exemplifies both a sharp deterioration in relative performance after the Second World War with the introduction of thorough-going socialism and then a dramatic turnaround since 1979 as free markets were reintroduced. It is an unusual test case of the free-market thesis about the power of incentives. However, much else has been going on in the world economy over the past few decades that has a bearing on the same thesis. In the next three chapters, we examine four factors, namely:

1. the spread of monetarism;
2. the liberalisation of world trade;
3. the acceptance of the discipline of world markets by an increasing band of less developed countries and their consequent 'emergence'; and
4. the acceptance of most developed countries in the OECD of the need to adjust to the resulting change in comparative advantage and concentrate on new technology.

We shall see how these four factors have created an environment in which less developed countries have had the capacity to grow rapidly, while developed countries have enjoyed still-rapidly rising living standards, low inflation and low unemployment.

The only cloud in th... f capitalist progress has been the ill-considered reaction by some countries of the North (the OECD) to the problems this progress has created for Northern unskilled workers. Instead of encouraging them to accept lower wages in order to retain their jobs, while giving whatever assistance is possible in retraining and transitional living support, a number of countries, mostly those on the European continent, have pursued 'social' policies that have had the effect of creating minimum levels for wages and pushing up non-wage employment costs, partly through employment taxes but mainly through regulation and workers' rights. This reaction has had disastrous effects on unemployment and growth.

In the rest of this chapter, I discuss the origins of the macroeconomic success now being seen in combating inflation across the developed countries of the world and ask whether it is durable; has inflation 'died', as some have claimed? In effect, we extend the sort of discussion above of UK monetarism to the broader world experience.

We then turn to growth and microeconomics in Chapter 7. I attempt to piece together the main factors driving trade, growth, and employment in the world economy since 1970. How far has trade from emerging markets had an impact on them and on the North? How far has technological change, and any bias in it towards skilled labour (notably because of computers), been responsible for growth and the plight of unskilled workers? What has been the role of higher education? How far have those social policies altered the picture? These and other questions must really be answered before we can comment seriously on the mechanisms by which the obviously encouraging record of the period has come about. We conclude it by drawing out these mechanisms and the main policy conclusions.

I then revert to the cloud just mentioned. Europe's policy reaction to the problems of unskilled workers has created difficulties not merely for its own economies but indirectly also for those closely involved in trade with it and with other shared institutions – most of all for the UK, which having pursued free-market policies finds itself yoked to a continent with a very different, regulated or 'stakeholder', approach. In Chapter 8, I discuss first the continent's problems and secondly the UK's consequential problems and options. It is obvious that this book's preferred solution to both problems is for continental policy to change, much in the way that British policy changed after 1979. That may yet happen; some political parties on the continent are seized of this need, for example Mr Aznar's Spanish conservatives, most sides in Irish politics, and in Germany the Bavarian CSU and the Free Democrats. Should this not happen, however, it seems unlikely, and certainly undesirable, that the UK should continue in its European relationship without renegotiation. Furthermore, the prospects for long-term stagnation on the continent would be seriously worrying for all OECD members.

THE CONQUEST OF INFLATION – IS THERE A NEW ERA?

There is one aspect of modern developed economies in which they do not much differ (unlike in growth and unemployment), and that is the effective elimination of inflation. That may seem to be an exaggerated description, given that inflation lies between zero and 3% for virtually all OECD countries (Fig. 6.1 and Table 6.1(a)). But the measurement of inflation is biased upwards because of the inadequate allowance for quality change and, in some countries, for the changing pattern of consumption towards lower-priced goods (for example, in hypermarkets as opposed to corner stores) – termed, respectively, quality bias and substitution bias. In the US in 1996, the Boskin Report to the US Senate put the two together at a central estimate of 1.1% per annum with a range of 0.8–1.6% per annum (William Nordhaus gives a broad and witty account of recent findings in the September 1997 issue of the *Economic Journal*). This implies that price stability, even falling prices, may hold across the bulk of OECD countries today.

How has this come about? And is it, as some have argued, bound to continue so that we are in a new era in which inflation is dead? I shall argue in this chapter that it has come about because of a shift in policy based on new thinking about the workings of the economy: thinking that I will call 'new classical monetarism'. Assuming that there is no reversal of this thinking, then the new policies will continue because they are optimal within this sort of thinking and with their continuance inflation will not return.

Some have argued that inflation has died because of liberalising changes in labour market institutions, but this could not be true because many countries' institutions have not been liberalised – indeed in some the reverse has happened and yet their inflation has gone away too.

A variant of this argument is that the increased competition from emerging market countries and the technological shift produced by the computer have together undermined unions' bargaining power, particularly those of unskilled workers, and that this has eliminated inflation (Roger Bootle argues along these lines in his *The Death of Inflation*, although his thesis is more general and, indeed, thoroughly eclectic). I will argue in the next chapter that these factors have certainly both been

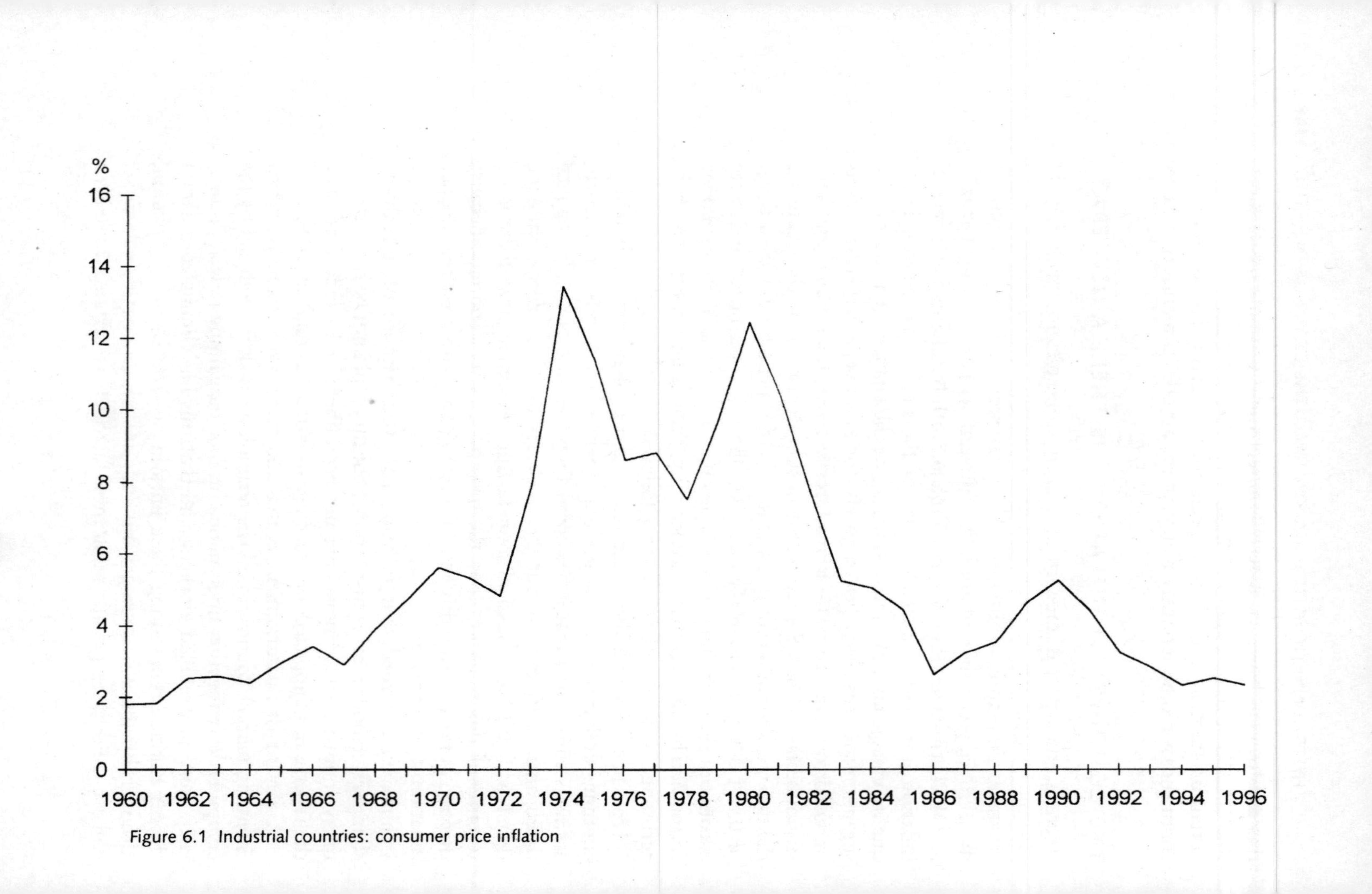

Figure 6.1 Industrial countries: consumer price inflation

strongly at work in the past two decades, and also that they clearly have had their impact generally across all OECD countries. However, this explanation faces a different problem with the facts. It seems to have been a powerful force since around 1970 at least and possibly earlier. Yet inflation peaked in the OECD as a whole at the end of the 1970s after two oil price crises (in 1973 and 1980). It has only fallen to the sort of low levels being generally seen in the late nineties at the start of that decade, and the recorded falls did not become widespread before 1996. Now, there might be long and variable lags in the process, but the length (up to three decades) and the variability (across countries – from 5 to 30 years) are both quite implausible.

But it is not just recent figures that go against these 'new era' theories; after all, inflation as a systematic tendency, decade after decade, is only a post-war phenomenon. Before the war, it had occurred in bursts, often around wars, and then been reversed; there was price stability over very long periods – as far as we know, the price level was roughly the same in 1939 as in 1839. During this period, there were many changes in labour market and other institutions, and it would therefore be odd to account for price behaviour in terms of these. And, indeed, we have a theory of inflation that looks in a quite different direction. In this theory we account for it in terms of money supply – the creation, that is the printing, of money.

Prices are the exchange rate between goods and money. So, thinking in terms of simple demand and supply, for inflation to occur (ie, prices to rise steadily for a long period) either the supply of goods must steadily contract or the supply of money must steadily rise. Alternatively, vice versa, the demand for goods must steadily rise relative to the demand for money. The most plausible candidate of these four possibilities is normally the steady rise in the supply of money. The supply of goods tends to rise gradually over time; and the relation between the demand for money and goods is again a fairly static one, subject to occasional once-for-all shifts. But we now go into these matters in more detail.

By money I mean the currency that a government has printed on its behalf, usually by the central bank (and equivalent liabilities that a government has that can be converted at face value into currency – mainly deposits with the central bank held by commercial banks). We distinguish between this and deposits with banks and other intermediaries that are supposed to be exchangeable at face value into currency. Under highly controlled or monopolised systems of intermediation – for example where there are just a few banks entitled to take deposits – there will be a close link between the supply of currency and the quantity of deposits through credit creation. Extra currency printed will be deposited interest-free in banks, which will increase credit; this will be in turn deposited and lead to more credit creation, and so on until the (credit-multiplier) process has converged on a higher level of deposits and credit. In these systems, it is usual to consider the total amount of currency and deposits as 'money'; effectively the banks as a monopoly have become an extension of the money-printing process. Banks do not compete for deposits through interest rates (they may be allowed to compete in a limited way through add-on services); hence no interest is paid on deposits and they are entirely like currency except that there will be some division of transactions between currency and deposits and some difference of security. These factors will mean that some proportion of money is held in currency. Add to that some proportion of deposits that the banks need to hold in their tills or at the central bank as backing for their deposits (in case of fluctuating demand), and you can work out the likely deposit multiple of currency.

However, today, due to deregulation, there is widespread competition among banks and between them and a whole range of other intermediaries (including building societies, unit trust companies, and institutions of all kinds taking deposits in the 'wholesale' market), each such institution offering to take deposits or their close substitutes such as unit-linked income bonds. We discussed this earlier in the chapter on UK monetary and fiscal policy; and we showed there that this will lead to a potentially most unstable stock of wider money measures, however defined. Clearly, currency plus bank deposits (often called 'M1' – see Table 6.1(d)) will be affected by the terms on other deposits and substitutes; so people have widened the definition steadily to include more and more deposit-substitutes. This does not remove the problem for two reasons. First, there are always other actual or potential substitutes just outside the definition; nowadays, when competition has led to interest being payable on virtually all types of deposits, the competition is fairly close between all forms of deposit. In addition, there is nothing to stop new entry by an intermediary into the deposit business. Secondly, there is the instability of the competition between deposits and the stock market: as prospects for the stock market change, portfolio investors move between 'cash' (interest-paying deposits) and stocks and also firms move between borrowing and issuing stocks to finance their operations.

So in these competitive systems I focus solely on currency as the money supply; the effects of printing more of it are then widely diffused through the financial system. Unfortunately for our measurements, currency too has been affected by the abolition of financial controls, including exchange controls. Currency of the major countries is often used widely by foreigners; for example, the Federal Reserve Board estimates from its research that around three-quarters of the dollars in existence are held outside the United States. And so, when estimating how much impact extra dollars printed will have on the US economy, we have to know how much of it will be absorbed outside the US by foreigners using it in their own economies.

The point nevertheless remains that prices are the rate of exchange between currency and goods. As I argued earlier, the simplest supply-and-demand theory tells you that this exchange rate depends on the relative supply of money or goods versus the relative demand for money or goods. Hence, given demands people have for money and goods, an increase in either goods or money supply will alter this exchange rate – there is money chasing goods or vice versa. As stated earlier, I shall focus mostly on the supply of money as the determinant of prices over long periods of time because the supply of goods grows in a steady way in the long term and the demand for money (currency) for transactions depends on the generally slow evolution of technology, as well as to some extent on the interest or inflation cost of holding it rather than converting it into a deposit.

This is not to say there are not sharp variations in this demand that are hard to explain, let alone to predict in advance. As we have seen above, in the UK with its shadow economy, falling inflation and shifting technology, and in the US with its foreign demand, the measurement of the appropriate (non-inflationary) supply of currency is hard. In practice, central banks have to resort to a wide variety of measures of the effects of their interest-rate policies in order to estimate whether they have got the supply right. Nevertheless, it the supply of money that is having the effects on prices, and that remains the theory of how prices are formed, whether it is easy or not to estimate how much money should be printed.

In Chapter 4 on UK monetary policy, I also went into some depth on the theory of how fiscal policy (budget deficits) had also to be geared to monetary objectives. So what we have here is a theory of monetary and fiscal restraint that we can loosely call monetarist. Add to it a theory that market participants use information intelligently (their rational expectations) and you have 'new classical monetarism', in which it is not merely what the government does today that matters but also what it is logically expected to do tomorrow. This nevertheless also implies that there is a most unfavourable trade-off between the printing of money and the health of the economy: if people anticipate the issue of extra money before it happens, prices will already be rising beforehand and will have risen in full by the time the issue is complete, and so it will have no impact on output but all the extra money will have been absorbed in higher prices. If people do not anticipate the issue, then some will spill over into higher output – but the effect will be only temporary: once people realise what has happened, prices will rise in line with the extra money. Governments then find that they have increased prices (and usually inflation) with either no or some merely temporary gain in output. To reverse the rise in inflation that has become generally expected is a hard process involving managing people's expectations downwards – what we have described earlier for the UK after 1979. The game no longer is worth the candle.

It is this general set of ideas – which we went into carefully in Chapter 4 – that has underlain the sea change in the behaviour of inflation. Governments and the popular opinions that fuel them are no longer attracted by the trade-off offered by inflationary policies. They and their central banks have therefore emphasised caution in deficits and interest-rate setting. This has been true generally across the OECD, whatever the state of labour markets, growth, or unemployment.

We may add that the vogue for independent central banks has emerged from this theory also – we discussed this in the context of Gordon Brown's decision in 1997 to give the Bank of England operational autonomy. However, central bank independence is a consequence (an evolution, as we saw) of the new policy environment; it is the latter, not central bank autonomy, that is the cause of lower inflation. This can easily be understood by a thought experiment. Suppose that Western public opinion had wanted to pursue inflationary policies because it thought them beneficial through a pleasant trade-off with lower unemployment – even, perhaps, as was once thought by post-war Keynesian policy makers and opinion leaders, producing permanently lower unemployment for modestly higher inflation, kept down by incomes policies. Could we believe that these democratic countries would have pursued non-inflationary policies because they notionally had independent central banks? If we did so believe, we would be negating the very concept of democracy!

There are several statistical studies purporting to show that inflation is the result of central bank independence – for example Alesina and Summers (1993), Cukierman (1992) and Grilli et al (1991). But, as so often happens, we have a *post hoc ergo propter hoc* problem: 'which is cause, which effect?'. In this particular case, we also have a problem in measuring independence; varieties of criteria are put forward to measure 'effective' independence. Conveniently these are correlated with lower inflation, yet there is more than a suspicion of circularity – would we really judge a central bank as effectively independent if it did not produce low inflation? Take Japan: according to the Japanese constitution, its central bank is as wholly owned a subsidiary of the government as you could ever wish, yet these studies manage to classify it (necessarily so for their purposes, because it has a very good inflation record) as highly independent. Thus do clever people deceive even themselves perhaps with their own sophistication?

From the alternative point of view, can we tell that it has been the change in monetary and fiscal policy that has been responsible for the drop in inflation, when we cannot properly measure the growth in money supply? This is indeed something of a problem. However, the measurement problem should not obscure a general gear change in money-supply growth, however measured. Measurement for the setting of interest rates in the short term is one thing, evaluation of long-term trends in retrospect is another and a bit easier. Furthermore, the trend to fiscal soundness is also clearly visible (Table 6.1(c)). Finally, we can point to another measure of monetary pressure or monetary ease, namely real or inflation-adjusted interest rates. In easy money, these can go negative as nominal interest rates fall and inflation picks up; that was pre-eminently the case in the mid-1970s during the first oil crisis and the money expansion that both preceded and accompanied it. In tight money periods, real interest rates can go high as the opposite occurs, but once inflation has come down through the corrective monetary pressure, real interest rates should normalise. If one looks at Table 6.1(e), which shows real interest rates, one sees that they have been uniformly positive since the early 1980s, went to painfully high levels in the mid-1980s, and have now generally subsided to rates (2–5%) that are not entirely normal in historical terms (the average over the past century for the UK and the US has been around 1.5%) but are nearly so – and a higher-than-historical-level could be rationalised in terms of capital scarcity, with emerging markets competing with developed countries for savings largely generated by the latter. The point is that real or inflation-adjusted interest rates have at no time been negative, indicating that monetary policy has throughout this period been, if anything, restrictive; Japan is the exception now because its policies were so highly restrictive in the early 1990s.

This indeed brings us to the last question, also related to the difficulty of money-supply measurement. Is there now a tendency for monetary policy to be over-cautious? Our discussion of the UK (in Chapter 5, on

		1971–80	1981–90	1991–96	Latest[†]
(a)	**Inflation**				
	USA	7.2	4.7	2.8	2.2
	Japan	8.7	1.9	1.0	2.1
	Germany	5.2	2.6	2.9	1.9
	France	9.8	6.2	2.2	1.3
	Italy	14.6	9.9	5.4	1.4
	UK	13.3	6.0	3.9	2.7
(b)	**Growth**				
	USA	2.7	2.7	2.3	3.7
	Japan	4.5	4.1	1.7	0.9
	Germany	2.7	2.2	2.0	2.4
	France	3.3	2.4	1.2	2.0
	Italy	3.8	2.2	1.0	1.2
	UK	2.0	2.6	1.4	3.5
(c)	**Government deficit as % of GDP (+)=deficit**				
	USA	1.0	2.8	2.8	0.3
	Japan	2.3	0.7	1.2	3.0
	Germany	2.1	2.0	3.2	3.1
	France	0.5	2.3	4.4	3.1
	Italy	7.6	11.2	8.8	3.2
	UK	3.2	2.3	5.6	0.8
(d)	**Money growth (M1)**				
	USA	6.9	6.9	5.0	-1.5
	Japan	12.5	5.6	7.8	9.1
	Germany	8.9	8.5	8.1	6.7
	France	n.a.	7.7	1.3	6.5
	Italy	19.0	11.0	4.5	7.7
	UK (M0)	11.0	4.6	5.2	6.8
(e)	**Real interest rates**				
	Nominal short run interest rate minus current inflation				
	USA	-1.0	3.7	1.3	3.4
	Japan	-1.6	3.7	2.0	-1.6
	Germany	1.7	4.0	3.3	1.8
	France	-0.7	4.4	5.3	2.4
	Italy	-2.8	5.3	5.9	4.1
	UK	-4.1	4.6	3.8	4.8

[†] Inflation: latest 12 months (Winter 1997)
Growth: (Q3 1997)
Deficit: Liverpool Group estimate for 1997 (UK: 1997/8)
M1/M0: latest 12 months (Winter 1997)
Real interest rates: interest rates end – 1997 less inflation over previous 12 months

Table 6.1 (a–e) OECD The last three decades

supply-side policy) suggested that this has been a UK problem since 1992, holding back the natural pace of recovery and causing a downward-biased perception of the success of the Conservative government's reform programme. Whether the same is true in other countries would require a case-by-case analysis. But, briefly, the impression of my research team is that it seems to have been avoided in the US; that in Japan there clearly was massive and excessive deflation in the early 1990s but policy since has moved to massive ease, unfortunately with limited effect in restoring recovery so far; and that on the European continent there is currently unquestioned monetary ease and the problem lies on the supply side, as argued above.

It is a measure of how far thinking on monetary policy has changed that someone like me who campaigned vigorously for monetary discipline in the early 1980s should be concerned about an excess of zeal in recent episodes, such as in Japan and the UK (chapters 4 and 5). These episodes have served to remind us of the problems to which Keynes drew attention: how severe downturns can generate and in turn be fed by a flattening of 'animal spirits' (or 'confidence') and a 'liquidity trap' (whereby interest rates reach a floor and so can no longer spur recovery). It is possible to have too much of a good thing: the control of inflation must be combined with intelligent reactions to the business cycle. Indeed the original attraction of money supply targeting (Friedman and Schwartz, 1963) was that it incorporated just such reactions, ensuring that interest rates would automatically fall in recessions and rise in booms. Unfortunately, as we have seen, difficulties of measurement now mean that money supply targeting is no longer easily useable *tout simple*.

CONCLUSIONS

What we have seen in this chapter is that across the OECD both monetary and fiscal policy have been tightened in the past two decades, as dictated by monetarist theory, in order to control and if possible eliminate inflation. The success in this has been impressive, so much so that people have spoken of the death of inflation. In this they are probably right, because there is no reason why intelligent democratic peoples, having tumbled to the poor trade-off offered by inflationary policy, should go back to such policy.

Some people have also pointed to technological change or labour market liberalisation as the reasons for low inflation, but movements in these factors fit neither the timing of inflation changes nor the theory of them, which requires a shift in the relationship between the growth in the supply and in the demand for money. The fact is that there has been a sea change in public attitudes to inflation as a result of a better understanding of how poor is the trade-off that it produces; this sea change first drove politicians into the monetarist policies that we have described, and has since changed further into the spreading independence of central banks, much as in the UK in 1997.

The spread of market liberalisation into financial markets has made the money supply difficult to measure and so undermined the original idea of pure money supply targeting. This means that setting interest rates needs to take careful account not merely of the inflation target but also of the state of the cycle, as monetarists always intended.

References

Advisory Commission – Boskin Report (1996) *Toward a More Accurate Measure of the Cost of Living*, Final Report to the Senate Finance Committee from the Advisory Commission to study the consumer price index, Michael J. Boskin, chairman, December 4, updated version.

Alesina, A. and Summers, L.H. (1993) 'Central Bank Independence and Macroeconomic Performance: Some Comparative Evidence' , *Journal of Money, Credit and Banking*, 25, 151–62.

Bootle, R. (1996) *The Death of Inflation – Surviving and Thriving in the Zero Era*, Nicholas Brealey Publishing, London.

Boskin (1996) – see Advisory Commission above.

Cukierman, A. (1992) *Central Bank Strategy, Credibility and Independence: Theory and Evidence*, MIT Press, Cambridge, US.

Friedman, M. and Schwartz, A. J. (1963) *A Monetary History of the United States, 1867–1960*, Princeton University Press (for the National Bureau of Economic Research), Princeton.

Grilli, V., Masciandaro, D. and Tabellini, G. (1991) 'Political and Monetary Institutions and Public Financial Policies in the Industrial Countries', *Economic Policy*, 13, 341–92.

Keynes, J. M. (1936) *The General Theory of Employment, Interest and Money*, Macmillan, London.

Nordhaus, W.D. (1997) 'Traditional Productivity Estimates are Asleep at the (Technological) Switch', *Economic Journal*, September, 1548–59.

CHAPTER SEVEN

The triumph of global capitalism – Free trade, globalisation and the world economy

IN THIS CHAPTER, we consider what the effects of globalisation have been in the past two decades or so, what the implications may be for the future, and the effects of different policy responses to these trends within the OECD. In politics and in economic journals, debate has flourished in the last decade over whether the problems of rising unemployment and the falling relative wages of unskilled workers can be linked to the growth of emerging market economies with their extremely low labour costs. Some politicians (such as Ross Perot in the US and the late Sir James Goldsmith in Europe) have claimed that they can, and a number of recent studies support their claims to varying extents – Wood (1994, 1997), Rowthorn (1995), Feenstra and Hanson (1995), Sachs and Schatz (1994, 1996), Leamer (1993, 1994), Oliviera-Martins (1993), Borjas et al (1992).

Others have contested such claims vigorously: a majority of politicians on both sides of the Atlantic, and academic studies including Bound and Johnson (1992), Katz and Murphy (1992), Lawrence and Slaughter (1993), Krugman (1995), Krugman and Lawrence (1994). These have tended to suggest that the problems of the labour market could be accounted for by an increasing bias in technology (due to computers) away from unskilled workers, as documented by Berman et al (1994), Machin (1994), Krueger (1993), and van Reenen (1994).

A major overtone of this debate has been protectionism, stridently demanded by both Perot and Goldsmith. However, such a policy is by no means an implication of their causal claims – see, for example, Minford (1996), where, in line with this book, I suggest that trade pressures may importantly explain these problems and argue strongly for a certain sort of negative income tax. Furthermore, even if technology were the cause of the OECD's labour problems, protectionism (of manufacturing) would also be a policy candidate since it would raise the wages of unskilled workers in which manufacturing is intensive. We begin in this chapter by focusing purely on the positive issues of causation; after that we reflect on the policy lessons.

Many authors have examined the evidence for particular countries and markets (especially the labour market) and attempted to explain the effects of globalisation in terms of one or other of these two hypotheses. The huge length of our list of references acknowledges the important detailed work performed. As so often when broad hypotheses are debated in economics, there will be a multitude of studies of parts of the picture, which do not necessarily all point in the same direction. The method herein is different. I propose to draw together and characterise the main trends in the world economy and in key markets and then to see whether I can explain them with a fair degree of accuracy by using an economic model of the world economy – albeit a necessarily simplified one whose coefficients are estimated from other information (and are thus 'calibrated'). Into this model I inject technological, trade and other candidate shocks to check whether they can account for the observed trends taken as a whole. I am, therefore, starting from the other end of the spectrum as it were – from the big picture – and hoping to make some progress there. Perhaps this can shed some light on these detailed studies at the opposite end of the spectrum.

I begin by describing the main trends of the past two decades that require explanation, and discuss how they can be explained in terms of the theory of international trade, applied here in the form of our model of the world economy, North and South. In particular, I consider how far the process of 'emergence' among developing countries and technological bias against unskilled workers in developed countries may have contributed to these trends.

THE FACTS OF THE LAST TWO DECADES

In Table 7.1, left-hand column, are shown the key facts of 1970–90 for North and South, expressed as average change per annum over the

Change per annum	Actual	Simulations							
1970–90		**1**	**2**	**3**	**4**	**5**	**6**	**7**	**8**
North									
Unskilled/Skilled:									
Wages	-0.9	-0.75	-1.08	+0.25	+1.84	+0.61	+0.03	+0.28	-0.355
Employment	-4.2	-0.48	-0.66	-0.34	-2.89	-0.43	+0.02	+0.15	+0.019
Shares of GDP:									
Manufacturing	-0.22	-1	+0.3	-0.09	-0.45	+2.19	-0.01	-0.16	-0.049
Services	+0.195	+0.1	-0.2	0	+0.47	+1.07	-0.05	-0.48	+0.12
Primary	-0.075	+0.92	-0.07	+0.08	-0.07	-3.27	+0.06	+0.63	-0.048
Non-traded	+0.1	-0.02	-0.03	+0.01	+0.05	0	0	+0.01	-0.012
Unemployment:									
Unskilled	+0.4	+0.1	+0.12	+0.47	-0.18	-0.13	0	-0.02	-0.314
Total	+0.2	-0.02	-0.05	+0.38	+0.1	-0.02	0	+0.03	-0.285
Living standard	+2.2	+0.25	+0.29	-0.32	+0.14	+0.31	0	0	+0.786
South									
Unskilled/Skilled:									
Wages	+2.3	+0.76	-1.07	+0.26	+1.83	+0.5	+0.03	-1.04	-0.096
Employment	+1.3	+0.47	-0.11	+0.03	+0.18	-0.08	+0.12	-0.08	-0.004
Shares of GDP:									
Manufacturing	+0.1	+1.31	-0.48	+0.16	+0.66	-2.44	-0.11	+0.18	-0.058
Services	+0.14	+0.05	+0.36	-0.06	-0.69	-1.63	0	+0.69	+0.046
Primary	-0.55	-1.23	+0.07	-0.09	+0.13	+4.37	-0.21	-0.86	+0.002
Non-traded	+0.36	-0.13	+0.05	-0.01	-0.1	-0.3	+0.32	-0.01	+0.01
Living standard	+1.1	+0.32	-0.01	0	+0.02	+0.12	+0.12	+0.01	-0.008
World									
Relative Prices:									
Manufacturing/Services	-0.8	-0.27	-0.39	+0.09	+0.67	+0.06	+0.01	+0.11	-0.042
Primary/Services	-0.3	-0.16	-0.3	+0.06	+0.54	-0.35	-0.01	+0.1	-0.032
North Trade Balances/GDP:									
Manufacturing	-0.025	-0.93	+0.32	-0.11	-0.43	+1.93	-0.01	-0.12	+0.047
Services	+0.005	-0.01	-0.26	+0.04	+0.5	+1.31	-0.05	-0.51	-0.018
Primary	+0.02	+0.94	-0.06	+0.07	-0.07	-3.23	+0.06	+0.63	-0.02

Simulations:

1. Simulated effect of 0.5% p.a. rise in Southern manufacturing productivity
2. Simulated effect of 1% p.a. fall in Northern unskilled share across all sectors
3. Simulated effect of 1% p.a. rise in Northern unemployment benefit rate
4. Simulated effect of 1% p.a. fall in Northern unskilled labour supply due to rise in higher education
5. Simulated effect of 0.5% p.a. rise in Southern primary productivity
6. Simulated effect of 0.5% p.a. rise in Southern non-traded productivity
7. Simulated effect of 0.5% p.a. rise in Southern services productivity
8. Simulated effect of 0.5% p.a. rise in Northern general productivity (distributed 0.5% manufacturing, 0.28% primary, 0.625% services, 0.395% non-traded)

Table 7.1 Actual data 1970–90, and simulated shock effects

period. The North is the OECD; the South is all developing countries, namely all non-OECD countries except the former Soviet bloc. While some of the ex-Soviet countries are now plainly emerging, their history within the free world is too recent and their data too patchy to include. Many of the statistics embodied in the table are usefully reviewed in Gundlach and Nunnenkampf (1994) and Nunnenkampf et al (1994), whose view of the processes involved also broadly coincides with mine here.

In the North, there has been 'deindustrialisation': the share of manufacturing in GDP has fallen. In the South, there has been industrialisation mainly at the expense of agriculture. Notice, too, how sharply non-traded production has expanded there, and how large has been the shift to traded services.

For the North, our data for wages comes from Nickell and Bell (1995) and Nickell (1995), gathered by them from other OECD economists. It shows that the wages of the skilled have risen virtually across the board. 'Skilled' are defined here as those with higher education (preliminary university education or equivalent), which seems appropriate in view of the emphasis in modern technology on knowledge-based, rather than craft-based, skill. 'Unskilled', then, becomes the rest of the labour force.

In the South, unskilled real wages appear to have risen both relative to the skilled workforce and in absolute terms. However, we have no data on skilled wages as such; we have had to infer skilled wages from per capita GDP, assuming this grows at the same rate as average real wages. Unskilled wages we have identified with general manufacturing wages. Our ratio of skilled to unskilled wages is consequently of doubtful accuracy.

Employment of unskilled workers has fallen everywhere in the North, relative to skilled workers. Skilled employment averaged about 14% of the total in the North as a whole at the start of the period, but had risen to around 30% by the end. In the South, if we treat manufacturing employment as a proxy for unskilled employment, we find that it has risen both relative to total employment and in absolute terms. As with wages, however, we have no data on skilled employment directly and have inferred it from total employment. Again, our ratio of skilled to unskilled employment is of doubtful accuracy.

Per capita GDP growth in the North has been roughly double that in the South during the review period, a well known fact.

Unemployment rates among the least skilled have risen everywhere in the North. Absolute rates of unemployment are in the low or high teens across the OECD, virtually without exception. Unemployment rates among skilled workers, again as measured by upper-secondary education or above, have risen too, so that overall unemployment rates have risen.

There has been a rise in the average skill-intensity of output in the North (documented, for example, by Lawrence and Slaughter, 1993). This of course must be so, given the large rise in skilled employment cited above. But it may well not reflect a genuine rise in skill intensity of particular firms engaged in given activities. It might merely reflect 'outsourcing' of those activities that require less skill to parts of the firm abroad or to foreign suppliers, or indeed these activities may just have closed down in the North and been substituted explicitly by imports. Unfortunately there is no way of telling which of these is happening with the data we have; however much we are able to break it down by industry and sub-industry, we still encounter this problem. Feenstra and Hanson (1995) have tested for such an effect indirectly, by checking whether the share of imports from less developed countries (LDCs) in trade is significant in explaining rising skill intensity; they found it was. Bernard and Jensen (1994) find that the share of exports also explains rising skill-intensity in US manufacturing.

World prices of manufactures exported by LDCs have fallen relative to those of services and complex manufactures, denoted 'services' here in Figure 7.1. Some uncertainty surrounds this index in the years up to 1975 owing to the effects of sharp movements in non-ferrous metals prices (Rowthorn, 1996; Athukorala, 1993; Sarkar and Singer, 1993). Our index gives an estimate of the trend from 1960 that is in the middle of this range of possibilities.

Primary product prices rose in real terms in the 1970s and fell during the 1980s. This applies particularly sharply to oil, but it applies also – if far less dramatically – to other primary products. The net effect of these two decadal swings has been an overall increase of about one-third in real oil prices but a real drop of some 40% in other primary product prices. Thus, depending on exactly how one weights these two components, one could say that for primary products as a whole there has been little net real change since 1970. For the record, we have created a joint series, using 50:50 weights based on shares in world exports: relative to the index of complex manufactures and services described above, this index shows a moderate decline of aggregate primary producer prices over the period 1970–90 – see Figure 7.2.

Throughout this period, the North has been a net exporter to the South of complex manufactures and services, while the South has been

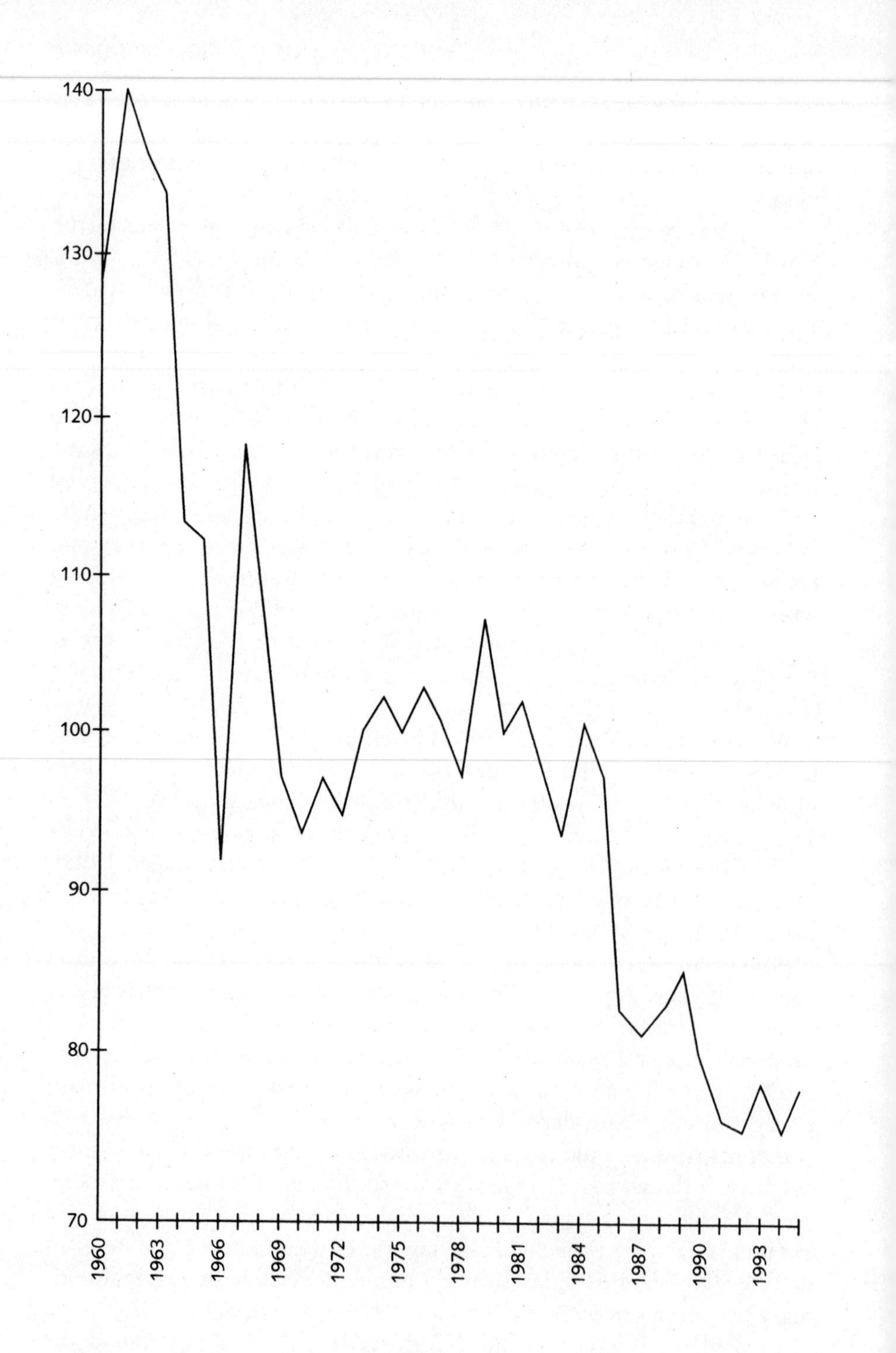

Figure 7.1 LDC manufacturing prices relative to services and complex manufactures

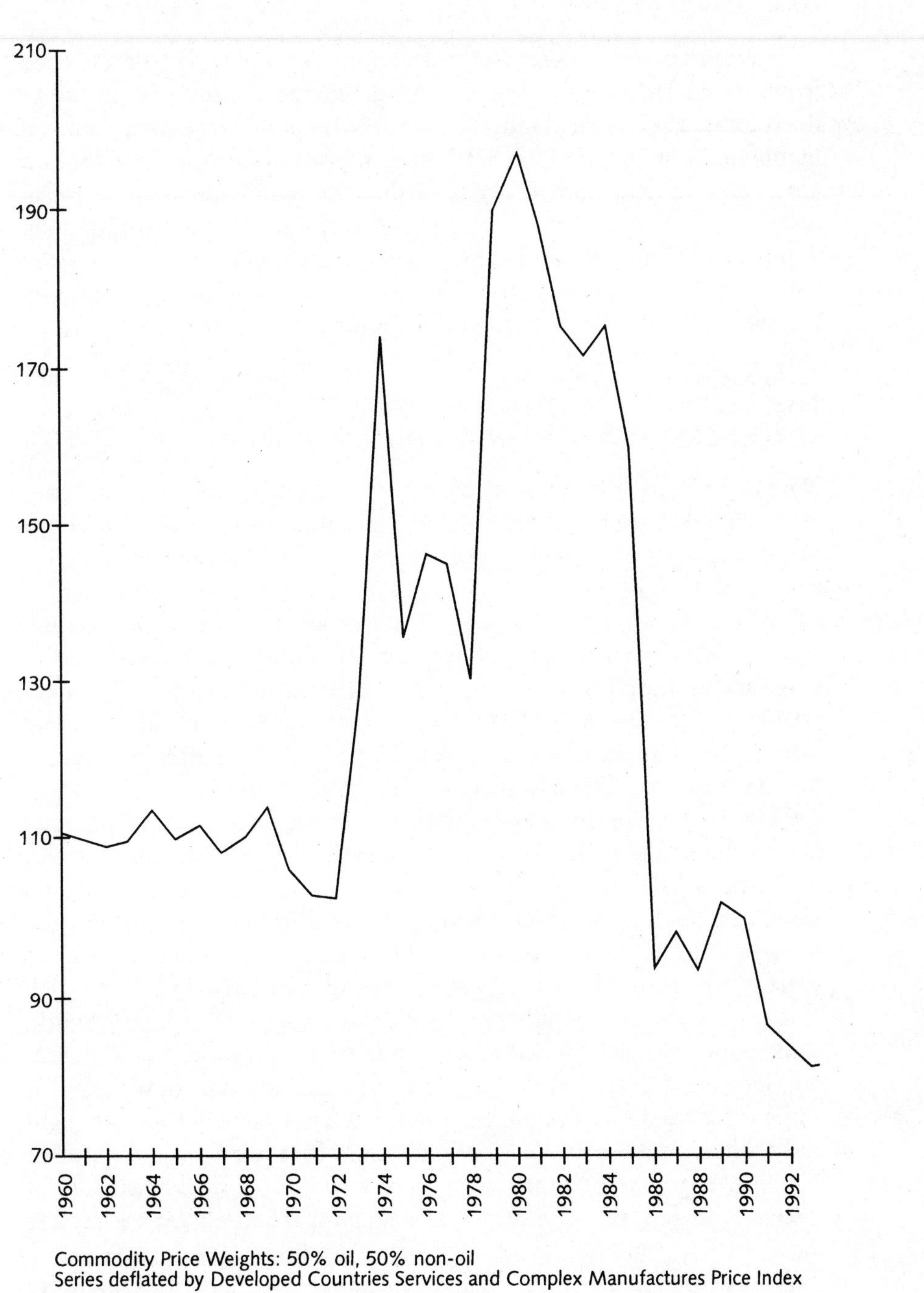

Commodity Price Weights: 50% oil, 50% non-oil
Series deflated by Developed Countries Services and Complex Manufactures Price Index

Figure 7.2 Real commodity prices

a net exporter to the North of primary products. The North switched from being a net exporter of basic manufactures to being a net importer during the 1980s. This shift in comparative advantage goes hand in hand with a huge growth in total trade between North and South, as a percentage of Northern GDP, such that the South has become much more important as a trading partner for the North. In particular, Southern exports of manufactures (basic and complex) have risen from a negligible 0.2% of Northern GDP in 1970 to 2% in 1992, accounting for over 10% of all Northern visible imports of goods.

THE RELEVANT MODEL OF TRADE IN TODAY'S WORLD: THE HECKSCHER–OHLIN–SAMUELSON MODEL

Having described the key facts of the world economy over the past couple of decades, we now consider how we might try to explain them. It turns out that international trade theory has well-developed tools for dealing with all of this. The recent explosion of growth in the emerging markets and the process of wage competition that Goldsmith rightly highlighted are neatly captured by the model that my team and I owe to two Swedish economists writing in the inter-war period, Eli Heckscher (1919) and Bertil Ohlin (1933), which was later put in mathematical form, with its implications carefully mapped out, by Paul Samuelson of MIT (Stolper and Samuelson, 1941; Samuelson, 1948).

Consider two linked open economies, 'North' and 'South'. The basic idea in the model is that these have different stocks of resources fixed, so to speak, within their borders. These stocks are notably land and labour, the second of which we may divide into unskilled (or with no skills that are in special demand) and skilled. Although labour can to some extent migrate, in practice this migration is strictly limited: rich Northern workers generally do not want to move to the poorer South, while poor Southern workers face severe political barriers to immigration into the North. Capital and raw materials are not, however, geographically fixed in supply in the same way because they can be bought and sold on an international market – they are 'traded' or 'mobile'. For example, if you want capital, you can borrow at a world real rate of interest and buy the capital goods you need from whoever produces them.

These resources are then employed in competitive industries that have fully exploited all increasing returns to scale: hence each has constant costs, and its price is driven to equality with those costs. Full employment is usually assumed in this theory, but this can be relaxed to account for unemployment: if an economy is willing to pay a resource more to be idle than it is worth at work, then there will be unemployment. So, most importantly, unskilled workers who find that the wages they can get are not attractive relative to the benefits they can claim when unemployed will remain unemployed. Their 'supply' is therefore affected not merely by physical availability but also by such social policy.

The main implication of this theory for our purposes here is that for any country producing some agriculture, some basic manufactured goods, and some complex manufactures and traded services – in other words, all three categories of traded goods and services – wages of both skilled and unskilled workers, and also land prices, will ultimately (once the same technology can be realistically applied anywhere) be equalised. This is known as the Factor Price Equalisation Theorem, first demonstrated by Paul Samuelson (1948).

Of course, it is this that our neo-protectionists have seen, and from which they have recoiled in horror: it is indeed a startling result, and one might think that it implies the impoverishment of the Northern countries if they allow it, through free trade, to happen. But we can show that the gains from free trade still occur – indeed, they are huge because of the great initial disparity of costs – and that, while unskilled workers in the Northern countries will indeed very probably be worse off, citizens as a whole there will be better off and therefore able to compensate, at least to some extent, those of their number that are worse off. In time, the supply of unskilled workers in the North will shrink, correspondingly shrinking the losing class and the need for compensation.

Furthermore, the whole process will take time – a long time probably – because of another feature that we have built into this model: initial differences of technology between North and South. We assume that 'emergence' (considered in more detail below) is basically the process by which Southern countries make themselves attractive to foreign investors from the North that have better technology, for these investors can make large profits under suitable conditions by transferring production to countries with much lower wages. Everything else should cost them the same – capital, raw materials, management – and yet they can use the same techniques, at the same productivity therefore, with a substantial saving in labour cost. Land, too, will be cheaper because its productivity in poor countries will be lower because of their less advanced technology.

In a recent paper (Minford, Riley and Nowell, 1997), my colleagues and I set out the model framework in its full detail, including the mathematical version of the model we use in what follows. But in the limited space I have here I turn next to the relevant, indeed vital, predictions of the model under plausible quantitative assumptions.

APPLYING THE MODEL

It is plain that this model confirms many of the worst fears of protectionists. Wages in the North for unskilled labour (that is the bulk of ordinary people who have no special skills in this context) fall to the same level as in the South once technology is easily transferable anywhere; but growing demand for the products that most use unskilled labour (basic manufactures) will raise the general level of wages in the South too. At the same time, land prices and skilled wages in the South are driven up to the levels in the North; but these too will be driven up yet further by rising demand and growth.

This is a vague statement and it will not satisfy our antagonists. We need to know some rough orders of magnitude for who will gain, who will lose, and by roughly how much. Both countries must gain individually from the opening of trade and also the world as a whole must gain from the rising technical proficiency of the South. But is it possible for one group in the North to lose catastrophically? Can there perhaps be 'immiserisation' of the North from the growing technical prowess of the South (echoing the fears expressed by UNCTAD's Raul Prebisch two generations ago about the effects of the South's growth in primary commodity production on its terms of trade) because this turns the terms of trade against the North, with the prices of its exports falling relative to the prices of its imports? Both of these are theoretical possibilities, but rather unusual assumptions about the responses of demand and supply to relative price changes would be needed to produce them, because in most applied work we find that the gains from trade and from growth are so large and widespread, relative to the effects of relative price movements, that they swamp them.

The way we tackle the issue is first to construct a world in which the North is rich in technology, as just set out above, and the South is poor. Trade exists and takes the following form: the South exports (net) labour-intensive (basic) manufactures and agricultural goods, and the North exports skill-intensive (complex) manufactures and services. To explore explanations of the trends described above, we 'simulate' this model; that is, we take the relationships built into the model and apply a change in the assumptions – a 'shock' – to discover the changes occurring to the economic environment as a result.

SIMULATIONS OF THE NORTH–SOUTH MODEL

We summarised the key facts in Table 7.1, left-hand column, as discussed earlier. In the next eight columns are shown the simulations we now proceed to discuss.

The first two have been adduced as particular reasons for the plight of unskilled workers in the OECD: in order, the 'emerging market' shock of low-wage competition that has so worried politicians in Europe and the United States (column 1), and technology bias against unskilled workers in the North (column 2). Then we consider the effects of other shocks that we know were occurring over this period: first, rising social protection of unskilled workers (column 3), a policy shock that is closely connected with our discussion of European social protection and labour inflexibility; and then in column 4 we simulate the huge expansion of higher education evident in our data on OECD skilled versus unskilled workers in the labour force. In columns 5–7, we simulate productivity growth in other sectors of the South; and, lastly, in column 8 we simulate the OECD's own productivity growth, which we identify as the result of technology creation as opposed to the technology transfer of the emerging market hypothesis. This full menu of shocks, though not all are of primary interest here, must be included to give a convincing overall account of the facts. No doubt others could be adduced, but these appear to be the main influences likely to affect the key trends examined here and, indeed, we find that together they give a pretty good fit to observed facts. We go through each of the shocks and their simulated effects in turn.

1. The simulation of emerging-market shock

When a country 'emerges', we mean that it enjoys:

- a high rate of inward investment;
- fast growth, primarily in manufacturing; and
- low labour costs.

The countries involved include many in South-East Asia and Latin America, as well as in other parts of the developing world.

Japan was at one time an emerging market on this definition, but in this book the focus is on events since 1970, and especially from 1980. Most of Japan's phenomenal post-war growth had happened by 1970, and it was by then a rich country. It is now as affected as other OECD countries by the locational attractions of the Pacific Rim. We therefore include Japan throughout within the OECD or 'North'.

We assume in what follows that the three elements (above) of emergence are linked: that the inward investment is profitable because of low labour costs allied to the investor's own techniques of production, and is devoted to the production of manufactured goods, which thereby grows rapidly. Before their emergence, these countries were ordinary 'developing countries'. Why would they change, as if by taking some elixir of growth? I suggest that it is due to a combination of property rights, a basic infrastructure, easier communications technology, and greater computer control of factory processes. Clearly, that suggestion – close in spirit to the 'openness' of Dollar (1992), the 'business capital' of Parente and Prescott (1995), as well as the 'transactions-reducing features' of North (1994) – would require much to establish. For my purposes here, let me appeal to some such set of factors that turn an economy from one in which inward investment is relatively unattractive (despite the low labour costs), to one where the high profitability of using low-wage workers becomes a magnet.

Given such conditions of emergence, we can visualise the process of inward investment as using the parent firm's technology by transferring it to the emerging market economy. This transfer raises the labour productivity of the host sector, and hence if wages are lower there, creates an excess return for inflowing capital.

This view implies that previous technology in the country was backward, compared with the technology in advanced economies. It also implies that there was some barrier to its transfer to indigenous firms – for instance, because of licensing requirements or an absence of indigenous management skills. Emergence then is technology transfer where the investing firm puts in machinery and management with the technology embodied in it. The managers need not physically be there, but they must direct the project remotely at least. This process takes time, there being some frictions such as identification of sites, negotiations of terms with governments and so on. Furthermore, such technology transfer is confined, it is supposed, to products whose production processes require few skilled workers, these being in short supply in emerging countries in the South. If skilled workers in the North are immobile, then their technology will also be immobile if it is embodied in them, through some implicit team knowledge. By contrast, computerised manufacturing will be easily transferred.

The first shock we consider is that of progressive technology transfer to the manufacturing sector of the South. The results of a 0.5% pa (maintained from 1970 to 1990) rise in Southern manufacturing productivity are shown in column 1 of Table 7.1.

The outline of the simulation is as follows. Suppose manufacturing productivity in the South rises steadily for the less complex manufactures that it can produce. Southern wages rise, drawing unskilled labour (usually out of low-productivity tasks in the agricultural sector) into manufacturing, whose supply rises, driving down the prices of these less complex manufactures on world markets. As OECD producers of these goods compete with this new output at falling prices, they are willing to pay lower wages for the unskilled workers that are heavily required for such industries. Meanwhile, rising demand from the emerging markets for the things the OECD has an advantage in supplying – namely, complex manufactures such as machine tools, and traded services such as merchant banking or the film industry – drives up their prices on world markets, and as a result OECD producers bid up the prices of the skilled labour they need to supply them. The overall result is an improvement in the terms of trade of the OECD vis-à-vis the emerging markets and a fall in the wages of unskilled workers relative to those of skilled workers.

Turning to the details and comparing column 1 with the facts, we can see that the effects are, strikingly, all in the same direction, suggesting that – at least qualitatively – we have the basic elements explaining world behaviour in this period. The North shows falling relative unskilled wages and employment, deindustrialisation and rising unemployment; the South shows industrialisation, rising relative unskilled wages and employment. At the world level, prices of basic manufactures fall relative to those of services, while the North's trade balance in basic manufacturing with the South deteriorates.

However, we must also consider orders of magnitude, rough as our estimates of many of these magnitudes necessarily are. Here there are difficulties, especially in the case of production and trade volumes – a point made trenchantly by Paul Krugman (1995) – but also in the case of relative unskilled employment in the North. Column 1, for a 0.5% pa rise in Southern manufacturing productivity, fits the other elements roughly. But it shows a decline in Northern manufacturing about five times the actual, a rise in Southern manufacturing thirteen times, and a manufacturing trade balance decline nearly forty times; in addition, the decline in relative unskilled employment in the North is

of the actual.

2. The simulation of technology-bias shock

We now turn to the main alternative explanation of rece

that there has been a shock of technology bias whereby

shifted away from unskilled to skilled labour in the advanced Northern countries, mainly due to the rise in the use of computers.

Let us think about the impact, or first-round, effect of this shock, where all prices remain unchanged. The technological shock shifts input usage in all industries away from unskilled labour, creating an excess supply of it. This excess supply stimulates (by downward pressure on wages) a rise in the production of unskilled-intensive goods – basic manufacturing. The expansion in the North of basic manufacturing leads to an excess supply of it on world markets, and the opposite for services and agriculture. Manufactured prices fall, driving down the wages of unskilled workers and raising those of skilled workers and land, in both North and South. The result is a familiar contraction of unskilled employment in the North, but also in the South. In the South as well, manufacturing output falls in consequence, while services and agriculture rise.

The results, in column 2 of Table 7.1, show considerable variation of direction compared with the facts in the table's left-hand column. They correctly predict falling world relative prices of manufactures. But although they also correctly predict falling relative unskilled wages and employment in the North, they indicate the same in the South, contrary to the facts. Their predictions of the production and trade effects are similarly contrary: the North's production of basic manufacturing is predicted to expand, that of the South to contract, and the North–South trade balance in manufacturing to improve. The orders of magnitude on trade and production are also both contrary and substantial.

We should not conclude from this that technological bias plays no role, far from it. As I shall argue below, a combination of column 2 with column 1 and other shocks to the world economy can fit the facts where no individual hypothesis can.

Let us now turn to consider some of those other such shocks.

3. The simulation of a labour-market regulation shock

So far, we have mainly commented on common features of Northern labour-market experience, except to note that if countries resisted the drop in unskilled wages by regulation of the labour market (such as minimum wages, strong unions, and high unemployment benefits), they would produce a disequilibrium collapse of those traded industries facing global competition because the workers displaced would be prevented from reducing wages. A way of simulating this process is to raise unemployment benefits: this raises the alternative rewards to working for unskilled workers and contracts their supply, so raising the unskilled wages that will prevail in the market and in turn reducing labour demand in line.

Clearly, some countries have followed such policies more than others. Even among the Anglo-Saxon/Oriental group, social policy has varied from little intervention (the United States) to considerable involvement (Australia, with a policy of consensus with strong unions). All have some intervention, taking different forms. For example, in the US there is a minimum wage; in Japan there is a cartelised non-traded sector with regulations enforcing high labour use; in the UK, benefits have risen because of rising house rents, entirely compensated for by the state amongst the unemployed. While the norm among European countries has been consistently for a high degree of intervention, again it has varied, with Italy for example having no effective unemployment benefit system.

Column 3 of Table 7.1 shows the result of a 1% pa rise in Northern unemployment benefits. This reduces unskilled labour supply. Because unskilled wages are bid up, there is a knock-on 'wage differential' effect on skilled wages. This also produces a decline in skilled labour supply, as skilled wages permitted by global competition cannot keep pace with the higher skilled wages demanded. Because the economy shrinks with reduced labour supply, non-traded demand and production fall and there is an absolute contraction of the traded sector. Because the supply of unskilled labour contracts by the largest proportion, the manufacturing sector contracts disproportionately. Overall, therefore, the policy raises real wages for unskilled workers – but at the cost of rising unemployment both of unskilled and skilled workers.

We have here an explanation not merely of high unemployment generally in the North but also of the divergent unemployment in the continental European countries, much worse than elsewhere as we have seen in earlier chapters. These countries, by attempting to hold up wages of unskilled workers, have raised unemployment across the board, not merely among the unskilled, because the upward pressure on unskilled wages has spilled over into the skilled labour market. We can think of the North as an average of the European and Anglo-Saxon/Oriental, with the former grouping suffering a disproportionate amount of the effects given in column 3.

4. Two other OECD labour-market shocks – technology creation and education – and productivity in other Southern sectors

Columns 4 and 8 of Table 7.1 show respectively the effect of a 1% pa fall in the supply curve of unskilled workers in the North (matched by a 3% rise in the supply curve of skilled workers) arising from the spread of higher education; and of a 0.5% pa rise in general Northern productivity (total factor productivity, namely productivity after allowing for the contribution of capital and other inputs), with a slight bias against primary and non-traded products dictated by the constraint that it has similar effects on the size of all four sectors of industry (three traded and one non-traded) in the model.

Column 4 shows the effect of the shift of supply towards skilled workers due to the spread of higher education. This shifts Northern resources out of manufacturing into services, driving down world service prices and raising the relative wages of unskilled workers whose unemployment in the North also falls accordingly. The rise in relative manufacturing prices shifts resources in the South out of services into manufacturing, replacing that in the North. Living standards rise in both North and South – in the North because skilled workers earn more, and in the South because of the favourable movement in the terms of trade.

The general productivity increase (column 8: 0.500% in manufacturing, 0.625% in services, 0.280% in primary, and 0.395% in non-traded, amounting to 0.5% overall) was restricted to be approximately neutral across sectors, in other words to leave sector output shares constant, with the added restriction that non-traded productivity growth should be less than that in manufacturing (a well-documented phenomenon). It has its effect very largely in the North: because, by construction, it leaves sector shares broadly unchanged similarly has a minimal effect in disturbing relative prices and so also production shares in the South. However, within the North it raises living standards and, by raising wages relative to benefits, reduces unemployment both generally and among unskilled workers particularly.

In addition, we need to examine the effects of possible productivity growth in other sectors of the South – primary, non-traded, and complex manufactures and traded services ('services' for short), and these are shown in columns 5–7. All of course raise living standards in the South but have contrasting effects on sectoral shares.

Productivity growth in the South's primary sector depresses the relative price of primary products and primary supply in the North while boosting that in the South, with corresponding offsetting movements in the other two traded sectors. Productivity growth in the Southern non-traded sector expands the South's non-traded sector at the expense of primary and manufacturing, but effects on relative prices and other factors in the North are minor. Southern productivity growth in the services sector expands Southern services and also manufacturing at the expense of primary production, but relative prices of services fall, causing a reverse movement of output shares in the North.

ASSESSING THE IMPORTANCE OF THE VARIOUS SHOCKS

We have identified eight key shocks disturbing the world economy in the two decades 1970–90. What are the contributions of each? In the economic literature devoted to them to date, they have been assessed in relation to partial data, even when a full model has been used as it has here; for example, Krugman (1995) looks solely at trade flows, and Lawrence and Slaughter (1993) solely at American data (some of it rather idiosyncratic – Minford, 1996). I have made an attempt in this chapter to show data on all relevant aspects of the world economy – prices and use of production inputs, production shares, unemployment, living standards, trade patterns, and relative prices of products. The data has its deficiencies but it is the best I and my co-workers could find. In principle, we would like to give all of it at least some weight in our assessment.

In Table 7.2 I present an unrestricted least squares regression of the facts on the various shocks in columns 1–8. This procedure finds the best-fitting size and combination of the shocks for the set of facts. It can be seen that all shocks are estimated to make a contribution to the explanation, only Southern service productivity being almost insignificant.

Table 7.3 shows the prediction of this unrestricted regression for the key variables. Certain important facts are not picked up well, notably all those relating to Northern output and trade movements. These failures could be remedied by using weights on the facts for importance and reliability. We may note that we doubt the reliability of the Southern relative unskilled employment and wage estimates, while clearly we must give great weight to the output movements not just because they are reliable but mainly because a 0.1% error on an output sector's share of GDP is more serious proportionately than a 0.1% error on living standard growth.

Table 7.3 also shows, in its final column, the predictions of a weighted regression that recognises such considerations. These predictions appear to remedy the failures of the unweighted regression. The best-fit regression identifies the following factors as being at work (Table 7.2):

Simulation	Unweighted regression coefficients	(S.E.)	Weighted regression coefficients	(S.E.)
1 Trade	1.46	(0.65)	1.61	(0.75)
2 Technology	1.23	(0.36)	1.55	(0.36)
3 Benefits	2.17	(1.28)	1.76	(0.99)
4 Higher education	0.65	(0.19)	0.62	(0.19)
5 Southern primary productivity	0.53	(0.36)	0.76	(0.42)
6 Southern non-traded productivity	3.64	(1.13)	2.99	(1.02)
7 Southern services productivity	0.25	(0.86)	1.36	(1.00)
8 Northern general productivity	2.25	(1.05)	1.66	(1.03)
R^2	0.92		0.88	
$\overline{R}^2$	0.87		0.81	

Table 7.2 Regressions of actual on simulated (standard errors in parenthesis)

% Change per annum 1970–90	Actual	Unweighted regression predicted	Weights for weighted regression	Weighted regression predicted
North				
Unskilled/Skilled:				
Wages	-0.9	-0.984	2	-0.96
Employment	-4.2	-4.209	1	-4.216
Shares of GDP:				
Manufacturing	-0.22	-0.604	8	-0.262
Services	+0.195	+0.738	8	+0.351
Primary	-0.075	-0.079	8	-0.042
Non-traded	+0.1	-0.038	8	-0.037
Unemployment:				
Unskilled	+0.4	+0.418	3	+0.414
Total	+0.2	+0.155	4	+0.172
Living standard	+2.2	+2.051	1	+1.918
South				
Unskilled/Skilled:				
Wages	+2.3	+1.437	0.5	+0.062
Employment	+1.3	+1.097	0.5	+0.936
Shares of GDP:				
Manufacturing	+0.1	+0.318	3	+0.038
Services	+0.14	-0.649	3	-0.116
Primary	-0.55	-0.478	3	-0.444
Non-traded	+0.36	+0.809	3	+0.522
Living standard	+1.1	+0.952	1	+0.963
World				
Relative Prices:				
Manufacturing/Services	-0.8	-0.242	2	-0.31
Primary/Services	-0.3	-0.391	1	-0.493
North Trade Balances/GDP:				
Manufacturing	-0.025	-0.418	9	-0.123
Services	+0.005	+0.421	9	+0.082
Primary	+0.02	_0.024	9	+0.065

Table 7.3 Actual and predicted, with and without weights

- a 0.8% pa rise in Southern productivity in manufacturing (the 'trade' or 'emerging market' shock);
- 1.5% pa fall in the factor share of unskilled labour in all Northern sectors ('technology bias');
- 0.8% pa rise in general Northern productivity;
- a 1.75% pa rise in Northern benefits (or equivalent social intervention);
- a 0.6% pa fall in unskilled labour supply; and
  percentage annual productivity growth for sectors in the South: 0.4% in primary, 1.5% in non-traded, 0.7% in services.

What this implies is that both trade and technology play a large and significant role in explaining Northern labour market problems. For example, two-fifths of the collapse in Northern unskilled employment is explained by these two factors (higher education explaining the bulk of the rest); and of that two-fifths, just under 60% is due to technology and just over 40% due to trade. If we take the fall in relative unskilled wages, the downward pressure exerted by these two factors is in the same proportion of 60:40. The same is true of unskilled unemployment, where the rest of the explanation is due to the effect of benefit-equivalent changes, partially offset by higher education in shrinking unskilled supply.

These two explanations of the plight of unskilled workers, and indeed other productivity changes that we have identified, may well be linked together in a more general description of the technological changes going on in globalisation. Ronald Jones and Henryk Kierzowski (1997) have suggested that the progress of the computer and related communications has increased optimal 'fragmentation' of the production process: before, different stages of manufacturing had to be done all together in one place, whereas now they can be unbundled, outsourced, and so on because of better (computer-based) communications. This unbundling may mean that skill-abundant countries now have higher productivity in skill-intensive goods, while those countries abundant in unskilled labour now have higher productivity in goods intensive in that.

Globalisation, in other words, increases both sorts of countries' productivity in the sorts of goods they are best at producing. This idea fits rather well into the picture we have been trying to set out of what may be behind the combination of the shocks that we have identified. These deeper sources of the productivity shocks themselves are obviously of great interest for future exploration.

HOW SERIOUS IS THE PROBLEM OF UNSKILLED WAGES?

What of the future? Are the trends we have seen in the past couple of decades likely to continue? Are we to be left with the problem of a group of unskilled workers and their families, with wages too low to support their family needs and hence permanently dependent on welfare in order to avoid serious poverty? This is the most difficult part to confront. The failure of unskilled wages to rise in the 'trickle down' manner that we previously assumed has created a concern about the ability of capitalism to generate outcomes that avoid social conflict. In the UK, unskilled wages have in fact risen, albeit modestly; in the US, they appear to have fallen on most measures. Will this continue, or even worsen?

The pessimistic view on this matter is that they will, because of competition from low wage countries and because of technological bias against unskilled workers. The optimistic view is that productivity growth in the West will be sufficient to raise wages steadily; a further argument is that the increasing scarcity of unskilled workers will enable them to be employed outside sectors competing with low-wage countries, and especially in the non-traded sector.

A useful starting point for consideration of these two opposing views is to review the behaviour of absolute real wages of unskilled workers over the past two decades, for so far we have focused on their relative wages rather than absolute living standards. Table 7.4 shows that, on average in the OECD (and the table also shows the experience of a large number of individual countries), the experience has not in fact been too bad. Real wages of even the very least skilled males (the lowest decile) have risen between 1970 and 1990, although they admittedly fell in the UK, the US, Canada and Australia – the Anglo-Saxon world, broadly speaking. However, the lowest decile is an odd group; it seems that the real wages of 'starter jobs' (the ones people take first when entering the labour market without any particular skill) have fallen in these countries, and it is people with these jobs who will be in the lowest decile. Yet they should in time get better jobs, in which case their poverty and poor wages will be transitional.

In all the countries given, apart from the US, real wages for the average male worker have risen over the period. The fall in average real wages in the United States is peculiar and may disguise rising other non-wage compensation such as spreading health insurance – even the ninth decile's real wages (the wages of those just below the top 10%) in the US apparently grew exiguously, which hardly seems plausible.

	USA	UK	Australia	Canada	Japan	Anglo-Saxon /Oriental	France	Germany	Italy	Sweden	European	OECD
Initial year	**1975**	**1973**	**1975**	**1973**	**1979–81**		**1973**	**1979–81**	**1979–81**	**1973**		
Real wages												
a. D1	85	96.1	96.1	98.1	115.5		175.6	135.1	114.1	101.0		
b. Average-D5	92.4	110.8	103.0	116.2	119.3		165.0	127.5	105.0	105.1		
c. Skilled-D9	102.0	129.9	109.2	121.2	126.9		173.9	143.7	114.1	105.2		
Terminal Year	**1989–90**	**1991**	**1991**	**1989–90**	**1989–90**		**1991**	**1991**	**1987–88**	**1991**		
% per annum rate of change of:												
a.	-1.1	-0.2	-0.2	-0.2	+1.5	-0.2	+3.2	+2.8	+1.8	+0.1	2.5	0.5
b.	-0.5	+0.6	+0.2	+0.9	+1.8	+0.3	+2.8	+2.2	+0.6	+0.3	+1.8	+0.7
c.	+0.1	+1.5	+0.6	+1.1	+2.4	+0.9	+3.1	+3.4	+1.7	+0.3	+2.6	+1.4

The top half of the table shows real wage levels in the terminal year as a percentage of the initial year. D1, D5, D9 = first, fifth and ninth deciles respectively. D5 identified with average, D9 with skilled.

Table 7.4 OECD Real wage growth among males

If we look at the share of the most 'unskilled' workers (defined as having no education beyond high school), it has fallen among men in the OECD astonishingly from a range of 23–73% in the early 1970s to one of 7–40% in the early 1990s (estimates from Nickell and Bell, 1995). According to UK estimates, the non-traded sector, which accounts for about half of a typical OECD country's GDP, requires unskilled labour to the extent of 39% of added value. This would suggest that the UK is already close to being able to absorb unskilled workers entirely into the non-traded sector.

So, to summarise, if one means by 'unskilled' those who are not highly skilled (this latter being defined as having received a university education), which is our definition in this chapter, then the real wages of unskilled workers have risen steadily on average across the OECD, with the exception of the US where they have marked time. Even there, it seems clear that our figures understate the rise in living standards; there has been a rise in non-wage compensation (such as health insurance) and the rise in the consumer price index has been estimated (by the Boskin Committee's 1996 Report to the US Senate) to be overstated by 1.1% pa. For the very least skilled, there is evidence of declining real wages in the Anglo-Saxon countries. But their numbers have dwindled massively, and this means both that the size of the problem has become smaller and that the UK may be getting close to the point where they become fully absorbed into the non-traded sector. Furthermore, their jobs are largely starter jobs from which most will graduate with work experience.

From the model I have described above, the effects of a variety of shocks on unskilled wages are clear, namely that there appear to be very substantial offsetting effects on the sharp downward pressure on unskilled wages exerted by low-wage competition and technological bias (Table 7.5). If nothing else had happened, unskilled wages would have fallen more than 1% a year over the last few decades. Yet powerful offsetting forces have been at work – principally, Northern productivity growth and rising Northern higher education – which have both boosted real unskilled wages sharply. Rising social benefits have also contributed somewhat, but this is unhealthy as it raises unemployment by reducing wage flexibility. It is also unnecessary because even without this influence there is plenty to buoy up unskilled wage growth 'naturally'.

While this picture hardly suggests rapid growth for unskilled wages, it is not the disaster the pessimists paint. We may have seen an exceptionally bad period for unskilled labour in the past twenty-odd years

Actual	**0.5**
Predicted by:	
Low-wage competition in manufactures	-0.47
OECD technological bias	-0.63
Rising OECD social benefits	0.20
Rising OECD higher education	0.36
Rising productivity Southern primary sector	0.28
Rising productivity Southern non-traded	0.03
Rising productivity Southern traded services	0.05
Rising productivity Northern (general)	1.06
Total predicted	0.9

Table 7.5 Effects on real unskilled wages (% pa, 1970–90) in OECD

(yet even that was not as bad as it might have been), but there are indications from this model that the steady contraction of unskilled labour through education and Western innovation in new technology are enough to more than offset the effects of low-wage competition and technological bias. Trade theory further suggests that this protection of unskilled workers is likely to increase once their share of GDP has fallen to levels that could be largely absorbed into the non-traded sector.

POLICY CONCLUSIONS

What our elaborate calculations show is that the emergence of developing countries and their low-wage competition has on its own produced a huge impact on the wages of unskilled workers, both relative to skilled and in absolute terms. An impact of a similar size has come from technological change biased against unskilled workers. However, these impacts have been more than offset by other developments: general productivity growth in the North and the expansion of higher education. Looking to the future, we have speculated that, so low now is the pool of unskilled labour, normally rising demand for it in the non-traded sector (the indirect effect of general productivity growth being fastest in the traded sector) may start to provide a powerful offset.

However that may be, the policy implications for a Western country are clear. Policies that stimulate productivity growth are helpful. Not only do they raise unskilled real wages but they also reduce unemployment both generally and particularly among the unskilled. Such policies are those of free markets, as we have argued throughout this book so far.

So are policies that raise higher education and skill levels. These, by inducing scarcity among unskilled workers, lower their unemployment and raise their real wages, while also raising living standards overall.

Policies that raise social protection are damaging. They raise unemployment not merely among unskilled workers but overall. They lower living standards overall, even if they do slightly raise the real wages absolutely of unskilled workers who retain their jobs. These policies have their effect by increasing the inflexibility of the labour market, as argued earlier in this book.

When we apply these ideas to the policies adopted on the European continent, we find that it is no real surprise that in the face of the severe shocks to the world economies of the past two decades, European unemployment has risen so sharply and productivity growth has slowed down. Even though there has been a large rise in higher education, this has been accompanied by policies of heavy state regulation, intervention and taxation and, in particular, strong social protection in the labour market.

Though we must hope that our speculation is correct that these trends will not be so powerful in the future, European policy still has to undo the effects to date, besides facing any further future challenge. There is no sign of any such policy change. It is hard to avoid the conclusion that the prospects for growth and unemployment on the European continent are grim.

But the policy conclusions do not stop with Northern countries. The South, too, has much to learn. The huge rewards for 'emerging' that have underlain the average trends in the South do not come without intelligent and disciplined policies. There must be conditions that can attract foreign investors. Not only must the advantage of low wage costs be preserved – by avoiding expensive worker rights and limiting unions' strike powers, for example – but also there must be a reliable framework of law, good infrastructure and political stability. Many Southern countries, especially in Africa, have signally failed to meet these conditions; consequently their chances of fully emerging are slim indeed.

Let us end this chapter, then, by noting that for those who are willing to submit to the disciplines of free markets, whether in the North or the South, the rewards, as evidenced by the past two decades, are substantial. Both the process of emergence and technological change have brought huge and widespread advantages to the world economy. It has not been aid but trade and global capitalism that have raised the living standards of poor countries dramatically where they were willing to enter the capitalist system convincingly. And in the North, those countries willing to accept flexible markets – especially in labour – have done best, and have experienced less of the difficulties of adjustment to rapid change and more of the rewards.

References

Advisory Commission – Boskin Report (1996) *Toward a More Accurate Measure of the Cost of Living*, Final Report to the Senate Finance Committee from the Advisory Commission to study the consumer price index, Michael J. Boskin, chairman, December 4, updated version.

Athukorala, P. (1993) 'Manufactured Exports from Developing Countries and their Terms of Trade: A Re-examination of the Sarkar–Singer Results, *World Development*, 21,1607–13.

Berman, E., Bound, J. and Griliches, Z. (1994) 'Changes in the Demand for Skilled Labour within US Manufacturing Industries: Evidence from the Annual Survey of Manufactures', *Quarterly Journal of Economics*, 109, 367–97.

Bernard, A.B. and Jensen, J.B. (1994) *Exporters, Skills Upgrading and the Wage Gap*, research paper 94-13, Center for Economic Studies, Bureau of the Census, Washington, US.

Borjas, G., Freeman, R. and Katz, L. (1992) 'On the Labour Market Effects of Immigration and Trade', in G.J. Borjas and R. Freeman (eds), *Immigration and the Workforce*, University of Chicago Press, Chicago.

Boskin (1996) – see Advisory Commission above.

Bound, J. and Johnson, G. (1992) 'Changes in the Structure of Wages in the 1980s: an Evaluation of Alternative Explanations, *American Economic Review*, June.

Dollar, D. (1992) 'Outward-oriented Developing Countries Really Do Grow More Rapidly: Evidence from 95 LDC, 1976–85, *Economic Development and Cultural Change*, 1992, pp 523–44.

Feenstra, R.C., and Hanson, G. (1995) 'Foreign Investment, Outsourcing and Relative Wages', in *Political Economy of Trade Policy: Essays in Honour of*

Jagdish Bhagwati, R. C. Feenstra, G.M. Grossman and D.A. Irwin (eds.), MIT Press, Cambridge, MA, pp. 89-127.

Gundlach, E. and Nunnenkampf, P. (1994) 'Globalisation and Structural Unemployment, *Konjunkturpolitik*, 40, 202–25.

Heckscher, E. (1919) 'The Effect of Foreign Trade on the Distribution of Income', *Economisk Tidskrift*, 497–512; reprinted as Ch. 13 in *AEA Readings in the Theory of International Trade* (Blakiston, Philadelphia, 1949), pp 272–300.

Jones, R.W. and Kierzowski, H. (1997) 'Globalisation and the consequences of international fragmentation', paper presented at the Robert Mundell Festschrift Conference, Washington DC, October 1997.

Katz, L. and Murphy, K. (1992) 'Changes in Relative Wages, 1963–1987: Supply and Demand Factors', *Quarterly Journal of Economics*, 113, no1.

Krueger, A.B. (1993) 'How Computers Have Changed the Wage Structure: Evidence from Microdata 1984-89', *Quarterly Journal of Economics*, 108, 33–60.

Krugman, P. (1995) 'Growing World Trade: Causes and Consequences', *Brookings Papers on Economic Activity*, 1:1995, 327–77.

Krugman, P. and Lawrence, R. (1994) 'Trade, Jobs and Wages', *Scientific American*, April 1994, 270:4, 44–9.

Lawrence, R.Z., and Slaughter, M.J. (1993) 'International Trade and American Wages in the 1980s: Giant Sucking Sound or Small Hiccup?', *Brookings Papers: Microeconomics* 2, 161–226.

Leamer, E. (1993) 'Wage Effects of a US–Mexican Free Trade Agreement', in P.M. Garber (ed.), *The Mexico–US Free Trade Agreement*, MIT Press, Cambridge, US.

Leamer, E. (1994) 'Trade, Wages and Revolving Door Ideas', working paper 4716, April, National Bureau of Economic Research, Cambridge, US.

Machin, S. (1994) *Changes in the Relative Demand for Skills in the UK Labour Market*, discussion paper no. 952, Centre for Economic Policy Research, London.

Minford, P. (1997) 'Unemployment in the OECD and its Remedies', in D. Snower and G. de la Dehesa (eds), *Unemployment Policy – Government Options for the Labour Market,* for the Centre for Economic Policy Research and the Consorcio Zona Franca de Vigo, Cambridge University Press, Cambridge, pp. 501–533.

Minford, P., Riley, J. and Nowell, E. (1997) 'Trade, technology and labour markets in the world economy 1970-90: a computable general equilibrium analysis', *Journal of Development Studies*, vol. 34, no. 2, pp. 1–34.

Nickell, S. (1995) 'The Distribution of Wages and Unemployment across Skill Groups', mimeograph, December, Institute of Economics and Statistics, Oxford.

Nickell, S. and Bell, B. (1995) 'The Collapse of Demand for the Unskilled and Unemployment across the OECD', *Oxford Review of Economic Policy*, 11(1), Spring, 40–62.

North, D. (1994) 'Institutional Competition' in *Locational Competition in the World Economy* (ed. H. Siebert), Kiel Institute of World Economics, J.C.B. Mohr (Paul Siebeck), Tübingen.

Nunnenkamp, P., Gundlach, E. and Agarwal, J.P. (1994) *Globalisation of Production and Markets*, Kieler Studien, Kiel Institute of World Economics, J.C.B. Mohr (Paul Siebeck), Tübingen.

Ohlin, B. (1933) *Interregional and International Trade*, Harvard University Press, Cambridge, US.

Oliviera-Martins, J. (1993) *Market Structure, International Trade and Relative Wages*, Economics Department working paper no. 134, OECD.

Parente, S.L. and Prescott, E.C. (1995), 'Technology Adoption and Growth', *Journal of Political Economy*, vol. 103, no. 5.

Rowthorn, R.E. (1995) 'A Simulation Model of North–South Trade', *UNCTAD Review 1995*, United Nations, New York and Geneva.

Sachs, J.D. and Shatz, H.J. (1994) 'Trade and Jobs in US Manufacturing', *Brookings Papers on Economic Activity*, 1:1994, 1–84.

Sachs, J.D. and Shatz, H.J. (1996) 'US trade with Developing Countries and Wage Inequality', *American Economic Review*, papers and proceedings, May, pp 234–9.

Samuelson, P.A. (1948) 'International Trade and the Equalisation of Factor Prices', *Economic Journal*, 58, 163–84.

Sarkar, P., and Singer, H.W. (1993) 'Manufacture–Manufacture Terms of Trade Deterioration: A Reply', *World Development*, 21, 1617–20.

Stolper, W. and Samuelson, P.A. (1941) 'Protection and Real Wages', *Review of Economic Studies*, 58–73.

Van Reenen, J. (1994) *Getting a Fair Share of the Plunder? Technology, Skills and Wages in British Establishments*, discussion paper no 881, Centre for Economic Policy Research, London.

Wood, A. (1994) *North–South Trade, Employment and Inequality – Changing Fortunes in a Skill-driven World*, Clarendon, Oxford.

Wood, A. (1997) 'Openness and Wage Inequality in Developing Countries: the Latin American Challenge to East Asian Conventional Wisdom', *World Bank Economic Review*, vol. 11, no. 1, pp. 33-57.

CHAPTER EIGHT

Europe and the new world order

THE CONTINENT OF Europe, henceforth Europe, is organised in a particular way that is markedly different from that of the UK (as it now is) or the US or indeed virtually all Anglo-Saxon countries. Let us call it 'stakeholder capitalism'. Various other names have been given to it, such as Rhenish capitalism, the German social market, and continental social democracy. But our name is most apposite because of the recent use in New Labour circles of 'stakeholding' and the clear admiration associated with it for the ways of the continent, particularly Germany.

Among economists, this continental model is classified as having a high degree of social insurance. What this means is that household income variations arising from the operation of the market (not just over time but absolutely, compared with some social norm of a decent living standard) are smoothed out by taxes and social transfers. As part of this mechanism, firms are heavily regulated, as well as having to pay high taxes to help fund the direct transfers. The regulation, to provide worker rights and security, is a system of hidden taxes and transfers.

How does this differ from socialism? Under fully fledged socialism, incomes are supposed to be entirely dictated by 'need', and production is entirely directed by planners. The market is replaced entirely by planners' prices and a direct allocation of resources. Under stakeholder capitalism, the markets exist but prices and incomes are controlled, taxed and supplemented to get as close as possible to some satisfactory social outcome; this mechanism of social insurance is the result of the continental democratic process and although a number of continental politicians have proposed programmes of reform, they have been markedly unsuccessful in attracting support at elections. This resulting system is a 'third' or 'middle' way between socialism and laissez-faire capitalism.

There are many detailed differences in the systems of particular countries. For example the Dutch are strongly in favour of free trade and freely competitive product markets, but their labour market is heavily regulated with extremely generous unemployment benefits and 'disability pensions' that effectively act as permanent unemployment benefit. At the other extreme, the French are intensely protectionist and intervene extensively in product markets (most notoriously in agriculture), yet in their labour market they have quite low levels of unionisation and their unemployment benefit rates are by continental standards ungenerous and decline sharply with the length of unemployment. Nevertheless, in spite of the differences there is a general similarity that distinguishes them from far more limited Anglo-Saxon social insurance and still more from the negligible social insurance practised in most Far-Eastern countries (where individual and family action is expected to insure the household).

Like most social insurance mechanisms, the origins of the continental form go back far in the history and philosophical thought of the continent of Europe. The present system can be seen as a direct descendant of mediaeval practices, such as the just price or wage, and guilds or cartels of producers and workers operating under settled conditions and strict regulation of entry into the market. This mediaeval system had the sanction of the Roman Catholic Church. Thinkers such as Hegel (in *The Philosophy of Right*, 1821) and Kant (in *The Critique of Practical Reason*, 1788) underpinned it philosophically with theories of Order, both social and moral. Bismarck took over this thinking when he formalised his state-wide system of social insurance.

By contrast, Anglo-Saxon capitalism can be traced to the Protestant rejection of Roman Catholicism in favour of free individual choice. This rejection began in the Low Countries and Britain, and it is consistent with this fact that the most free-market country on the continent is Holland. The fact that it is not thoroughly Anglo-Saxon in approach reflects the long history of struggle between Protestant and Catholic factions in the Low Countries, with frequent spells of external imperial intervention. As for that quintessence of Anglo-Saxon capitalism, the United States, its origins are clearly seen in the ultimate rejection of even British Anglicanism by the Plymouth Brethren. With no mediaeval baggage in tow, these pioneers were able to create a new culture of individual freedom and self-reliance.

How well can stakeholder capitalism work with its heavy-handed social insurance mechanism? It was Hayek (1988) who pointed out that socialism was the translation to the level of the state of the instincts and practices of the tribe and equivalent small communities, such as the mediaeval town. It is obvious that, in a close-knit community, people may well give of their best even though they do not directly reap the reward in monetary income, because they are closely observed, judged and rewarded in non-monetary ways (esteem, status etc) by their peers. If they do not perform, they risk ostracism. Responsibilities are honoured in return for insurance in times of need.

One may ask whether, even under such ideal circumstances of close-knittedness, efficiency in its fullest sense can be achieved. Static efficiency no doubt can; effort will be great, and resources distributed to good effect – perhaps even maximum effect allowing for indirect effects ('externalities') and as monitored sensitively by the community. But dynamic efficiency? The theory of high social insurance can in principle embrace high incentives for the innovator. Monetary rewards are necessarily limited, but status rewards could be large. However, there are two problems: innovators may not always be the sort of people who value such rewards and, more importantly, since innovation necessarily disrupts existing social and economic relationships, these rewards may not be easy to deliver – the leaders might decree general approbation but the people will mutter. The history of mediaeval society suggests that innovation was not often rewarded, indeed rather the contrary.

This lack of dynamic efficiency is extended to static efficiency when the community within which social insurance is delivered is widened to the level of the state. For then that close observation of delivery of responsibilities is no longer possible. State rules and policing are no substitute for local monitoring. People can rig their activities to conform to the letter of any rules, even if they do not actually break the law, and still avoid delivering the required effort.

The size of this problem of static inefficiency will generally depend on the gap between the free-market price that would prevail in the absence of intervention and the de facto price that the insurance system puts in place. Economists have a measure of the lost value of production due to this gap in lost 'consumer surplus'; this measure increases with the square of the gap. Consequently, for small gaps it will be trivial but for large gaps it can become immense.

Nevertheless, it is important to realise that the loss of static and dynamic efficiency does not show itself up as a total or even partial breakdown of an economy. As Adam Smith once observed, 'There is a great deal of ruin in a nation', and the loss of static efficiency is some percentage, probably in single figures, of the nation's output. It will be most obvious in the level of unemployment (including 'concealed unemployment', such as the extent of disability pensions or the rate of work-sharing). As for dynamic inefficiency, which is not even easily measurable except with long hindsight, it will show up as a slightly lower rate of productivity growth (a quarter of one percent, say) that will accumulate to a serious reduction of living standards but only over several decades.

The proponents of heavy social insurance argue that people will be generally happier and also work more effectively because of the security created by the system. Security, one may concede, is something people prize. The difficulty is to assess how much extra security is delivered by heavy social insurance as compared with lighter social insurance and indeed private insurance. The extra depends not only on the intention of the system if the economy maintains its efficiency but also on that very efficiency of the economy. To put the point in an extreme and unreasonable way, the Soviet Union may have delivered a high degree of social insurance in terms of reducing the variability and inequality of incomes, but so great was its inefficiency that it delivered a far lower average living standard than a comparable but less developed country such as Malaysia.

Hence the probability of having a low income may well be less in such a country, both because the average is so much higher and because private and residual public insurance delivers some reduction in variability. Indeed, it may well be the case, by the same token, that in such a country there is both a higher probability of being well-off and a lower probability of being worse-off, a situation illustrated in Figure 8.1, which shows a population distribution by income level. It is referred to as being 'stochastically dominant', by which is meant that anyone of given characteristics could expect to be better off in the one country rather than the other. One can think of these characteristics as giving someone a certain productivity level for which there is some internationally set wage under the best available technology; then social institutions redistribute money to and from that person, reducing variability and imposing an efficiency cost in lost average living standard. Plainly, a rational electorate will prefer a stochastically dominant system (as although they may get a kick from all being poor together, this would be irrational), but a choice of systems like that illustrated in ure 8.2 could generate dissent because it involves – at least for the g – losers as well as winners.

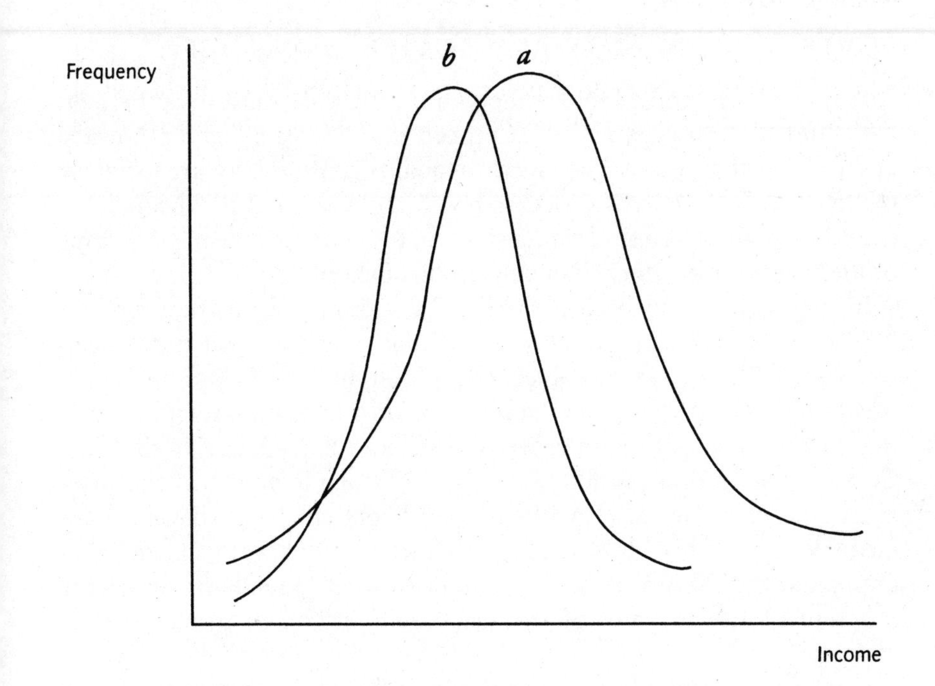

Figure 8.1 Income distributions where there is no stochastic dominance

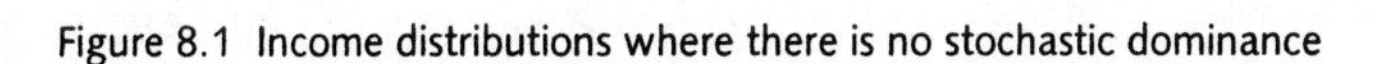

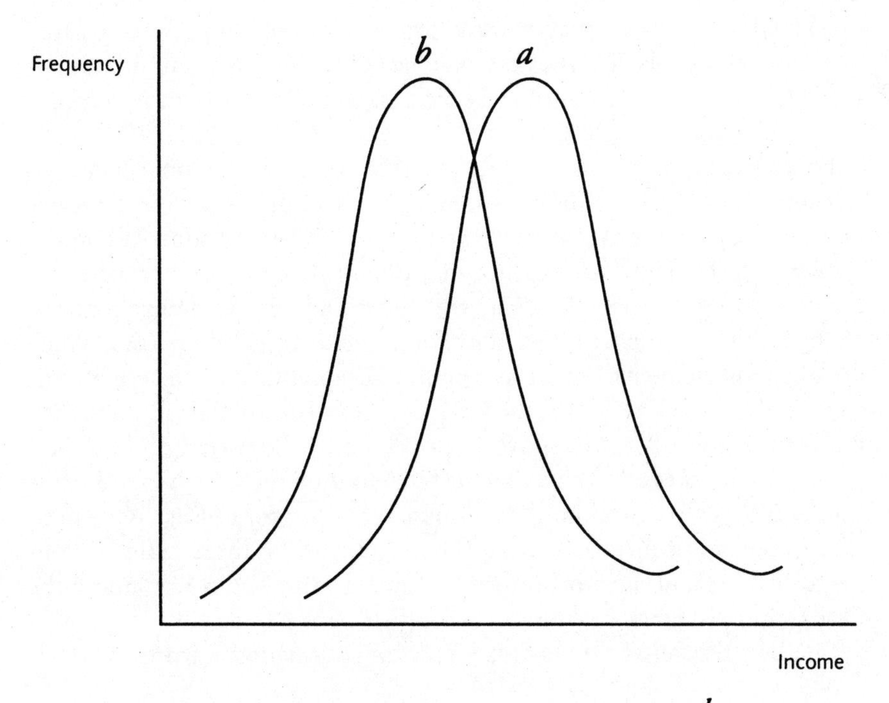

Figure 8.2 Income distributions: *a* stochastically dominates *b*

POVERTY, INEQUALITY AND SOCIAL INSURANCE

Although many people bracket the two together, we must insist here on the difference between social insurance that protects against poverty and policies that aim for equality. Inequality and poverty are different things. Plainly, poverty is concerned with the bottom of the income distribution; it also has a time dimension, that is to say it is defined in terms of lifetime income rather than current income only.

Inequality concerns both the top and bottom of the distribution and it is usually measured by current income only (or current financial wealth). Now, I can see no objection, indeed much in favour, of people becoming very rich in income terms; nor do I know of much evidence that people generally resent riches and success. Indeed, during the UK's Conservative reform programme from 1979, the lowering of top marginal rates of income tax (to 40%) was deliberately designed to increase inequality in this way. It is a notable fact that so far was this from being unpopular that New Labour has committed itself to retaining this lower top rate of tax in spite of the usual Labour voices demanding its increase.

One of the effects of union power was to flatten the wage distribution and hold back the pay of skilled workers. Again, the UK reduction of union power was intended among other things to increase the earnings of skilled workers so that market pressures were properly translated into market signals. There is no evidence that this has been unpopular; indeed, once more the contrary is the case and New Labour is committed to maintaining the union laws.

Poverty alleviation is another matter altogether. Going back to Rowntree (1901), it has been usual in the UK to define poverty in terms of an ability to survive as a participant in society at some minimum (poverty) level. This is a measure that obviously contains a relative element in so far as such things as transport and entertainment patterns change, but it is heavily affected by food intake and shelter costs, which are absolute elements. As far as popular acceptability is concerned, this – certainly in the UK – is the measure that commands interest, unlike the many measures of relative poverty proffered by the poverty lobby.

In a free market economy, there is by definition the possibility of some households (the natural unit) becoming very poor for at least some period of their adult members' lives. There seem to be three main responses to this around the world: the Continental, the Anglo-Saxon and the Oriental approaches.

The first response, that emanating from continental Europe, involves a high degree of regulation of labour-market outcomes – it is the stakeholder approach that we have spent a lot of space on and concentrate on further in this chapter. The second involves little intervention in labour market outcomes, but quite a bit through the tax/transfer system: benefits are paid to poor households in cash and kind to make up for what wages cannot deliver. This is at present the standard capitalist model of the non-stakeholder variety. We tend to refer to it as 'free market' – but we should not forget that it remains highly interventionist in the welfare area, and in the next chapter we will consider whether that cannot be changed too, in favour of more private provision. We come, thirdly, to the Oriental model of welfare, which is the least interventionist of all, at least in terms of state spending. Under it, the individual and the family are expected to provide for themselves through high saving, insurance and mutual support. As a result, tax rates are much lower.

It is natural to wish for some measure of the poverty generated by these three systems to set against their efficiency achievement. The problem is that we need a measure of lifetime poverty as opposed to purely episodic poverty, and most countries have little data on how incomes move over people's lives. Only the US has long runs of 'panel studies', where the same people are checked out for a long period. These studies suggest a high degree of mobility between income groups over time, but there is enough persistence for it to be clear that some at least of the poor at a point in time do indeed remain poor throughout their lives.

However, what we do not know is how this persistence itself is affected by welfare payments. We have little data on Oriental poverty or mobility; plenty on Continental poverty, little on Continental mobility. This is an unsatisfactory situation for making decisions about welfare and social insurance. What we can say is that there have been steady rises in living standards for the poorest fifth of society throughout the western world in the past four decades. Table 8.1 shows the trends in the living standards of the lowest quintile in a variety of these countries; while not completely up to date, it shows clearly that the poor are not getting poorer anywhere in the developed world. Take, for example, the vexed case of the UK since 1979 ('Thatcher's Britain'). Table 8.1 estimates that a lowest-quintile household's real disposable income rose by 17% between 1979 and 1995. As David Green (1998) has recently reminded us, real expenditure trends for the poor are likely to measure their living standards more accurately than income, given all the benefits they receive as well as the problems of income definition. Similarly, Richard Pryke (1995) found that income measures used to establish the

		Bottom quintile share of disposable income (%)	Per capita real disposable income (Index)+	Estimated per capita real disposable income of bottom quintile
USA	1966	4.3	100.0	100.0
	1976	4.3	128.9	128.9
	1985	4.7	155.1	169.5
Japan	1969	7.9	100.0	100.0
	1979	8.7	149.9	165.1
Italy	1969	5.1	100.0	100.0
	1977	6.2	125.1	152.1
	1986	6.8	161.0	214.2
Germany (West)	1968	6.2	100.0	100.0
	1974	6.9	131.7	146.6
	1988	7.0	178.2	201.2
France	1970	4.3	100.0	100.0
	1979	6.3	131.6	192.8
	1989	5.6	158.8	206.8
UK	1968	(10.7)	100.0	100.0
	1979	9.4	133.3	117.1
	1989	7.6	171.2	121.6
	1995	7.9	185.4	136.9

+ For Japan, Italy and France real consumer expenditure

Table 8.1 Estimated real disposable income per capita of bottom fifth (quintile) of households

Sources: World Bank World Development Report, OECD National Accounts; for UK Office of National Statistics Economic Trends (bracketed figures for 1968 obtained by splicing World Bank Income share series onto Economic Trends series)

extent of poverty were highly misleading, exaggerating it by a factor of nearly four. Goodman and Webb (1995) found that the expenditure of the lowest quintile (by income) rose by 27% between 1979 and 1992; the equivalent growth for 1979–95 was 28% (DSS, 1997).

These figures unfortunately do not get us very far in terms of policy. We examined in the last chapter the pressures exerted by the global trends of low-wage competition and technological bias against unskilled workers. We saw that in fact the vast mass of unskilled (ie, not highly educated) workers managed nevertheless to improve their living standards steadily, if only moderately. This was the result very largely of strong Northern productivity growth, aided by the rapid expansion of higher education. While rising social protection (mainly concentrated on the continent) also raised their wages, it did so only by raising unemployment sharply: a very poor bargain.

Hence, while we should expect some rise in episodic poverty, it should induce us not to intervene any more through social wage protection but rather to stimulate productivity growth and training. This still leaves the question of how far one should go with income transfers to poor households, a method of social insurance that, by permitting wages to fall and create jobs, is more efficient than the direct social fixing of wages and workers' rights. If we then compare this system of income transfers with the widespread Oriental system of privately funded insurance, we are on more difficult ground, which I go on to discuss at much greater length in the next chapter.

STAKEHOLDER CAPITALISM – AN INTERIM ASSESSMENT

There is in general, therefore, no easy way to weigh up the gains and losses of stakeholder capitalism. There should be some gain in security, as measured by income variability and inequality, but there is also likely to be some loss in efficiency, showing up in reduced average living standards. In different societies, security as reduced variability may be prized relatively more or less compared with average living standard; hence it is rational for some to have more or less social insurance in line with these different preferences. Nevertheless, if there is a shift in the trade-off – for example a sharp rise in the efficiency losses associated with heavy social insurance – we would expect to see a corresponding shift in popular attitudes away from social insurance, even in countries like those of the continent predisposed towards it.

There is evidence of some such shift in the past couple of decades. By the early 1970s, the continental system of social insurance had become very generous, rather like that of the UK following its post-war social consensus. Increasing generosity had accompanied three decades of rapid post-war growth. However, the oil price crisis of 1973 ushered in two and a half decades of slower growth and rising unemployment. The continental welfare state has consequently had to absorb a sharply increasing share of GDP in tax funding, and this is being exacerbated by the demographic trends of falling birth and death rates that make the state pension promises unfundable without a further sharp rise in taxation.

Behind this crisis lie trends in world trade (notably the growth of the emerging market economies) and in technology (computer substitution away from unskilled workers) within a world market tightly integrated by modern communications and the sweeping away of barriers to trade and capital movements – globalisation for short. These trends, as we saw in Chapter 7, enforce substantial changes in prices and wages through international competition. Countries amongst those in continental Europe that attempt to prevent these price and wage changes create a large gap vis-à-vis free market values and are consequently a source of large efficiency losses. These show up in high unemployment, low participation, high taxes to pay the resulting benefit bills, and slowing productivity growth rates.

Tables 5.1 to 5.6 in Chapter 5 showed many key figures for the labour market and productivity, and here we complete the picture. Table 8.2 shows two measures of systemic difference: government spending relative to GDP, and the index of general economic freedom (compiled by 47 free-market institutes around the world) used in Chapter 1. Table 8.3 shows the recent behaviour of state deficits and of public debt – the public finance problems of European countries, in spite of massive efforts at retrenchment to meet the Maastricht Treaty criteria, are still severe.

Figure 8.3 shows pension projections made recently by the OECD (Roseveare *et al*, 1996) of which (except the UK, whose reforms were discussed above in Chapter 5 and will be reverted to in Chapter 9) have worsening imbalances between state pensions and contributions on present policies, chiefly because of demographic trends. For continental Europe, this bankruptcy of the state pension system comes on top of overt fiscal difficulties and at existing levels of taxation of around 50% of GDP, where tax resistance is already strong.

It is striking that, among OECD countries faced with these common trends, the Anglo-Saxon and Oriental approaches have generated much less unemployment and lower taxes than those of Europe. This is because their wages, costs and prices are more flexible in response to

Anglo Saxon/Oriental	Gov't spending as % of GDP	Economic Freedom Index*	Rank in world†
USA	36.7*	7.9	4
Japan	36.7*	6.7	18
UK	43.5**	7.3	7
Continental European			
Germany	51.0**	6.4	25
France	54.3*	6.1	36
Italy	53.2**	5.5	55

* 1995

** 1996

† based on Economic Freedom Index

Table 8.2 Systemic differences

Source: J. Gwartney and R. Lawson (1997) *Economic Freedom of the World*, Fraser Institute, Canada, with 46 other institutes worldwide

	1995	1996	1997 (projected)	Public debt (gross) end of 1996*
USA	2.3	1.4	0.3	63.1
Japan	4.4	4.9	3.0	82.6
Germany	3.4	3.8	3.1	60.7
France	4.2	3.7	3.1	56.2
Italy	7.0	7.0	3.2	123.7
UK	4.4	3.1	0.8**	54.8

* General Government consolidated gross debt (for EEC, Maastricht definition)

** 1997/8 Financial year

Table 8.3 Fiscal balances and debt (as a % of GDP)

Source: Liverpool Research Group projection, December 1997

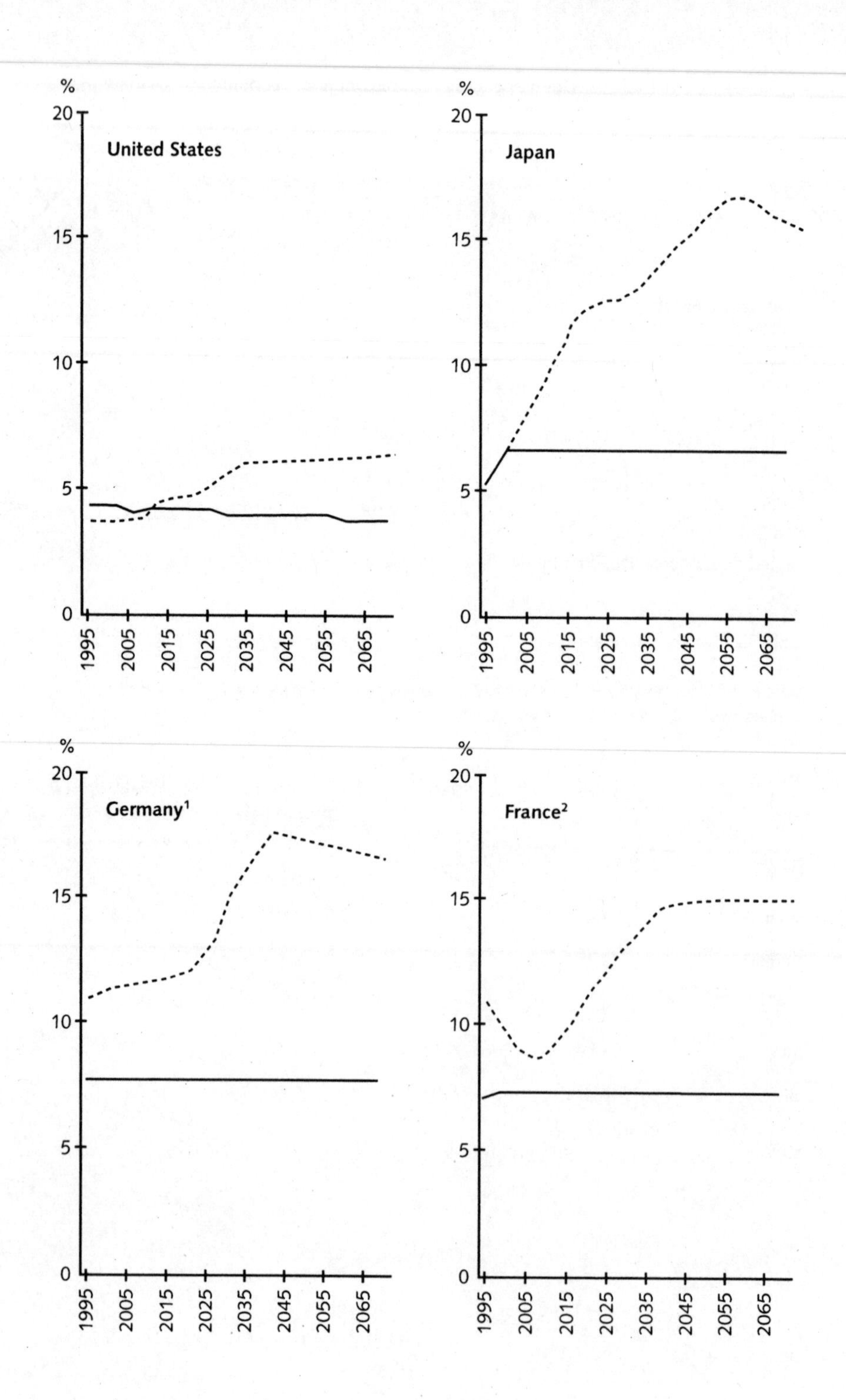

%
20
15
10
5
0
United States
1995
2005
2015
2025
2035
2045
2055
2065
Japan
Germany[1]
France[2]

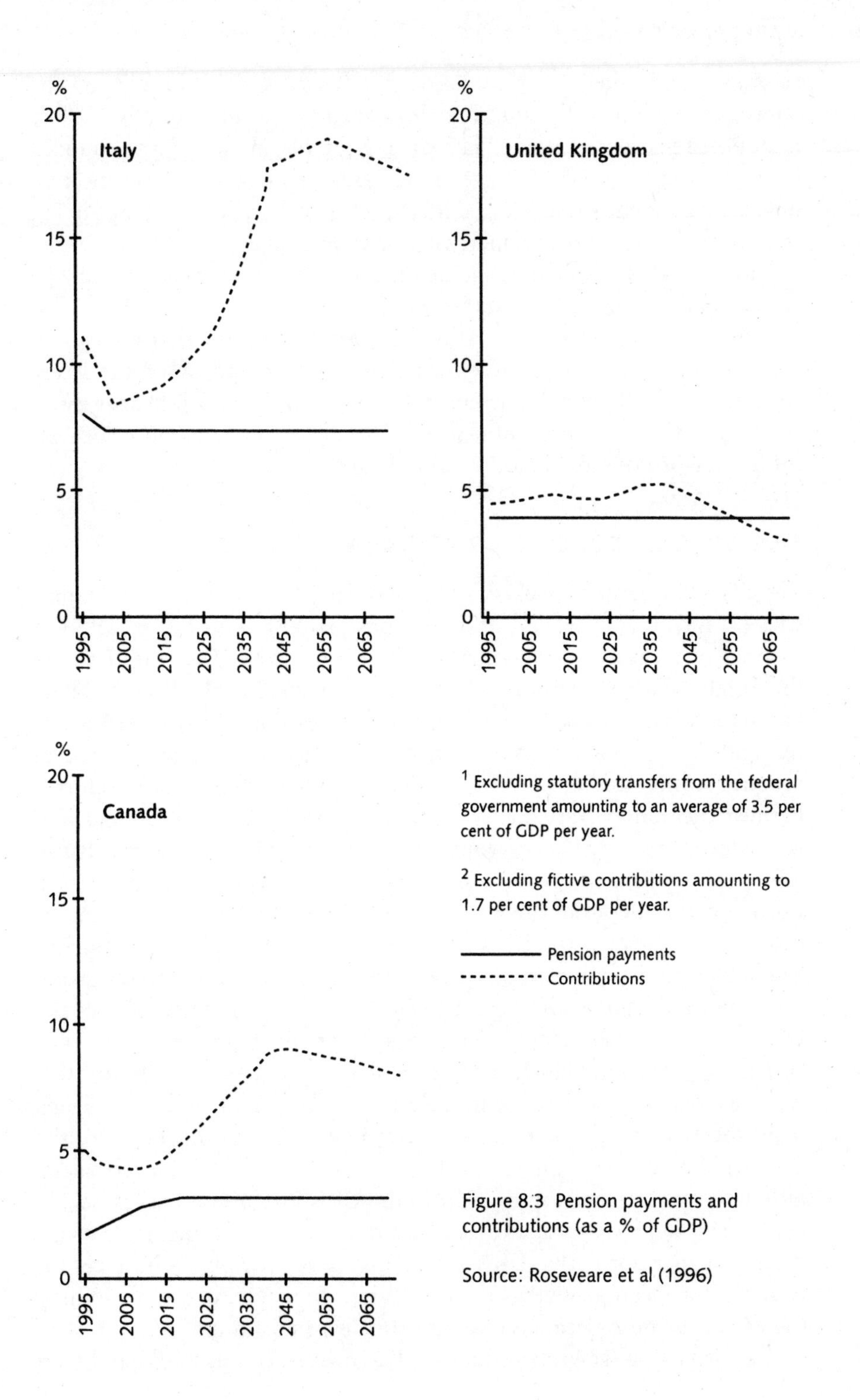

Figure 8.3 Pension payments and contributions (as a % of GDP)

Source: Roseveare et al (1996)

economic and other shocks, whereas the heavy social insurance on the continent operates by limiting this flexibility substantially. While undoubtedly it has succeeded in reducing the rise in inequality produced by these trends – which have quite badly damaged the position of unskilled workers – it has levied a large efficiency cost on average living standards, largely through increased unemployment.

I now turn to the dilemma facing the UK in its relations with a Europe whose social insurance and stakeholder capitalism are, in my view, so at odds with the relatively successful free market economy that it has now established. I consider the dilemma that would be posed by the likely continuation of Europe's current policies for the UK: will it drift away from close ties with the continent in order to preserve its more successful framework of Anglo-Saxon capitalism?

THE UK AND EUROPE – THE BALANCE SHEET

The EC Commission, backed by the vast majority of continental countries (in most instances, all of them), has proposed during the 1990s a number of measures to be taken by the Community. These are notably the Single Market, the Single Currency, and the Social Chapter. These measures would achieve a much higher degree of integration within the EC and create pressure for still further integration; yet they could in practice stultify and even reverse many of the UK's free-market reforms because the dominant regulative structure of the resulting EC could well be – indeed most probably would be – Continental in approach. It follows that one cannot consider the policy needs and prospects of Western Europe without considering those of the EC and how the conflict that is now visible between the UK's Anglo-Saxon system and the continent's Rhenish capitalism can be resolved. This section discusses these issues. For maximum clarity, the argument proceeds from the viewpoint of the UK and its relations with Europe. For better or worse the continent's system appears unlikely to change much in the next decade or two, whereas that of the UK, being relatively recent and under challenge from the EC's proposed new structure, may well do so. Therefore the active policy choices appear to lie mostly with the UK. Nevertheless, although this section is written from the UK's viewpoint, it is as deeply concerned with what makes economic sense for continental Europe itself. Furthermore, the UK's problems have obvious relevance for Eastern European and other countries that, they intend, will be joining the EC in the next decade or so into the new millennium.

The discussion is purely economic, like the rest of this book, and I am implicitly treating political sentiment as something that adjusts in the end to economic interests. Although I have been labelled 'Eurosceptic', my attitude is essentially pragmatic about the forms of economic co-operation that the UK should have with Europe, and how far these would then reduce political 'sovereignty' then becomes a consequential matter to be put up with. This section attempts to judge the pragmatic basis for different aspects of that co-operation, together with the balance sheet of our present and possible future involvement. It considers in turn agriculture, money, the social dimension, and non-agricultural trade and investment. A much fuller account, with details backing up the calculations set out below, is contained in Minford (1996).

The position of the UK government (both current Labour and previous Conservative) on the country's balance sheet has depended on the crucial proviso that we can effectively limit the scope of (or, from the Conservative viewpoint, keep out of the highly damaging) social chapter and single currency until some balance of advantage appears in it – say because we become greatly more integrated with the continent. With that proviso, it appears to believe that the net gain, from our existing free-ish trade links with a Europe that has quite substantial barriers to trade with the rest of the world, is sufficient to outweigh the costs of the agricultural programmes. This apparently quite sane assessment is the basic position I wish to test.

Agriculture

I look first at the by-now familiar costs of the Common Agricultural Policy (CAP) and the Common Fisheries Policy (CFP).

The cost to the EC as a whole of the CAP and other agricultural support has been estimated by the OECD for 1990 at £48 billion to consumers, plus £27 billion to taxpayers; of these amounts some £46 billion is a transfer to farmers, even if badly targeted (going largely to landowners and part-time farmers). Hence the net cost of the CAP and related arrangements is £29 billion, or about 1% of EC GDP at that time.

Our concern here is with the cost to the UK of the CAP itself (the costs above also include those of national programmes of assistance to farmers). The CAP is a system of implicit tariffs on imports and subsidies to exports both of which are set in order to raise food prices inside the EC up to the CAP intervention levels. As the UK is a net importer of food, it can treat the CAP as a variable tariff, which, the OECD estimates, is of the order of 40% in a typical year. This tariff implies that the consumer pays more for food than the world price, the extra going partly to the UK farmer and the rest going to the central CAP fund in Brussels. The implied cost to the UK consumer net of the receipts of UK farmers is probably around £3 billion at 1990 prices in a typical year.

On top of this we must add further effects of the higher prices: the consumer's loss of welfare due to reduced food purchases and the extra costs that farmers incur from increased production. These costs are the 'excess costs' or the 'pure waste' from the CAP, so called because they result from the misallocation of resources compared with what consumers and producers would do if prices were at their true world levels. These costs could run to another £2.5 billion at 1990 prices.

Total costs to the consumer net of gains to farmers would therefore be some £5.5 billion at 1990 prices, or £6.5 billion at today's prices, for a typical year. In any particular year, the gap between CAP and world prices, from which these costs stem, can vary: in 1995, for example, the gap virtually disappeared as world food prices surged, but this is highly unusual; from 1979 to 1993 it varied between 31% and 49%.

To these net costs must be added the UK's net budgetary contribution to the EC in support of the CAP's running costs and deficit (the latter coming about because the CAP possibly pays out subsidies on food exports that may exceed receipts from food imports). The vast bulk of the EC budget is devoted to the costs of agricultural support and administration. Hence we may, for convenience, include all our fiscal contributions under this head. As the 'solidarity' dimension – the programme to spend on the poorer regions of the EEC, stemming from Maastricht – expands, the UK is scheduled to spend more in years to come on this. But at this stage it is small. Our budgetary contributions are running at around £3.5 billion net.

In sum, then, a typical year's cost at current prices is some £10 billion, around 1.5% of GDP. This still understates the true loss to the UK because the amounts received back by farmers and in regional subsidies are poorly 'targeted'. They also exclude ownership losses of UK fishermen under the CFP. Nevertheless, this ratio of 1.5% gives a rough order of magnitude.

The Single Currency

The advantages of a single currency are the lowering of transactions costs (of currency exchange) and the elimination of exchange rate uncertainty against currencies in European Monetary Union (EMU). The main disadvantage is that the government loses the use of interest-rate and exchange-rate movements in response to shocks that are 'asymmetric' (ie, differ from those of other countries in EMU). A number of other issues have also been raised, but these are, I will argue, less central: inflation control, fiscal matters, and possible protectionism by EMU members against non-members.

On the key issue, the estimates available of transactions cost savings are extremely low. A survey by the Commission found that in advanced countries with a high degree of computerised credit transactions, it could amount to as little as 0.1% of GDP. As for exchange-rate uncertainty, theory suggests it is diversifiable and therefore that the risk premium for those wishing to insure the risk (by buying currency 'forward' and 'hedging') will be negligible. Empirical work looking for some link from exchange-rate uncertainty to trade has found nil or minimal effects, confirming this view.

On the other hand, empirical work on the effects of abandoning independent monetary policy has suggested there would be a serious increase in macroeconomic instability. My own work with my research team, using the Liverpool Model, has suggested an approximate doubling of both inflation and output variability, Figure 8.4 shows our calculations, which are derived by applying large numbers of typical past shocks to EC countries within the model and working out the resulting variability of output and prices under different exchange-rate regimes. This is consistent with other studies, noting the low degree of integration between European states (compared, say, with that of US states), particularly in relation to a tiny central budget and little labour mobility.

Should EMU nevertheless go ahead in continental Europe, there are considerable risks. Unemployment is already high, as we have seen, and unlikely to fall much, which will be a source of popular resentment. Furthermore, either tax rates will have to rise or expenditure, including state pension entitlements, be cut in order to deal with the poor state of public finances, and this will be another source of popular resistance. The new European Central Bank, the ECB, will have less power to stabilise the business cycle and unemployment of the many disparate regions of the EC, so that (for example) in the next recession in France, unemployment may well go up far more than normal, on top of its existing level of around 13%.

The strains that these likely events will produce in political terms will have consequences impossible to predict. They range from EMU break-up through more protectionism to serious social disorder. This obviously suggests that the UK would be most unwise to get involved, not merely because of the problems it would cause us directly in our economic management but also because the spill-over of these problems, bad enough anyway, would be worsened if we were inside EMU.

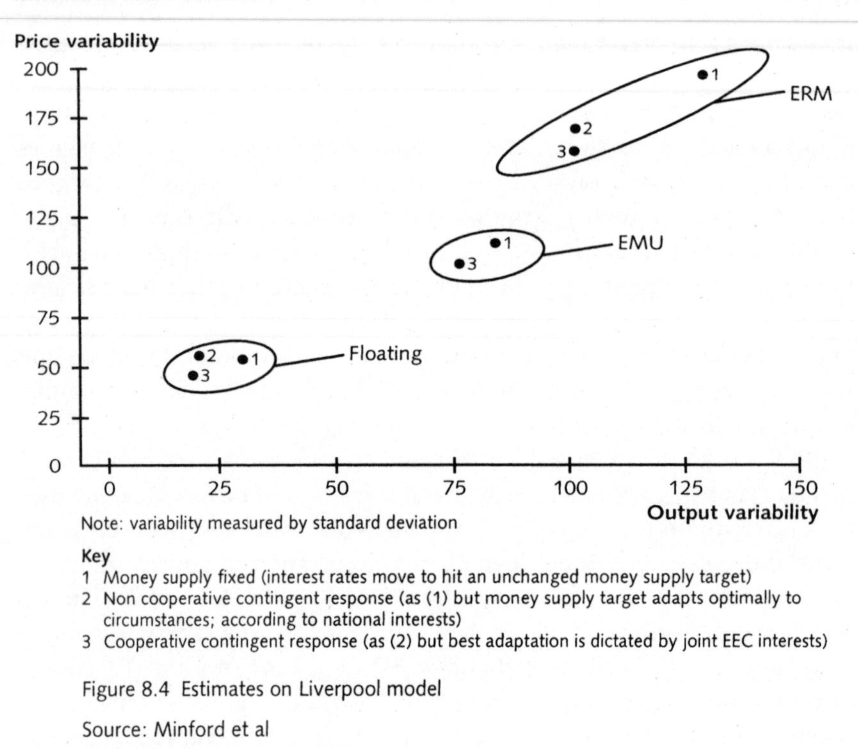

Figure 8.4 Estimates on Liverpool model

Source: Minford et al

I now turn to the other issues mentioned above, namely inflation control, fiscal matters, and possible protectionism by EMU members against non-members.

Inflation control is sometimes urged as an advantage of EMU. However, such control can be achieved domestically if it is popularly desired – and if it is not, then it is unclear how a country could join EMU or, having done so, stay in it. Further, it is not clear that the proposed European Central Bank will offer secure inflation control, given its board composition, lack of political backing in individual countries, and the pressure on it to fund country deficits.

The lack of fiscal co-operation that could well occur under the Maastricht agreement is widely considered to be a problem. In fact, the way that fiscal policy would work is unclear at present because there is no agreement on how rigorously the Maastricht fiscal criteria will be applied by the monitoring committee.

Thirdly, EMU members could levy protectionist measures against non-members on the grounds of 'competitive devaluation'. However, these would have to be non-tariff measures permitted by the Treaty of

Rome Single Market regulations, but there is none of any si
and anything attempted could be referred to the European (
attempt illicit measures would endanger the Treaty and would
be unlikely. In fact, already most continental countries prac
ever protectionism of this kind that they can (for example, the subsidi-
sing of airlines such as Iberia) and there is a constant effort by the EC Commission's competition directorate to stop or at least limit this activity. In or out of EMU, a level of protectionism exists and the pressure for it is intense. It is quite possible that the pressure would be still greater were the UK to enter EMU at any conceivable exchange rate, since with its low labour costs (measured in Euros) it would appear to be at least as much a competitive magnet for foreign investment.

It is my conclusion that the best course for all EC members would be to continue with monetary co-operation in the European Monetary Institute; and for the UK to stay out of EMU should it go ahead in some form, as looks likely at the time of writing in autumn 1997.

The Social Chapter

The Social Chapter is somewhat vague in its formulation, which makes assessing its impact difficult. However, qualified majority voting governs both Articles 2 and 4 of the Chapter, respectively on worker rights and pan-European bargaining. More importantly, the Chapter commits the EC to pursuing the objectives of the Social Charter – a long shopping list of demands for regulation and workers' rights intended to make the EC as a whole as regulated as the most regulated member; and it hands over sweeping powers of interpretation to the Commission and the European Court, both of which are committed to increasing the EC's role in regulation. As a consequence it is likely to have a serious impact on UK business costs, although the extent of this is hard to gauge as it will depend on just how far this programme is pursued in practice.

We examine the effects on the UK in low- and high-impact scenarios for the three main aspects of minimum wages, union powers, and worker rights. The effects, which all come about because employer costs are raised, are summarised in Table 8.4 (all of them derived from the Liverpool Model of the UK).

It can be seen that these are dangerously large costs, even in the least-cost scenario with its cost at 9% of GDP and 10% on unemployment. The high-cost scenario is obviously so damaging, at 20% of GDP and an unquantifiable rise in unemployment, that we must assume any UK government would prevent it occurring even if only by invoking the Luxembourg Compromise with its implicit threat of leaving the EC.

I. A minimum wage

	A minimum wage of:	
	50% of male median	*66% of average*
Long term effects on:		
output (%)	-1.5	-5
unemployment		
(% of labour force)	+1.8	+5.0
million	+0.5	+1.4

II. Union power simulation

	Union power rises:	
	to mid-80s level	*to 1980 level*
Long term effects on:		
output (%)	-3	-5.8
unemployment		
(% of labour force)	+1.3	+4.3
million	+0.4	+1.3

III. Rise in the social cost burden on employers

	Social cost rise:	
	by 20% of wages	*by 60% of wages*
Long term effects on:		
output (%)	-4.4	-11
unemployment		
(% of labour force)	+3.0	+18
million	+0.9	+5.5

IV. Combination of minimum wages, union power rise, and higher social cost burdens on employers (combination of I–III)

	Least	*Most*
Long term effects on:		
output (%)	-9	-20
unemployment		
(% of labour force)	+10	(extreme value)
million	+3	(extreme value)

Table 8.4 The effects on UK output and unemployment of social measures

Non-agricultural trade and investment

There are three main questions to ask about these central arrangements of the EC that are summarised as 'The Single Market'. The first is: does it pay the UK to belong to them? The second is: does it pay the EC for the UK to belong? And the third is: does it pay the EC to have these arrangements at all; and, if not, how long are they likely to last?

Going into a little more detail, by the 'arrangements' I mean the common external tariff and non-tariff barriers against the rest of the world (including anti-dumping actions or threats and voluntary export restraint), combined with their intended absence inside the EC under the Single Market. While the tariff is generally low, the non-tariff barriers are high for a wide range of sensitive products, especially consumer durables such as electronics and cars, where 'sensitive' means 'vulnerable to world competition'. Capital goods – of which Germany is a large exporter – are generally less protected because they are (as yet) less threatened by competition.

Studies of EC prices for consumer durables are few, but the UK's Monopolies and Mergers Commission found in its Cars Report that car prices were some 40% higher in the EC on average than in Japan, whose industry is the world's most competitive, and some 20% higher than in the US. And in its report on compact discs it found from a number of surveys that on a wide range of goods and services, including CDs, EC prices were some 30% higher than US prices. In our calculations, we take this effect of protection to be around 30% on average.

We are now faced with a paradox. The UK is a low-cost producer relative to mainland Europe; it is therefore attracting large amounts of inward investment from those who wish to produce behind Europe's protective wall. The UK in Europe is like the Southern states within the US, which have captured large segments of US car production, for example.

It therefore pays the UK in a narrow sense for Europe to be protective while it pursues low costs – a flexible labour market, low regulation and no Social Chapter. One theoretically possible outcome of this would be for these protected industries to migrate from the mainland to the UK, until they had either disappeared from the continent, or had used up all available UK labour and driven wage costs in the UK up to those in the EC mainland.

However, I argue that the process will be stopped by political forces inside the EC well before either of these events occurs. In the case where the UK stays outside the Maastricht Social Chapter, the tolerance for our dissent will continue up to the point at which we displace imports into the EC only; thus, for example, on cars, the EC agreement is that Japanese UK output of transplants will be offset by a contraction of imports from Japan. In the case where we join the Social Chapter, the process would more likely be stopped by a rise in our costs – of this more below. I shall assume for now that the UK will not join, or will do so in a highly qualified way – as seems to be the intention of the New Labour government.

My team's calculations then are that the UK consumer durables industry would expand by some 50 billion Ecu, or £40 billion – the extent of EC imports – and would generate £30 billion of net UK exports. The benefit of this to the UK is estimated to be 30% of this, that is £9 billion. This benefit could be more if a significant number if those so employed would have otherwise been unemployed. The order of magnitude of this benefit is astonishingly similar to the cost of the CAP.

If we now ask whether this situation is of net value to the EC, we find that the answer depends crucially on whether or not the EC retains the Social Chapter policies now in being. If it does, then protection enables it to keep people in jobs in these consumer durable industries who otherwise would be unemployed; this is probably a net benefit. Meanwhile, provided the UK output is at the expense of imports, as I have assumed, the EC mainland is undamaged by UK production and their imports merely switch from Japan, etc, to the UK. However if the EC realises the damage done to its job prospects by the Social Chapter policies and duly abolishes them, it then will have no need of protection to maintain jobs. The large cost to consumers of protectionism will then lead it to abolish that too – a policy we could hardly oppose with any logic. That abolition would in turn eliminate our gain from the EC in non-agricultural trade.

Hence the EC's gain rests on unstable foundations. I have argued that continental Europe will wish to keep protection in being as long as the Social Chapter continues; but that Chapter itself is deeply damaging to the EC members on the continent because of its job destructiveness. Sooner or later it must crumble. However, continental politics is on the whole consensual, and with unions holding great power there, the crumbling will at most be gradual. We can see from the extraordinary longevity of the CAP that strong pressure groups can keep costly arrangements in being for decades in the EC. The Charter's cost is an order of magnitude greater, and through unemployment more socially visible; the Charter should therefore be more at risk. It would be surprising if it did not last for at least another decade, taking it well into the next century, but I should be surprised if it lasted much longer than that.

What this means from the UK's viewpoint is that the excess returns from the industries that we are now building up will not last for too long. By around 2005 or so, we should reckon on prices dropping to world levels. Nevertheless, provided our labour market remains flexible, the future of UK production should remain secure – providing a normal if not excessive profit rate. The supply of unskilled labour will not have dried up by then: it will take several generations of changed incentives and more intense education to achieve that. Wage rates will therefore need to be low and tax burdens light to ensure that the continued employment of workers is competitive. But the UK approach of topping up poor households' income while allowing wages to be competitive should ensure this is viable.

THE CURRENT BALANCE SHEET – THUS FAR AND NO FURTHER

We have examined the key economic elements of our relationship with the EC. In sum, we have found the CAP is costly (to the tune of £10 billion a year), the single currency and the Social Chapter would be highly costly were we to join, and the non-agricultural trade arrangements may in due course generate a net gain to us of more than £9 billion a year as a result of enabling us to build up our consumer durables industry (notably cars) within the EC protective wall.

It follows that, if we leave aside for the moment EMU and the Social Chapter, the issue of whether there is a net long-term (discounted) gain or loss to the UK depends on how long the CAP and the protective wall each last. If we made the illustrative assumption that they both disappeared by 2010, we could lose somewhat on balance since the gain from the non-agricultural side would only recently have come in by then, while the CAP will have cost us more than a decade of full operation. However, any assumption is speculative, since it involves assessing the power of the various pressure groups involved and the ability of politicians and public opinion to assert the general EC interest – a task well beyond the scope of this book.

We have also seen that from the continental viewpoint it does not damage those economies to let the UK take advantage of these trade arrangements, provided it is limited to import-replacement as I have assumed. Hence their pressure on the UK to join the Social Chapter will be more precautionary than intense as long as this limit is observed, which it effectively is through the sensitivity of inward investors. Of course, the continent gains from our contributions to the CAP.

However, this situation is inherently unstable, since on the agricultural side the cost for us depends on protection and on the non-agricultural side the benefit for us depends on protection plus the Social Chapter. These policies are damaging to the EC and we should probably assume that eventually both will be eliminated. Whether CAP or industrial protection goes first clearly has a bearing on our net gain from our overall EC relationships.

Finally, I must reiterate that the assessment up to this point depends crucially on the proviso that the UK will not join either the Social Chapter or EMU, both of which would swing the balance of economic advantage in our EC membership strongly to the negative. Were the UK to join both, it would not merely be carrying the £10 billion CAP burden but would also lose much of the gain on the industrial trade side because the necessary inward investment would be deterred. It would also suffer from the direct added costs of EMU and the Social Chapter documented earlier.

Hence the present situation is extraordinarily fragile. The status quo is a sort of equilibrium: all three UK parties support EC membership, and even Eurosceptic Conservatives can justify it on the grounds that there is a rough balance of advantage, as discussed in this paper. But New Labour has (in its rhetoric at least) implied that it would like to go further. It has decided, but in the spirit of strict limitation, to join the Social Chapter; and it has now made clear its intention in the longer term to join 'a successful EMU', provided it is in the UK's economic interests and is agreed to in a referendum. The Liberal Democrats have, of course, for a long time committed themselves to both without reservation.

If Labour commits itself finally to EMU and fails to stem the Social Chapter, Conservatives would be bound to reconsider the balance of advantage, which I have argued would swing strongly negative – indeed Conservative policy has been close to this position in its strenuous opposition to the Social Chapter and now in its decision (in opposition) to stay out of EMU for at least two Parliaments. One could thus see a situation in these circumstances where the Conservatives could swing to campaigning for exit from the EC. However, Labour has recently shown increasing signs of caution, as the economic case against both the Social Chapter and EMU has become clearer to it. It may well be, therefore, that the UK's economic interests, as identified here, will be pursued fairly stubbornly by any likely future government.

LONGER-TERM ISSUES: THE LIKELY NEED FOR RENEGOTIATION

We have looked at the EC balance sheet in a deliberately narrow way, computing costs and benefits of each element over a fairly limited time horizon. However, we must now look at the longer term issues that this calculation has raised.

The UK has set out to liberalise its economy and it is from this policy that all its hopes of future growth stem, just as has its relatively good performance in conditions of sharply increasing competition for the old OECD economies. It may be that the rest of the EC will come to liberalise itself (in both the agricultural and industrial spheres) and will not attempt to compel the UK into restrictive policies. If so, the UK can continue within the EC with some balance of advantage – or at least no serious negative balance. True, the particularly favourable trade situation will disappear, but by then so too will the burdens of the CAP, as reforms of it gradually take a grip.

Should the EC decide, however, to remain a regulated and protected area, the UK can continue within that structure only if it manages to resist any EC attempt to regulate it similarly. Indeed, this basis does give the UK in a narrow way the substantial gains on inward investment discussed above. Nevertheless, it is not in the UK's broader long-term interest that the EC should continue in this manner. The EC is the UK's major market; for the EC to stagnate will be a problem for the UK too, at least until excess UK production can be directed elsewhere.

But there is a more fundamental problem. The continued difference of regulative approach between the UK and the rest of the EC will be a cause of permanent tension, which will have to be resolved. The UK's position would be that of a free rider on our partners' folly, hardly a tenable long-run policy although I have argued that it could survive for a reasonable while.

The reason such a situation could not survive indefinitely is that the firms locating in the low-cost UK cannot be expected to remain indefinitely sensitive to the concerns of the UK's EC partners. I argued earlier that these firms would exercise restraint in the medium term by restricting their production to the extent of existing imports into the EC, and in this way they would not displace continental producers. However, once these transplant industries were established, with fully conceded rights of access to the full Single Market, such considerations would be overcome by the competitive logic of the companies involved.

It follows that the UK's EC partners will not be happy to allow this possibility to continue for long. Until 2000 and perhaps a few years beyond, existing understandings may hold up. But beyond that, the continental members of the EC will wish to prevent possible competitive expansion. One means available to them is to inflict on the UK the same social burdens as they carry, thereby closing off the profitability of expansion.

The UK could resist this, but should such a clash occur, the outcome would be hard to predict. On the one hand, no treaty between independent nations can withstand a wholesale clash of economic interests, where the closure of swathes of continental EC production would be a possibility. On the other hand, to abandon the Treaty would create difficulties for all sides: for the UK, given that its industrial base would have been built up relying on the EC market; and for the continent, as it would lose UK contributions in other areas such as the CAP. It could well be that the UK, having become so dependent on the EC market, would be forced to agree to some compromise on regulation as the price of retaining its EC membership: that in turn could be highly damaging to the UK economy as a whole.

What this suggests is that, should Europe continue in a 'Fortress Europe' approach, the UK should strictly limit further inward investment designed for the European market. It should then stick rigidly to the existing Treaty and agree no further substantive changes. It could nevertheless indicate that it was willing to permit other EC countries to go further if they wished, but only on condition that the UK was interfered with no further by extensions to the law created by the European Court or the European Parliament.

However, should other members not be willing to proceed in this way and should the Court and Parliament continue to harass the UK with regulatory extension, then it should itself withdraw co-operation and veto any changes in the current Treaty. The UK should then propose that it would be willing to renegotiate its position in a trade and market Treaty, preserving the status quo (in trade access, the Single Market and related matters), and then leave the EC.

To conclude my argument, it is that in the longer term the UK must work for a free market in Europe; if it fails, it will then be forced to contemplate a future outside Europe, as a free-market trading nation. What we have seen above is that this option holds no terrors; there is no balance of advantage to speak of for or against the UK's European membership. It makes sense to try and make a success of that membership because so much has been invested in it, but if in spite of all efforts the UK's EC partners will not tolerate the conditions for that success, then the UK can walk away in confidence.

To put it in a nutshell, the UK's economic success as a nation depends on its newly revived free-market structure. If the EC in practice can tolerate this, then well and good; if it cannot, leaving the EC must be seriously contemplated. The price of staying in would be too high, namely the country's very economic viability.

CONCLUSIONS

This chapter began with a discussion of the difficulties that the continent of Europe is now having in dealing with the global economy because of its attachment to a stakeholder economy whereby there is substantial state-provided social insurance. Unemployment has soared there, taxes have risen, and growth has slowed. At the same time, these countries have actively been seeking closer integration, and by implication the imposition of a similar stakeholder system throughout the resulting European Union.

This poses a serious dilemma for countries that have a relatively free-market capitalist system. Such countries include the UK, and some of the countries due to join the EU, such as the Czech Republic, Poland and Turkey. Some other countries within the existing EU, such as Spain, Portugal and Ireland, where regulation either has already (as in the first two) or could (as in Ireland) do great damage, are beginning to realise they too face the dilemma – although so far perhaps the thud of EC cheques into their public accounts may have dulled the perception of this long-term threat. Finally, of course, the protagonists of both stakeholding and integration – Germany, France and Italy – may even themselves begin to change in order to lessen the self-inflicted damage they are suffering.

The logic of this book – that societies in the end find sustainable methods of organisation – points to these difficulties being resolved by a wholesale shift on the continent of Europe and in the EC towards free-market capitalism. At present, this seems 'politically impossible', much as the reform of the Soviet Union once did; the lessons of history are that the politically impossible yields in the end to the economically sensible.

This chapter has been entirely economic in its focus. Yet some, both on the continent and in the UK (notably in the Foreign and Commonwealth Office), argue that the economics is secondary to the political imperative for European unification, on the grounds that in a world of superpowers Europe too should be one. Such people are impatient, even contemptuous, of the 'sophists and calculators' who, like I do here, deploy economic arguments against their project. For them all these economic arrangements, such as social standardisation and a single currency, with the huge co-ordination of policies that that will make necessary, are part of the (backdoor) process by which a single state will be formed. The incidental costs to parts of the Union like the UK are simply irrelevant to them. Let me end, therefore, by addressing this political argument of theirs.

There are two issues I would raise with this argument. The first is: suppose we accept there must be threats of countervailing force against superpowers that might threaten the security of a small to middle-sized nation. Does it follow that such a nation must merge itself, merely for security reasons, within a superstate? Surely not: as we argued in Chapter 2, there are alliances on offer between nations that share an identity of interest in resisting such aggression. The UK belongs to NATO for this purpose, apparently to excellent effect.

The second issue involves a questioning of the idea that superpowers or superstates will, even can, launch such threats in the modern, interdependent world of increasingly democratic peoples. Britain is never likely again to wield the huge power (in relative terms) that it did in the nineteenth century. Yet is this a loss today? By analogy from Chapter 2, this country can afford to maintain small, efficient armed forces to deal with localised threats to its citizens and close allies, and it in fact does so by contribution to a nuclear club (run by the United States) and the NATO alliance. These are the planks of our security policy.

And so, if one asks whether or not these arrangements can deal with all conceivable threats, notably those from superpowers themselves, one is in something of a quandary. What might these be? Might the US threaten to annex the UK as its next state? The idea is absurd, but it would certainly cause NATO to react, or more likely collapse with consequences unpalatable to the US itself. Might China do the same? Well, no doubt then NATO and that nuclear club would take action; and then there is the UN, the international community that today is used by the US and NATO as a legitimate route by which to maintain a peaceful world.

But the point about all these questions is that they seem both stupid and irrelevant. The main aim of democratic humanity (even where it is not yet quite democratic) is to improve its lot by the most reliable means to that end, which is trade and investment. What scope is there in today's world for a foolish Kaiser, an idiot Tsar, or a megalomaniac Napoleon? None, of course.

In the light of this analysis, the idea that any self-governing people should feel compelled to submit themselves to government by a foreign power, however 'democratically pooled' with many foreigners that power may be, seems old-fashioned in the worst sense: that is, it is adapted to a world that has truly disappeared. Must Canada become part of the USA? Must Korea pool itself with Japan? To ask is to be ridiculed. If such political ideas appeal to Frenchmen or Spaniards, so be it, for it is their democratic choice – although it must be asked, for how long? The ideas themselves, though, appear to have no political logic, besides posing the economic problems to which we have devoted so much space.

References

DSS (Department of Social Security) (1997) *Households Below Average Income: a Statistical Analysis 1979–1994/5*, The Stationery Office, Norwich, p. 89.

Goodman, A. and Webb, S. (1995) *The Distribution of UK Household Expenditure 1979–1992*, Institute for Fiscal Studies, London, p. 25.

Green, D. (1998) *Benefit Dependency – How Welfare Undermines Independence*, Institute of Economic Affairs, London.

Hayek, F. A. (1988) *The Fatal Conceit – The Errors of Socialism*, collected works of F.A. Hayek (Vol.1), ed. W.W. Bartley III, Routledge, London and New York.

Hegel, G.W.F. (1821) *The Philosophy of Right.*

Kant, I. (1788) *The Critique of Practical Reason.*

Minford, P. (1996) 'Britain and Europe: the Balance Sheet (with a Japanese View by Noriko Hama)', *European Business Review*, autumn 1996.

Pryke, R. (1995) *Taking the Measure of Poverty – a Critique of Low-income Statistics: Alternative Estimates and Policy Implications*, Research Monograph No. 5, Institute of Economic Affairs, London.

Roseveare, D. Leibfritz, W., Fore, D. and Wurzel, E. (1996) *Ageing Populations, Pension Systems and Government Budgets: Simulations for 20 OECD Countries*, OECD Economics Department Working Paper No. 168, OECD, Paris.

Rowntree, B.S. (1901) *Poverty : a Study of Town Life*, Macmillan, London.

Smith, Adam (1831) *Correspondence with Sir John Sinclair.*

CHAPTER NINE

Western capitalism: can its achievements be built on?

WHAT WE HAVE seen so far is clear evidence of the success of economies where incentives have been given the most rein, in line with the general theory that incentives promote both static and dynamic efficiency. We have looked at summary measures of economic freedom and seen how they are highly correlated with economic growth. We have examined the case of the UK, which came close to catastrophe after three decades of socialism and has since restored monetary stability and economic dynamism by its reforms over the past two decades. Then we looked more broadly at the world economy since 1970 and saw how inflation has been curbed if not actually eliminated; growth has spread from developed to emerging market economies, a key factor in which has been the opening of their capital markets to foreigners and the pursuit of free-market policies internally. Finally, we have seen how in the OECD there has been a split between countries that allowed wages to be flexibly determined by market forces and those that propped up unskilled wages through social intervention, the latter group having seen much higher unemployment and a consequent reduction in growth.

Is there more that can be done to improve the workings of Anglo-Saxon capitalism, which we have identified as a better model than Rhenish or stakeholder capitalism? It so happens that the countries of South-East Asia that have led the emerging market group in the past two decades have an interesting thing in common: they have virtually no welfare state and – in its absence – exceptionally low levels of taxation, with people being encouraged (compelled, in some cases) to save substantially to provide for themselves for life's contingencies. This apparent connection between their growth performance and such low tax rates, made possible by their lack of state welfare provision, is exactly what would be predicted by our theory. I shall argue in the rest of this chapter that countries pursuing Anglo-Saxon capitalism can do much better by mimicking this aspect of Far-Eastern economies, so making possible a quantum leap downwards in their tax burdens.

The welfare state is, one might say, the last frontier of privatisation, discovered to be such a useful device across the OECD in the past twenty years. Welfare is immensely costly in tax burden; for example, in the UK it increases taxes by some 25% of GDP. Yet after many years of accretion under the pressure of politically left-leaning thinkers and a variety of pressure groups – mainly recipient and professional dispensing groups – it has proved to be most resistant to change. I shall focus the following discussion on the UK, partly because I am most familiar with it and partly because, in the course of a supremely radical programme by the UK's historical standards, the welfare state has so far been barely touched. Hence consideration of the UK's position – a country where reform has been achieved in so many other areas – may tell us why it is so difficult to make progress there.

CAPITALISM – THE FINAL FRONTIER: REPLACING THE WELFARE STATE

The idea of the welfare state, as originally set out by Beveridge, was to underpin people's lives with a safety net so that they should feel secure while pursuing their normal activities with undiminished enthusiasm and effort. The safety net was rigged up to provide for people's needs in a civilised modern society. So, for example, if a person became unemployed they obtained unemployment benefit topped up by income support to provide for necessary food, transport and so on. On top of this, the state would pay for education, health care, pension entitlement, rent and rates (now council tax), and a raft of other costs to which income support was a 'passport' (including school meals, milk, dental and optical care, and medical prescriptions). In effect, a person could live, bring up a family, and retire until death, entirely at state expense.

This cradle-to-grave concept of security was intended only to be used in emergency. It was expected that people would normally work, make their own pension contributions (to the state and to private additional occupational pension schemes), pay their own rent or own their own home, and lead healthy lives that would put only limited burdens on the NHS. However, this has not proved to be the case. The benefits system and its use have grown like Topsy. The logic has usually been impeccable. It was noted fairly early on that incomes in work could fall short of incomes on benefit and state support out of work. So benefits began to be paid to supplement low work income of households: nowadays 'family credit' (a general supplement for families with children) and housing benefit (a supplement to help with housing costs) are the two main types.

Categories of people in need widened as family breakdown increasingly occurred and also as unemployment rose to unexpectedly high levels. These included special benefits for children, for single parents, and for those 'disabled'. As more and more people fell into these benefit categories, local authorities, charitable trusts, bus companies and others followed the central government's lead and gave special discounts for those on benefits.

The result is that the Department of Social Security in 1997 has spent £90 billion (11% of GDP) on benefits, just under half of which is the basic state pension and support for the retired. Apart from ten million pensioners, another five million households (containing 11 million people) receive one or more of these means-tested benefits. This does not count the cost of all the discounts or benefits to which these basic benefits are a passport; nor does it include the cost of education and the NHS, nor child benefit, which is a lump-sum amount per child that replaced children's tax allowances.

The main consequences of these benefit transfers are twofold. First, they badly undermine recipients' incentives to work because necessary means-testing implies that the implicit marginal tax rate on extra earnings is extremely high in most cases – usually between 70% and 90%. Secondly, because the benefits have to be paid for out of general taxation and so raise marginal tax rates, they undermine ordinary taxpayers' incentives to work as well. When I say 'incentive to work', I include in that the incentive to innovate since any reward to innovatory efforts is taxed at the same marginal rates.

There are further consequences. First, to the extent that the state spends money on behalf of the consumer, there is a loss of incentive to get value for money – misallocation of resources in use. Secondly, for households on benefits whose notional pension contributions are partly or totally being paid by the state, there is no incentive to save in the form of extra National Insurance contributions; these will produce no extra pension and so are merely part of the tax disincentive. Thirdly, for those whose contributions records will entitle them only to a basic pension that would then be topped up by state support, there is a positive disincentive to save for a further (private) pension because this would remove their entitlement to that income support.

We have here a mechanism to reduce both static and dynamic efficiency on a large scale. It is controversial to maintain that it has also changed social and family behaviour – for example, increasing crime because work pays less, or the number of single parents because of the special benefits attracted by single parenthood. However, it would be surprising if it had had no effect in these directions. What is by now quite incontrovertible is that it contributes to unemployment (because the extra reward to work is low for low-wage workers – the 'unemployment trap') and contributes to lack of skill (because the extra reward to better pay from greater skill is low among such workers – the 'poverty trap').

An increasingly important twist in this argument is the effect on work by partners of unemployed people and on part-time work. This twist, as well as the general picture, is shown on the three-dimensional figure that follows (Figure 9.1) for a typical family/household, based on data and calculations of Paul Ashton in my Research Group. The figure shows total weekly income of the household on the vertical axis (the height of the mountain, so to speak) while the two horizontal axes show the hours worked and the wages at which they are worked by a household member. The flat plateau-like stretches on the figure are the areas of very low incentive, and they particularly affect part-time work because the household's benefits are means-tested stringently as extra income comes in. Similar figures can be drawn for other households.

A natural and widespread reaction to such figures is to suggest more liberal means-tests. But it is plain from inspection that if more liberal means-testing of one segment is introduced, the cost of benefits for that segment are increased (the height of the mountain is raised); then if incentives above that are not to be damaged, more liberal means-testing must be introduced there too. Proceeding in this manner up the income scale, more and more people are brought into the benefit net, so worsening their incentives, raising the cost of the whole benefit system, and increasing marginal tax rates for the general taxpayer. In its most extreme version, the suggestion of greater means-test liberality takes the form of the 'basic income' proposal whereby you give benefits at a flat rate regardless of income. This has a very large cost to the general taxpayer: Paul Ashton, has estimated that to give every one in the

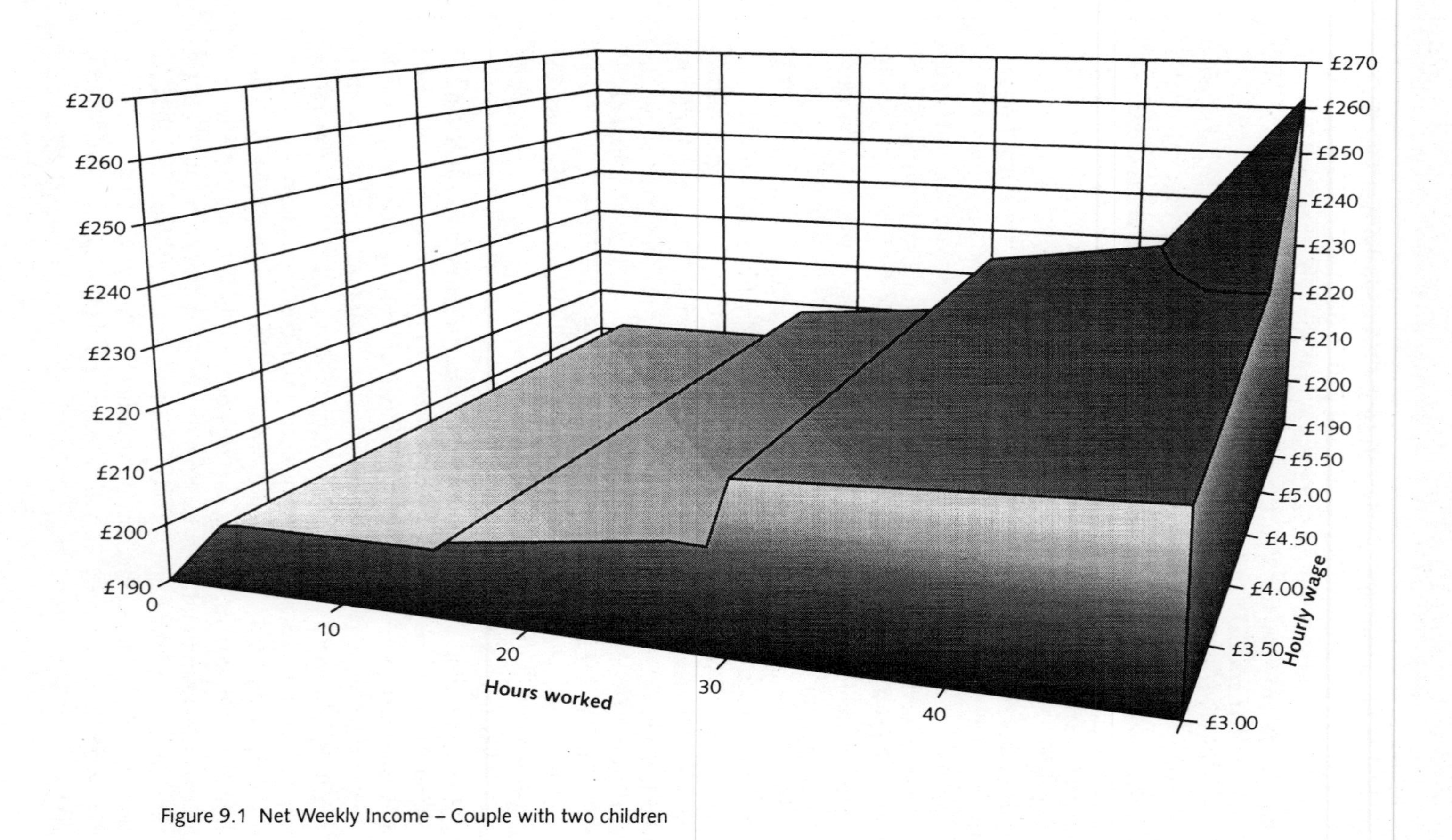

Figure 9.1 Net Weekly Income – Couple with two children

population a basic income (at current income support and housing benefit scales, but of course without means-tested withdrawal) would cost some £80 billion in 1998, making necessary a rise in standard and higher income tax rates of some 25 pence in the pound: in round terms, a standard rate of 50% and an upper rate of 65%.

We find, therefore, that once a system like this is in place, there is no way of improving incentives for people at one point in the system without worsening them for people at another point in it. One can tinker around to obtain an optimal shape according to some criterion (such as loss of efficiency); and I argued in 1990 that the reforms instituted then by (now Sir) Norman Fowler were probably well designed from that viewpoint. But however well tuned, the system creates a severe drag on efficiency.

In passing we should note that efficiency loss is not strictly the same as loss of work effort as such; when income is transferred between people, some may work harder and others less hard as their income changes; this is not an alteration in efficiency so much as the effect of changing income distribution and the consequent expression of personal tastes for work and leisure, on which economists cannot offer comment. Neither the distribution of income nor people's tastes for leisure are matters of efficiency.

Having struggled for many years to come up with a way of making this efficiency loss tolerable (with no success), I recently began to study more seriously the structure of alternative and radically different systems. It is my view that those who speak of 'integrating' the tax and benefits systems (in the manner of the assignment given by Tony Blair to Martin Taylor of Barclays Bank plc) delude themselves if they think that that approach is a solution to the problem. The two systems are designed for different purposes and, in fact, each allows for the other's operation as effectively as is possible. The benefits system deals with the poor, while the tax system deals with the average and the rich. In the same vein, the earned income tax rebate if introduced at US rates would merely be a dilution of in-work benefit provision, amounting to a worsening of the unemployment trap in order to improve the poverty trap – yet another example of the principle noted above.

The alternative system that is of most interest is that widely in use in the Far East. There, people are expected – sometimes compelled – to save large amounts during their working lives to provide for themselves during life's emergencies. Their wider families may also be involved as part of the process, but increasingly (as families there too become more 'nuclear') the emphasis is on the individual household providing through savings or insurance. This approach is highly promising because it removes the anchor point of the benefit system – the income provided for no work – and so enables incentives to be restored up the income scale. In terms of our 'net income mountain' metaphor, this can be seen as getting the household to start climbing from sea level instead of being helicoptered up to the unemployment benefit level. Climbing from sea level restores proper slopes (more upward progress from given amounts of – horizontal – effort in work) and removes the plateaux of high marginal tax rates. It is this approach we explore in the suggestions that follow. In the rest of this chapter I sketch out a proposal to replace welfare with self-provision through private saving and insurance backed up by state loans and a supporting system akin to the Elizabethan poor law – ie, a system that is intrusive in its monitoring of those who really cannot or will not cope.

A MODEL OF A NEW WELFARE SOCIETY – THE BASIC CONCEPT IN A RHETORICAL OVERVIEW

Imagine a new Prime Minister addressing the nation and attempting to attract its support for such a bold new approach to welfare. The following might be a first draft of his speech:

> 'The average household should pay for its own health and education needs. There are three advantages in this. First, those who pay also control, and have the power to get value for their money; when the state is the intermediate buyer, it is less sensitive to household needs. So the pattern of spending is less effective.
>
> Secondly, the amount of resources devoted to health care and education are no longer held back by arbitrary Treasury cuts. This is an inevitable effect of state buying because there is a divorce between the buyer (the department of state) and the financier (the Treasury, representing the taxpayer). The total spending is therefore not properly sensitive to household needs.
>
> Thirdly, and least appreciated, the marginal tax rate on the household can come down, so increasing incentives to work and take entrepreneurial risks. This applies even if there is no efficiency gain from the last two reasons: before, the household paid through a higher (marginal) rate of tax; now, the household will pay 'up front' through a school fees or health insurance policy, say, and the household tax rate is lower. The household's living standard is, of course, no higher since it now also has to pay the insurance premiums, but crucially its incentives are transformed: if, for example, the standard rate of tax came down from 20 to 10 pence, the household would now keep 90% of every extra pound earned.

How would people pay their own way? In education it is straightforward: everyone must go to an authorised school; and everyone must pay, either out of income, or savings, or borrowings. In health care it is more complicated. Everyone must insure in a minimum-cover policy, which would cover normal medical problems, going to the doctor, having a baby, the normal minor illnesses of old age, and non-emergency operations. And the state through National Insurance would, as now, cover emergency services and very serious conditions and operations. The result would be that our doctors and trust hospitals would mainly be dealing with privately-insured patients with a small element of state-insured activity.

Next, benefits. We want to see everyone standing on their own two feet. This is a rich country and it is absurd that we count people as poor and deserving of state help when in many other countries they would be regarded as immensely fortunate.

There must nevertheless be a safety net. By that, we mean that no one in our society should starve or be homeless if in spite of their very best efforts they cannot make ends meet. But in the first place, they should have made sufficient provision through their own savings and insurance. If that proves inadequate, we propose that the state will offer them loans in place of benefits, loans that they will be under the strongest pressure to pay back over the long term.

We have a huge bureaucracy administering the many benefits that the state provides: housing, unemployment, family credit, income support, and many others – not to speak of social work and community care workers. We propose to reorganise the system further. All those currently involved in benefit administration and social work will be placed in a single Agency, which will be made independent and given a budget for loans based on projected needs – 'privatisation' effectively, but subject to ultimate political direction (like the Child Support Agency).

The Agency will make local arrangements for keeping in touch with loan recipients and their circumstances – through a local charity, for example, or the local authority, or any other suitable body, but each loan recipient should have only one contact body to deal with. Recipients will have a file that will be kept by this body only. The body will negotiate with them a discretionary amount of repayment for each year, and draw up a contract under which they will undertake these repayments. We are, in short, proposing a return to the sensible system the Elizabethans had, but made manageable today by the computer. The government would set the maximum benefit rates against which loan entitlement would be assessed, and would operate an appeals system that would allow it to police the Agency's operations.

What of these benefit rates? We will review all the rates – which will now be maxima for loans – from the viewpoint of need, as defined. And we shall, of course, take into account the new costs of school fees and medical insurance.

This is a revolution in welfare; and many have planned on the basis of the old system. That is why there will be a reasonable system of transition as we implement these vital reforms. Older generations will retain their rights – call this 'grandfather rights' – much as they did when we abolished rent control. For those currently in the benefits system, we plan to cut benefits only at a rate that is at least compensated for by tax cuts or other fiscal changes for all groups – we shall ensure, in other words, that there are no significant losers in the short term.

The transitional arrangements will imply that nobody on low earnings is worse off than now over their lifetime. That has been, and will continue to be, a constraint on the parameters of the new system. We believe that once new generations are working with the new set-up, they too, being fully prepared for it, will be better off over their lifetimes than present generations on welfare.

Some people will nevertheless fail to meet the requirements of this new system, both in transition and once it is fully installed. There are always those who cannot, or perhaps sometimes will not, manage. For these people, there will be no immediate repayment of loans, but instead the Agency will operate a tough but understanding regime. Such people will have access to support under the present basic 'safety net' of benefit rates, but they will be required to co-operate in a plan for loan recovery, using all the information that they can provide, and if they do not so co-operate, they will be subject to normal judicial penalties.

We know that once we have a safety net – and we must – we cannot avoid an unemployment and poverty trap, if the safety net is made generally available with limited tests of need. That is why we are privatising benefits. Once upon a time, these benefits were the responsibility of families – extended families mostly. Families are notoriously vigilant in checking on – monitoring – their dependants, and we have first-hand experience of that from our own children, cousins and nephews. The state has been unable to do the same job of monitoring while paying the same sorts of benefits. But today's technology makes it possible to decentralise and privatise this task, so that the state too can operate a safety net built upon a loans system.

Finally, we propose to take the welfare element out of pensions. Everyone should provide for their own old age; the existing system is a combination of Pay-As-You-Go for the majority and welfare transfers to those who do not contribute and have no incentive to save for themselves. We will turn it into a funded system, by allowing all to 'opt out' much as has already been done with the State Earnings Related Pension Scheme. At the same time, the basic pension for those who do not contribute will be withdrawn for new generations of workers; they will thus have to contribute, if necessary by drawing a loan to do so from the Agency.

Putting this all together enables us to cut tax rates sharply, so underpinning the improved incentives for the poorest members of society with generally improved incentives right up the income scale.'

I now follow this rhetorical overview with brief sketches of how health, education and pensions might be 'privatised' without sacrificing the essential element of public good in present arrangements. The aim will be to insert regulation for this element, just as has been done in the privatisation of nationalised industries, for example. I then confront the issue on which this chapter mainly focuses, the substitution of loans for welfare grants.

PRIVATISING HEALTH AND EDUCATION

So far in the UK there have been substantial steps towards an 'internal market' in health care and education. By this is meant that the government pays the cost for those using state facilities, but that there is competition in the supply of services. In so far as the cost is paid as a voucher given to an individual, that individual can select the supply directly. But some parts of the service are not supplied in return for vouchers; instead, the individual has only limited scope to choose where to obtain the service, while the state's agents buy it 'in bulk' from competitive suppliers.

In health care, for example, hospitals bid for resources from Regional Health Authorities (RHAs), the disbursing agents of the state. Having received an allocation, these health authorities then offer services to the general public, who choose where to go but do not pay. Also, some general practitioners act as 'fundholders', with the facility of buying a service from a hospital on behalf of their patients, the cost of which the state then reimburses on a scale. Other GPs send patients to hospitals for the service that has already been bought by the RHAs. Finally, these hospitals are allowed to offer services to private patients, in competition with private hospitals. The latter too may, in principle, offer services to the state, either bidding to RHAs or competing for the patients of fundholder GPs.

This description reveals how patchy the competition between healthcare providers is in an internal market. There is supposedly a 'level playing field' but in practice the private suppliers in this market are greatly disadvantaged; their ex-public-sector rivals get public capital and other funding through block grants for which they, as private suppliers, are effectively ineligible. Furthermore, the signals within the internal market are confused by public-sector politics: a hospital trust bids for funds from an RHA, which itself is vulnerable to Parliamentary criticism if its clients, the trusts, do not perform 'because of lack of resources'.

An internal market may well be an improvement on no market. But it is far from a proper market with external customers in the normal sense. Therefore it seems that the internal market is a half-way house that satisfies no one. It undermines the private sector while still politicising the ex-public sector.

Within education, similar problems are to be found. Parents intending to use state schools have a voucher of sorts, in the sense that they can take their 'custom' to a number of local schools. However, in practice, the choice is limited and little different from the system of neighbourhood allocation previously in existence. There are those children who could obtain 'assisted places' at independent schools – scholarships in effect, and to be abolished by the New Labour government – but otherwise 'vouchers' are not spendable except in the state sector. Hence, while there is some competition between suppliers of education in the state sector, it is limited and fairly ineffectual. It is a sort of internal market but it falls far short of a true market.

So we find that these 'internal markets' with quasi-vouchers are not even moderate approximations to markets in the true sense. The UK government has been unwilling to operate a full voucher system, under which, in principle, an internal market would become a full market with merely a direct subsidy paid on the demand side. The reason for this unwillingness is financial: to give a voucher adequate to pay for NHS-style health care and state-provided education would be expensive, since those who would otherwise pay for themselves privately would receive it too. Furthermore, people would spend their vouchers wherever they wished, so that the state would lose control both of the amount supplied and of the costs in the (ex-) public sector. Such a situation causes further financial pressure since there will be agitation for the voucher to be raised to cover whatever then becomes defined through the market as an 'adequate' service.

Even if vouchers were to be provided, so that there could be a full market, they would be a transfer of the basic income variety, non-means-tested and implying a substantial rise in distortional taxation. They cannot therefore be considered as an ideal long-run solution.

I propose in this chapter, therefore, the idea that everyone should pay in full for health care (through insurance) and for education, although with some caveats. These would include: regulation (Minford, 1988/89) of medical insurers' pools of clients and policy cover in order to avoid well known problems of adverse selection and moral hazard; the state continuing to insure people 'socially' against very expensive and long-term conditions; and, in education, the free provision of schooling to children of parents who fall into the 'unable or unwilling' categories of welfare (mentioned above and discussed at length below). This list of caveats is not exhaustive but, rather, is intended to provide examples of the sort of supporting state action that would permit this total privatisation.

THE REFORM OF PENSIONS

While the ideas involved in privatising health and education are relatively familiar, the privatisation of pensions has only recently come to the fore in advanced countries, as a result of the funding crisis threatening their state pensions. We need therefore to devote more space to discussing the issues involved (what follows is based on Minford, 1997).

At present UK state pensions consist of a basic pension indexed to prices and an earnings-related portion known as the State Earnings-Related Pension Scheme (SERPS) and likely to be worth (by the early 2000s) 15% of average earnings. However, terms for contracting-out of SERPS (a reduction of National Insurance contributions of 1.8% for the employee and 3% for the employer) have induced many to opt out in favour of their own personal or occupational pension scheme; these opting-out terms have recently been enhanced by an additional age-related inducement designed to offset the attraction for people aged 40 or more to opt back into the SERPS. As a result, only 6.5 million people out of a potential 28 million are now covered by SERPS. Eleven million people contribute to an occupational pension scheme and 5.6 million to personal pension schemes.

This, of course, implies that some five million people of working age do not have occupational pensions, SERPS, or any personal scheme. For them, the state pension or other state old-age support ('income support') represents their only protection, apart from whatever other savings they may have. Income-support means tests, however, discourage such savings among those who do not have enough contributions to qualify for the state pension or for whom the state pension is inadequate to meet their state-determined needs. Groups relying heavily on the state pension are the low-paid and those with frequent job changes.

Groups relying heavily on income support are single women, the self-employed and those who have had frequent spells of unemployment – those who, in other words, have failed to reach a full contributions record or, in the case of the self-employed, who have failed to make adequate personal provision. Since income support is fractionally above the state pension, many with pensions qualify for income support, which therefore forms an integral part of the state pension system in its full sense.

This immediately makes it clear that there are two elements in the UK state pension system: the provision of a pension in return for NI contributions according to some scale of entitlements, and the provision of welfare quite unrelated to contributions. Because the relationship between contributions and entitlements even for full contributors is extremely loose, the element of welfare extends beyond income support to the basic state pension itself: contributions to the state pension are related to earnings whereas the basic state pension is a flat amount, so that there is redistribution from better-off to worse-off. Only the SERPS operates roughly like an occupational scheme with contributions related to earnings and pension related to final pay.

Objects of reform

Our concerns with this system are several.

First, the incentive to save may be reduced. If additional saving towards a state pension brings in no extra pension benefit, then the incentive to save is diminished. How much this is so depends on how far other savings, including private pensions (and including SERPS in this context), are in existence: if, for example, everyone had a private pension or SERPS in addition to their state pension, then the structure of the state pension is irrelevant to the (marginal) incentive to save. For those with their own private pensions, therefore, there will be no effect on the incentive to save from privatisation, but for those without, there may well be. Suppose a person has a poor contributions record, so that he or she will qualify for income support. By saving, that person will fail the means test and by contributing will get no extra support since he or she will still fail to qualify for a pension above the support level. Only those whose contributions have pushed their pension entitlement above the support level will have an incentive to save.

Secondly, the total rate of saving in the economy is also potentially affected by 'intergenerational transfers'. A Pay-As-You-Go (PAYG) pension scheme like the UK's collects NI contributions from the current generation of workers and pays pensions to the previous generation, now retired. A privatised ('funded') scheme makes no such transfers; every generation gets out what it paid in, grossed up by the real rate of interest. It may be that the current generation would save more if it did not expect to receive a pension from the next generation.

Whether it does so or not turns on whether it makes provision or not for the needs of the next generation in its bequests. If it does, it will take account of the extra taxation (NI contributions) its descendants will have to make and adjusts bequests upwards to offset this – hence saving just the same. This is the famous argument due to Ricardo (1817) and revived by Barro (1974) for why intergenerational tax or transfers might not affect total saving. Economists such as Martin Feldstein (1974, 1994) have argued that such bequest behaviour is far from widespread and that therefore shifting to funded pensions from PAYG pensions will raise private saving. They then go on to argue that this will benefit the economy by raising investment and so growth, an argument that requires that the higher savings rate lowers the real rate of interest even though the economy is tied to the world capital market by full scope for foreign inward and outward investment. We consider this channel of effects carefully later; but it must be distinguished from the previous argument about the marginal incentive to save, which is not directly linked to intergenerational transfers.

Thirdly, the incentive to work may be reduced. Compare a fully private pension system without welfare transfers with what we have. In a private pension system, extra work produces extra pay from which contributions may be paid to a pension voluntarily, with a full return to the payer – there is no taxation. Under the present state pension, those with full contributions who work extra time pay extra national insurance but obtain no extra basic pension. Those without full contributions who work extra similarly pay more but get no extra income support. (Notice that SERPS is not involved: when people work extra and pay more contributions, they do get more SERPS pension rights in the same way as in an occupational scheme.) So, overall, the present pension system levies a tax on work.

Finally, the state has to be kept solvent, with a necessary concern for the state's budget constraint. Clearly, abolishing the state's PAYG scheme would create a gaping hole in the public finances: current pensions would have to go on being paid while current contributions would stop. The resulting hole would have to be filled by raising taxes now or by borrowing (equivalent to raising them later, by a larger amount, so as to obtain the same present discounted value). The effect of such taxes would have to be factored in – both on the popular acceptability of the change and on its incentive effects. This concern is sometimes expressed as 'one generation having to pay twice' – for example with current taxes being raised, the current generation would not only have to pay contributions for a private pension but would also have to pay taxes towards the ongoing pensions of the previous generation.

Where we are

The NI Fund's future expenditures and payments have been recently projected by the OECD, in a comparative study of all major economies – Figure 8.3 in the last chapter sets them out. At current contribution rates and with pension rights as presently offered (as described earlier), the present discounted values of the two streams are roughly equal. This is the case in spite of a large projected increase in the population of state pension age over the next 50 years. The UK is in fact the only country in this position – for three reasons discussed in Chapter 5: it has indexed the basic pension to prices, it has reformed SERPS and it has raised women's retirement age from 60 to 65.

The UK government spends about £37 billion a year currently (ie, in the late 1990s) on old-age pensions and income support, equivalent to some 4.5% of GDP. The OECD's procedure was to project pension and support entitlements given the demographic picture, assuming current policy – ie, the indexing of the basic pension and income support to prices and the SERPS to earnings (but with entitlement falling gradually to 15%). Assuming other charges on the Fund are paid for out of general taxation, the Fund's NI contributions are then projected essentially as a constant fraction of GDP, since they are related to wages, which broadly grow at the same rate as GDP. As we saw in Chapter 8, a significant number of OECD countries face a pensions funding crisis.

SERPS contracting-out has lowered both contributions and expenditures in these projections for the UK. Since the contracting-out terms were determined in order to be just attractive for the large number of normal workers with scope for an occupational or personal scheme, we can roughly consider these streams to be the same in present value. Hence SERPS's partial privatisation has basically made no difference to the necessary NI contributions rate in the long term, ie, to present value – although in particular periods it will, because the NI Fund policy is to match current flows.

The implications of this situation are that those still remaining in SERPS are getting an occupational pension that would be more expensive to replicate for them in the private sector given their circumstances (such as variable, interrupted employment), while those paying full contributions for the basic pension are getting a very poor return, indeed a negative one in most cases in actuarial terms. In contrast, those paying less than full contributions and getting income support are getting a subsidised return.

The first step: contracting out of basic pension

We can immediately introduce our first step in privatisation: contracting-out terms from the basic pension. Because this pension is of modest value, the terms that need to be offered are small in cost. We calculate that for a man aged 20 on average earnings, the necessary NI rebate is only 1.5% of earnings (for a woman, with longer life expectancy, 1.8%). Since the pension is a fixed real amount, the contracted-out amount is also a flat amount, and consequently it varies in inverse proportion to earnings. It also rises with age, so that the closer one is to retirement the less does discounting work in one's favour – so for a 60-year-old man it would be 3.3% (4.0% for a woman).

We assume that the contracting-out in practice is calculated by the Government Actuary's Department (GAD) for each individual as a rebate on their NI contributions rate, given their earnings in the previous three years. To allow people flexibility of cash flow across good and bad years, the GAD would allow NI rebates to be carried over spells of unemployment and used up heavily in years of exceptional earnings. We assume too of course that, as with SERPS opting-out, the corresponding amounts are contributed to an approved private pension scheme.

Because these terms are calculated actuarially as the value that the basic pension gives the contributor, we thereby guarantee two important things. The state is indifferent to the contracting-out, the present value of the Fund being the same. So is the individual who contracts out, for the same reason. There is nevertheless an improvement for both parties, in that the individual's marginal tax rate on work is cut by the amount of the reduction in the NI rate; besides the marginal gain to the individual, the state gains from enhanced output and revenue.

Notice that all this implies there is no 'double burden' on one generation. Because the state rolls up debt, the present generation in effect pays for its private pensions out of reduced NI contributions, and its reduced future state pensions pay for the reduced contributions flow of the state.

This process will generate higher public debt until the flow of pensions being paid has caught up with the lowered flow of contributions. If 70% of contributors contracted out, my research team and I calculate that the loss of NI contributions would start at £12.5 billion pa, while the reduction of pensions would rise to £21.4 billion after 45 years. Extra debt would then level off at around £400 billion (around 16% of GDP at that time, assuming a 2.5% pa real growth of the economy). This debt would from then on automatically be rolled over and serviced by the Fund. It would in effect be 'paid for' without any rise in taxes: the existing 'taxes' (NI contributions) of everyone are sufficient to pay the interest and also to pay the ongoing pensions and income support of the 30% whose contributions are inadequate. The extra public debt poses no fiscal problem: it is secured on the reduced pension liabilities produced by the contracting-out. This can be seen formally in the fact that the present value of the Fund's debt tends to zero, because a constant debt tends in present value to zero as it is discounted further and further into the future. So we see that after contracting out, the same zero net present value of the Fund's net stream is maintained.

This arrangement parallels what has already been done with the SERPS. The difference is that when the 9.7 million (about two-thirds of those entitled) opted out of SERPS, the resulting roll-up in debt was not permitted because there was a roughly equivalent deficiency in the net present value of the state's pensions accounts. The opportunity was therefore taken to raise NI contributions.

Further steps on welfare

With this step out of the way, we have left in the state scheme:

1. those whom SERPS suits; and
2. those subsidised by the basic state pension and income-support system – those 'on welfare' in other words.

To induce group 1 to contract out would require a portable private sector product that is comparable in expense overheads to SERPS. There seems to be no reason for the competitive process between the state and the private sector for group 1's custom to be pre-empted. The state does have a first-mover advantage in dealing with mobile workers on low incomes – where contribution collectability and default are a problem – but very large private schemes could in principle also acquire them.

Group 2 poses a far more fundamental problem, of the same type as all welfare programmes. The aim is to abolish this welfare transfer altogether and put in place a system where these people, like everyone else, save for their own pension. In effect, these people would be contracted out of any NI contributions, and their entitlement to the basic pension would lapse totally. They would then have to contribute sufficient amounts to a private scheme to make up to the basic pension level. To do this, they would be eligible to borrow from the state's welfare loan fund.

I must stress that I see this sort of reform as requiring a very long time-scale, with a strong emphasis on changing the expectations and entitlements of new entrants into the labour market. It will also be greatly facilitated by the return of full employment, about which in an earlier chapter I have already explained my grounds for optimism: my estimate of the non-inflationary rate of unemployment is, it will be recalled, 2.5% (around three-quarters of a million workers).

A word before concluding on the framework of regulation and taxation. On regulation, I would opt for a minimal system, where people are required to save a minimum amount in approved pension and other long-term savings schemes. On the supplier side of the market, there is already substantial regulation which is gradually being refined, being excessive in some ways and inadequate in others. On taxation, I would opt uncontroversially for the existing system of full tax relief for all such approved schemes.

It is unfortunate in this context that in the July 1997 Budget Mr Brown abolished Advance Corporation Tax relief for pension funds; this has had the effect of creating a tax disincentive for private pensions and a relative tax advantage for SERPS. This change will need to be unwound one way or another in order to implement the ideas sketched out here – and apparently broadly supported by Mr Blair's pensions advisers. Otherwise there will be large-scale re-nationalisation of pensions as people contract back into SERPS, and there will be inadequate take-up of new private pensions.

In sum, therefore, what I propose for pensions is comprehensive opting-out immediately from the state pensions scheme in its entirety, with the consequent rise in public debt being absorbed against the fall in future unfunded liabilities. This is similar to Peter Lilley's Basic Pension-Plus proposal before the 1997 general election, except that his was confined to new entrants to the labour market. In my scheme, in the long term all would be compelled to fund their own pension but, as in the Lilley scheme, this would only apply to new entrants, so that the spread to all would be very gradual. There would be no further state help for new entrants except for those in the 'unable or unwilling' category that we will deal with next. Here again, then, I would abolish state welfare over time.

The new system to replace welfare

So far, I have discussed the elimination of welfare transfers while deferring detailed consideration of the key question of how need would be catered for. Until recently, it has been assumed in the West that some universal system of episodic benefits was the only practicable way of helping those in episodic need (unemployment, low wages with a large dependent family, unaffordable rents, and so on); however, so serious is now the evidence of incentive problems created by such universal systems, however finely tuned they are, that there is widespread willingness to consider radical alternatives. The incoming government of Tony Blair in the UK has used words indicating intentions to introduce these, but as yet no real flesh has been put on the bones.

In this section I set out a proposal of this sort. It borrows extensively from practices in Chile, Singapore and other Far-Eastern countries where there is no state welfare in the Western sense. It is similar to that of the Adam Smith Institute Fortune Account, set out in Butler and Pirie (1995); but unlike that proposal, it is accompanied by the proposition that everyone must pay for themselves, if necessary with loans – there is no benefit transfer to anyone.

The key assumption that underlies the proposal is that of full employment, by which I mean a flexible labour market generating jobs for all those who would normally wish to participate in work. This, as I have already argued, is now within reach in the UK. Even allowing for some minor effects of a minimum wage and slight strengthening of union powers (expectations for both of which are being managed downwards by the Blair government), my estimate of attainable unemployment of 2.5% will remain and buttresses the key assumption here of 'full employment'.

Without this assumption, my proposal will not work, for the obvious reason that one cannot easily compel people to take jobs even in a situation of high unemployment – officials at the sharp end will not co-operate, and there is strong political opposition. Never mind that the high unemployment itself is the result of inflexible wages due to unwillingness to take jobs; that point is never easy to establish in popular political discourse, because in the short term it manifests itself as a pure 'lack of jobs' – and of job offers also, since employers do not even advertise in such circumstances.

The proposal applies to new entrants. They should save and insure adequately to fund their own welfare needs: their children's education, their own and their family's health care, their pension, and their episodes of unemployment beyond some 3-to-6-month period of state insurance. To this end, they would be expected to put aside some substantial percentage of their income into a designated fund – for use by them for these specified purposes. The income within this fund would be tax-exempt as present pension fund income is in the UK.

There could be built-in allowances to use this fund for other purposes once primary needs were satisfied – via, say, 'contribution holidays' (as now available in corporate pensions). A regulatory office would be needed as usual to deal with this sort of problem. To buttress the set-up, there would be a system for loans and for dealing with those in default, outlined in the overview above.

What about the vexed issue, yet again as with opting-out from pensions, of public debt? As new entrants make their new personal contributions, they will of course be 'funding' their own future unfunded welfare liabilities; but the welfare of existing participants will go on being paid for out of current taxes. If new entrants receive tax cuts in respect of their future savings, then there will be a *pro tanto* current deficit and public debt will accumulate.

The difference in the case of non-pension welfare is that the unfunded liabilities are over the working life, often quite early on in it (for instance the young family's burden of education and health care), and so the pay-off of the debt comes fairly rapidly. Hence, if new entrants were to be given tax rebates of equal present value, as in the pension case above, the roll-up of debt would not be so large. If, for illustrative purposes, we supposed that new entrants start contributing on average at age 20 in respect of non-pension ex-welfare expenses at 5% of their income and that 40% of this stream of expenses occurred in their thirties with the rest spread evenly over their lives, then in the UK the debt would accumulate at only £0.2 billion per year and peak at £2 billion ten years later. In other words, this would be a trivial accumulation.

With new entrants being given tax rebates equal in present value to the stream of benefits they were forfeiting, we would be converting a tax stream with negative work incentives into a contributions stream with none in that, while extra work would attract extra contributions, these would all be going towards the extra benefit of the working individual (unlike the tax stream, for which there would be no corresponding marginal benefit, these welfare benefits being fixed by some scale of need.)

We are left with the problem of those in need, in this case with wages (since by assumption they are working) too low to support the family needs. Clearly, these proposals will fail if a large class of people are absolutely unable to cope throughout their lifetimes regardless of their best efforts.

In Chapter 7 we discussed the likelihood of a serious stagnation or even fall in real unskilled wages in the future. We concluded that, provided productivity growth was maintained and there was also a steady expansion of higher education and training, there should be sufficient growth in demand for unskilled workers in the non-traded half of the economy to absorb their declining numbers and even create rising scarcity. We should not forget that in the 1950s and 1960s this was the situation; that very fact may have helped to diminish the incentive to obtain good education and training in the succeeding two decades and so contributed to the relative decline of unskilled wages. Nowadays, with the lessons of this latest period fresh in the popular mind, there is every prospect that the trend in unskilled wages will revert to that earlier experience.

In a recent (1994) book, Richard Herrnstein and Charles Murray argued that lack of intelligence is the root cause of poverty through lack of skill, and it could thus effectively prevent unskilled workers from achieving an adequate living standard indefinitely. However, that is to assume that skill will indefinitely be rewarded in such a relatively generous way as has occurred in the past few decades. I am arguing here that this experience is not likely to be repeated, just as it did not occur in the period immediately after the Second World War.

Returning, therefore, to my proposals, it is reasonable to suppose that unskilled workers could deal with their own lifetime problems. No doubt there will be some who cannot; but there is provision for the exceptions in the scheme.

All these are speculations in any case about the future. But whether most people will or will not be able to cope, remembering that they will receive tax rebates equal to the present value of their lost benefits, is something that can only be settled by a trial of the new system, which will evoke new behaviour. 'Inability to cope' is a reaction itself to a system that subsidises such behaviour.

Will new entrants accept such a new system? The change will be 'regressive' compared with the existing system; yet it will also offer substantially lower marginal tax rates. A rough idea of this can be obtained by noting that the *average* tax rate can fall in the UK by the amount currently spent on welfare (25% of GDP). Political debate in the UK in the late 1990s suggests that this prospect may well appeal to the younger generation. What economists can say at least is that the lower marginal rates that it makes possible will increase efficiency in a number of dimensions, including higher incentives to save, to work, and to improve skills.

It is in fact hard to see any distinction in principle between the reforms so far undertaken in the UK and accepted, and this reform of welfare. The main practical difference is that the reforms involve three very different phases in people's lives – youth, old age and times of sickness. These phases are converted in political terms into three separate interest groups, each of which is extremely powerful, especially when allied to the professionals who cater for its needs. Reform, therefore, has to mobilise people generally in the cause of efficiency against formidable opposition, while also allaying their fears about their own insecure phases of life. However, the intellectual case is essentially no different from that against other forms of regulation, in the labour market and elsewhere.

Conclusion

I began by pointing to the severe and unavoidable incentive problems created by the existing welfare state in most Western countries. I have sketched out a proposal for the abolition of the welfare state as we know it in most Western countries and its replacement by private provision through compulsory saving and insurance, underpinned by a state loan facility (of last resort) and an ultimate safety net for those who cannot or will not repay such loans. In order to enable its introduction in an orderly way, it will only affect new entrants to the labour market and hence will be introduced over a very long time-scale. I suggest that the new entrants will be attracted by the lower tax rates and wider opportunities they face, even though the new system is more regressive than the old; and that there is no reason to expect that there will be the sort of immiserisation of the unskilled that would make such a system quite unworkable.

In line with the rest of this book, my general conclusion is that societies will in the end find a way of achieving the efficiency gains that welfare reform offers, substituting mainly personal saving and insurance, but also some residual state insurance, for the massively wasteful social insurance systems now in place.

References

Barro, R.J. (1974) 'Are government bonds net wealth?' *Journal of Political Economy*, 82, pp. 1095–1117.

Butler, E. and Pirie, M. (1995) *The Fortune Account,* Adam Smith Institute, London.

Feldstein, M. (1974) 'Social security, induced retirement, and aggregate capital accumulation', *Journal of Political Economy*, 82.

Feldstein, M. (1994) 'Fiscal policies, capital formation and capitalism', NBER Working Paper No. 4885.

Herrnstein, R.J. and Murray, C. (1994) *The Bell Curve – Intelligence and Class Structure in American Life*, Free Press, Simon and Schuster, New York.

Minford, P. (1984) 'State Expenditure: A Study in Waste', supplement to *Economic Affairs*, April/June.

Minford, P. (1988/9) 'A Policy for the National Health Service', *Economic Affairs*, Oct/Nov 1988, 21–8, and Dec/Jan 1989, 23–6; reprinted in P. Minford, *The Supply-side Revolution in Britain*, IEA/Edward Elgar, pp. 165–91.

Minford, P. (1990) 'The Poverty Trap after the Fowler Reforms', in A. Bowen and K. Mayhew (eds) *Improving Incentives for the Low-paid*, Macmillan for NEDO; reprinted in P. Minford, *The Supply-side Revolution in Britain*, IEA/Edward Elgar, 1991, pp. 112–31.

Ricardo, D. (1817) *The Principles of Political Economy and Taxation*, Dent, London, (1911, reprinted 1960), Ch. 17.

CHAPTER TEN

Conclusions

WE BEGAN BY setting out some principles of how people decide their priorities and how societies' organisation of themselves survives. We concluded that people have aims for the long term (the duty principle), to which they give greater importance than short-term gratifications (the pleasure principle). In consenting to public proposals and in accommodations with each other, they will therefore not block arrangements that promote general future efficiency, provided there is not too much current disadvantage to themselves. It therefore makes sense for politicians to propose efficiency-producing reforms, although ones designed to avoid current losses to groups with blocking power.

We have examined the record of free-market policies in the UK and of interventionist policies on the continent of Europe – two contrasting policy sets – in order to provide evidence on these ideas. We saw clear evidence of long-term revival in the UK and of long-term slowdown on the continent.

We have also looked internationally at the process by which world free trade and domestic policies of 'openness' (essentially free market activity) have spawned the rapid development of many developing countries. Previously, policies of protection in these countries failed to produce growth in spite of a generally open world-trade environment and large aid programmes: trade with free-market policies has achieved what aid and protection could not. Furthermore, advanced countries with flexible labour markets, amongst which we find the majority of Anglo-Saxon countries (and Far-Eastern ones such as Japan and Korea), have performed more impressively in the face of this globalisation process.

The policies that have achieved consent in these advanced countries and in emerging market economies are the free-market policies that have brought growth. Meanwhile, on the European continent there is evidence of social malaise and voter rejection of governments. The Italians, for example, have torn up their constitution and rejected with it the previous longstanding government of the Christian Democrats amid a torrent of corruption charges. The French threw out most of the Socialist party in their last-but-one election and with equal decisiveness have more recently rejected the Gaullists who replaced them. In Germany, as in France and Italy, there has been a sharp rise in support for fascist parties. Meanwhile, in the UK, the US and the Antipodes, while governments have indeed been rejected at the polls, they have been succeeded (most recently in the UK with New Labour) by governments similarly committed to market forces. Politics has been more about fresh people than about fresh policies.

This restiveness with the prevailing policies on the Continent and the relative policy tranquillity in Anglo-Saxon countries is occurring in spite of the fact that inequality (corresponding to the reduction in social insurance, implied by less intervention) has risen relatively in the latter countries. Why have people there put up with this rise in inequality? Mainly, of course, it is because it merely reflects substantial rises in the rewards to those with skill and good entrepreneurial fortune; and there is no evidence that ordinary people (as opposed to some 'left-wingers') begrudge others their good fortune. But it is also because these policies have generally raised, and at worst protected, their absolute living standards (no losers) while also offering better prospects in the long term. We have seen this recipe in practice throughout the UK's post-1979 reform programme in the buying-off of losers while enabling greater efficiency. The result is visible in the statistics for UK household real income: the living standard of the bottom groups has generally grown measurably since 1979 even according to estimated income figures and more so according to more relevant expenditure figures.

When we look further East, we see widespread acceptance of even less government intervention, with social programmes limited to government spending on education and health and negligible other state-funded social insurance: the all-embracing Western cradle-to-grave welfare state does not exist there. This Eastern model of capitalism, with the least social interventionism and hence the lowest tax rates of those we have looked at in this book, has generated impressive growth over several decades, first in Japan and then more generally on the Pacific Rim (whatever the short term problems produced by recent financial crises). Nor has this apparently generated a price in higher poverty or social discontent. It suggests that Anglo-Saxon capitalism too – though right to ignore a number of other facets of eastern capitalism, not least the dangerous lack of democracy in some countries – could move in particular to less social insurance, lower tax rates and greater efficiency.

We have concluded that societies are capable of reform towards more efficient arrangements; that these policies are not blocked when put forward in an intelligent manner; and that the absence of them, tending to stagnation, produces blocking of the existing policies. We should therefore anticipate reform as politicians react to these opportunities. For many, this will seem a optimistic message. For those who feel that greater equality is a moral imperative, it will be depressing. But the evidence suggests that most people are prepared to pay the price, if such it is, of greater inequality for the sake of a dynamic and efficient society.

It is not so much that capitalism has triumphed or that people have mostly seen through the stakeholder fallacy, though both are true. The encouraging thing is that people learn from experience and social institutions reflect that learning. Marx forecast the inevitable fall of capitalism; what we have seen is in fact the extinction of communism and the eclipse of socialism because people have discovered that only under free markets are human energy and ingenuity properly released and harnessed. Since economic freedom is also an important component of political freedom, people choose this capitalist mixture because it provides both economic success and personal autonomy.

INDEX